Transcendental Philosophy and Everyday Experience

Transcendental Philosophy and Everyday Experience

Edited by
Tom Rockmore
and
Vladimir Zeman

HUMANITIES PRESS
NEW JERSEY

This collection first published in 1997 by
Humanities Press International, Inc.
165 First Avenue, Atlantic Highlands, New Jersey 07716

This collection © 1997 by Humanities Press International, Inc.

Library of Congress Cataloging-in-Publication Data
Transcendental philosophy and everyday experience / edited by Tom
  Rockmore and Vladimir Zeman.
      p. cm.
    Includes bibliographical references and index.
    ISBN 0-391-04024-3 (cloth)
    1. Transcendentalism. I. Rockmore, Tom, 1942– . II. Zeman,
  Vladimir.
    B823.T69 1997
    141'.3—dc21   96-37869
                                                                  CIP

Printed in the United States of America.

In memory of M. I. L.

CONTENTS

vii

PART 4   TRANSCENDENTAL PHILOSOPHY AND THE EMOTIONS

Introduction

This volume of studies on transcendental philosophy and everyday experience focuses first on transcendental philosophy and second on the intersection of two central philosophical themes. The importance of the themes of transcendental philosophy and everyday experience, or everyday life, should be self-evident. Modern philosophy since René Descartes is dominated by the Cartesian concern with methodological rigor as the key to knowledge. Transcendental philosophy is a general term designating a particularly rigorous approach to knowledge usually associated with Kant and with such later thinkers as Edmund Husserl and the early Martin Heidegger.

It is at least arguable that transcendental arguments appear earlier in the tradition. Plato's brief in favor of what is routinely called the theory of ideas, roughly claims that we need to invoke an unchanging world of reality in order to explain cognition from our position within the changing world of appearances, can serve as an early instance. He seems to think that, unless we invoke the theory of ideas, we cannot understand the very possibility of knowledge. Yet we can date the modern view of transcendental philosophy from Immanuel Kant. Historically, Kant is the first thinker to insist clearly on the transcendental status of his theory. Every reader of the *Critique of Pure Reason* knows that in this book Kant advances a theory combining empirical realism and transcendental idealism. Influenced by Kant, beginning in *Logical Investigations*, Husserl later developed a theory of transcendental phenomenology.

In our time, the nature, scope, and viability of transcendental philosophy has become a "hot" topic. Numerous papers, conferences, books, and collections of papers have been devoted to discussing various aspects of transcendental philosophy.[1] In the 1960s and 1970s, attacks against transcendental philosophy narrowed their attention to studies of its nature and possibility. At the time of this writing, transcendental philosophy is still under heavy attack, but the eventual outcome of the discussion is far from clear. We are still a long way from being able to evaluate the arguments advanced against transcendental philosophy. Also there is no reason to think that these or other arguments will prove decisive even in the long run.

1

Philosophers, who practice argument as their main stock in trade, almost their only product with which to conduct business, are as resistant to argument, even of the highest quality, as the next person. Certainly, the mere appearance of an argument, or even a good argument, against transcendental philosophy, so far, has had no visible effect on the continued reliance on a transcendental approach. Even within pragmatism, which is notoriously resistant to transcendental thought, there has been a certain renewal of the transcendental orientation, for instance in Karl-Otto Apel's transcendental form of pragmatism, which builds on Charles Peirce.[2] Heidegger's theory has recently been described as transcendental pragmatism.[3] In his theory of communicative action, Jürgen Habermas has long relied on a so-called quasi-transcendental approach, perhaps most explicitly in his recent study of law.[4]

Regardless of the eventual outcome, critical discussion of transcendental philosophy is important for at least two reasons. On the one hand, at stake is the viability of one of the leading forms of modern philosophy. It would, for instance, be very difficult to salvage much of anything, say, of Kant's critical philosophy if it turned out that transcendental philosophy in all of its many variants, although not necessarily in Kant's writings, was not at least a potentially viable approach. On the other hand, if transcendental philosophy can be regarded as identical with philosophy as we know it; if there is no other plausible way to do philosophy, as Kant certainly contends; and if transcendental philosophy as such is not viable; then philosophy itself must be abandoned. This extreme conclusion has recently been drawn by Heidegger who, in his last period, simply seems to equate Kant's critical philosophy with philosophy itself.[5] So, depending on the attitude one takes toward transcendental philosophy, clearly the stakes in its examination and its defense are high, very high.

The situation, as concerns the analysis of everyday experience, is somewhat different, since this theme has only recently reemerged. The general theme of everyday experience, although not under that heading, and obviously not necessarily from a transcendental perspective that is often said to originate with Kant, comes into the tradition very early. Plato's *Republic* provides an ideal theory of everyday life. This theme later recurs in different ways in a great many important texts, including Augustine's *City of God*, Hobbes's *Leviathan*, Rousseau's *The Social Contract*, Fichte's *Closed Commercial State*, Hegel's *Philosophy of Right*, in many of Marx's writings, and in many works in this century, recently, for instance, in Rawl's *Theory of Justice*.

Kant's specific contribution is to raise the question regarding the conditions of the possibility of experience and knowledge in its most general, or properly transcendental, form. Although transcendental argument arguably exists earlier than Kant, for instance in Aristotle's well-known efforts to understand the possibility of science, Kant is obviously the first thinker to focus clearly on the very possibility of experience of objects and knowledge that others tacitly assume but never explicitly thematize.

Husserl, who was aware of the close link between his theory and Kant's, takes the latter's theory a step further in focusing, as Kant does not, on the link between transcendental philosophy, in his case transcendental phenomenology, and ordinary experience, particularly in his final period. His last, unfinished book, *The Crisis of European Sciences and Transcendental Phenomenology*, contains some very interesting discussions about the concept of the lifeworld (*Lebenswelt*).[6] In phenomenological circles, considerable attention has been given to elucidating Husserl's tantalizing, but insufficiently-clarified concept. Alfred Schutz and other phenomenologists influenced by Husserl, including Heidegger, have independently contributed to a phenomenological elucidation of aspects of the life-world.

This volume is concerned not only with transcendental philosophy but with the intersection of transcendental philosophy and everyday life, or experience. Over the centuries until, say, Husserl, the link of philosophy to social reality has more frequently been presupposed than critically examined. Transcendental philosophy as it developed in German idealism is officially a theory of experience. Yet, with the exception of Husserl scholars, interested in this topic as it emerges in Husserl's final thought, in view of the importance of this theme, no more than insufficient attention has been directed toward the relation of transcendental philosophy and everyday experience, as opposed to experience in general.

For Husserl's generation, this theme was directly raised, in the aftermath of the First World War, in Max Weber's celebrated lecture, "Vom inneren Beruf zur Wissenschaft" [1919]. Husserl was concerned with the social relevance of philosophy throughout his career, for instance in his programmatic analysis of "Philosophy as Rigorous Science" [1911]. But he turned more directly to this theme in the wake of the collapse of the Weimar Republic and the rise of National Socialism. To combat the rise of unreason, he proposed the defense of the ancient distinction between knowledge and opinion through transcendental phenomenology. His analysis of the life-world in his last, unfinished book is intended simultaneously to provide yet another introduction to transcendental phenomenology, to clarify the distinction between physicalistic objectivism and transcendental subjectivism, to elucidate its relation to psychology, and, in dire circumstances preceding the coming Second World War, to defend once more the social relevance of philosophy.

Obviously, the topic is not unprecedented. It is a perennial theme that emerges early in the philosophical tradition. Plato and Aristotle disagree about the relevance of theoretical philosophy, including by inference what later came to be called transcendental philosophy, for politics. Whereas for Plato theoretical philosophy is a necessary condition of the good life, for Aristotle theoretical philosophy is not relevant for social life. Their disagreement echoes through the later discussion, dividing many important thinkers. In our time, it separates two of the leading phenomenologists of our century: Husserl and Heidegger. The former insisted on the defense of reason as the only real alternative to National Socialist politics, whereas the latter, who joined his thought to his deed, maintained in obviously Platonic fashion that philosophy offered the acceptable grounding of Nazi practice.[7]

The importance of the intersection between transcendental philosophy and everyday life is obvious, now more than ever, in a period typified by rising skepticism about the social relevance of philosophy, or even its possibility. The ancient Platonic theme of the link between philosophy and politics has lost none of its interest. It remains important to determine how philosophy relates to the world in which we live, in particular to scrutinize the role a philosopher can reasonably expect, or be expected, to play within society; in short, the extent to which he can usefully contribute to enlightening us about our world and ourselves.

In our time, the traditional epistemological form of skepticism about the possibility of knowledge has been transformed into a rather different form of philosophical skepticism regarding the legitimate philosophical role within society. The traditional idea of philosophy as being the only source of knowledge, in the full sense, is the prerequisite for the further idea that it has a special social function that, as Plato holds, separates, say, the philosopher from the soldier and the farmer.

This idea, which was always controversial, was clearly easier to defend when philosophy was still understood on the basis of the old Platonic model as the science of sciences underlying all claims to know of whatever kind. According to this view, the various sciences are subordinated to the science of philosophy. Yet the gradual separation of philosophy and the sciences, due to the rise of the new science in the seventeenth century, has forever changed the understanding of the relationship between philosophy and science in fundamental ways.

This change is particularly apparent in the writings of the Vienna Circle thinkers and their U.S. allies, above all in analytic philosophy of science, arguably the leading form of analytic philosophy at present. Such thinkers uniformly reject the view that the natural sciences depend on philosophy for their claims to know, an idea still defended very clearly as late as Kant. The aim of the critical philosophy is often described as an effort to ground Newtonian science.[8] While rejecting the idea that natural sciences depend on philosophy, analytic philosophers of science hold that science is signally important, even, in extreme views, bordering on scientism, the main contemporary source of knowledge. For such thinkers, the role of philosophy is not to substitute itself for science, but to understand the relation of the sciences among themselves and to provide a logical reconstruction of the cognitive basis of the individual sciences.

Analytic philosophy of science rethinks the relation of philosophy to science in according to science a primary importance in respect to which philosophy recedes to a secondary, or meta-level, from which it can reflect on science, but not contribute to its success. Although it recasts philosophy as a secondary source of knowledge, and it is exceedingly skeptical about a traditional view of philosophy, it is not necessarily skeptical about philosophy itself. Yet a clear form of skepticism about philosophy as understood in the modern discussion has emerged recently in postmodernism.

Postmodern philosophy, which has become popular in the last decade in the writings of Richard Rorty, Jean-François Lyotard, Derrida, and others, is a loose appellation grouping together authors whose main point in common, other than the name, seems to be their disinterest in, even a disdain for, the traditional philosophical concern to justify claims to know. A typical instance is Lyotard's unargued suggestion, arguably intended as a refutation of G. W. F. Hegel, that there no longer is anything like a *méta-récit*.[9]

At the dawn of philosophy, Socrates got into trouble when he insisted on examining claims "to know" in ways that seemed to threaten the established political order. This "Socratic" concern is central to modern philosophy, which literally turns on the felt need to justify all assertions or contentions, to accept nothing on faith, to demand a reason for every claim to know. In modern times, an important part of the philosophical task has been seen as the unstinting effort to cover one's tracks, or even to leave no tracks at all, to give nothing away. It has been widely believed that to admit even the least space in the train of reasoning about knowledge is tantamount to admitting that we do not know that we can know, since knowledge itself cannot be shown to be possible.

In that precise sense, whether or not one finds postmodern thought convincing, it is clear that the tendency as a whole represents a revolt against the modern concern to legitimate philosophical claims, particularly claims to know. At least since Descartes, the idea that knowledge claims should and in fact could be legitimated, or justified against even the most remote theoretical possibility of doubt, runs throughout the discussion like a red thread. Descartes certainly believed that he was able to weave a seamless web of justification against the radical form of doubt that he raises against himself. Kant's transcendental philosophy, which was famously intended to limit knowledge to make room for faith, was in part also intended to justify faith in knowledge. This latter task is clearly renewed in the most rigorous way in Husserl's transcendental phenomenology.

A justification of claims to know is, obviously, not self-evident, but very problematic, or the extensive attention devoted to it over a period of centuries would not have been necessary. Since Husserl, the belief in the need for, and the capacity to provide for, anything approaching a rigorous justification of claims to know has been threatened in a least two ways. One is certainly the increasingly widespread conviction among recent philosophers of all stripes that efforts to provide an epistemological justification have now failed for epistemological reasons. Here, the demise of foundationalism is significant.

Foundationalism that dates from Descartes is the favored epistemological strategy of modern times. The attack on foundationalism launched within German idealism, for instance by Johann Gottlieb Fichte and Hegel, becomes a central concern in recent analytic philosophy. With the stubborn exception of Roderick Chisholm,[10] few analytic thinkers now contend that foundationalism is, or even, with appropriate modifications, could become, a viable option. This has led to a rash of doomsayers, perhaps the most prominent of whom is Putnam, who now simply contends that the analytic approach to reference has been shown to be a blind alley. An even more extreme reaction is Rorty's view, beginning in *Philosophy and the Mirror of Nature*, which seems to equate the very possibility of philosophy with the success of analytic foundationalism, leading more recently in *Contingency, Irony, and Solidarity* to the inference that truth cannot be defended.

The other is the much more disturbing turn, not against foundationalism, but against the very examination of claims to know for the apparent reason, for which arguments are simply not provided, that no ultimate justification is forthcoming. What is disturbing about this view is not the view itself, which is merely another form of epistemological skepticism—here directed, not to knowledge in general, but to philosophy—but rather the failure to provide any argument in favor of this conclusion that is far from self-evident. It is by no means clear that we can legitimately claim to know that we cannot know, although that seems to be the underlying assumption in much, perhaps all, of recent postmodernist thought, which is simply presented without argument. It is as if a conceptual fatigue had arisen in virtue of the long concern with knowledge that somehow dispenses contemporary thinkers from even the need to argue their claims, as if they had suddenly become self-evident.

Analytic philosophy has always been inclined toward technical analysis, since its origins in Gottlob Frege, a highly technical thinker. The apparent failure of the analytic effort to make out the foundationalist approach represents the perceived failure to present a viable form of epistemological foundationalism that is apparent in recent attention to anti-foundationalism.[11] In analytic philosophy, the battle has clearly been, and is still being, waged on an epistemological level. The situation is very different in so-called postmodernist philosophy, which, however, comes to a nearly identical conclusion.

To the observer, the opposition between earlier thinkers, concerned to justify their claims, and postmodernists, seemingly indifferent, or even opposed, to this task, is striking. As a group, the postmodernists are all influenced in various ways by Heidegger, who was increasingly unconcerned to justify his prophetic pronouncements. What in his early philosophy was depicted as an effort to overcome (*Überwindung*, from *überwinden*, roughly meaning "to overcome a difficulty") the history of ontology later became simply a turn away from it (*Verwindung*, from *verwinden*, roughly meaning "to come away from") as part of the famous, but famously obscure turning in his thought.

As part of the concern with scientific philosophy, there is a persistent stress on the rigorous deduction of a categorial framework in German idealism from Kant to Hegel. This stress vanishes without a trace in Heidegger, who, at least in *Being and Time*, is clearly still a categorial thinker. For many observers, he simply seems to invoke a series of categories that appear as it were to be plucked out of thin air. The idea that claims to know require a justification is never addressed in his thought, as if this theme no longer required any sustained treatment or even required no treatment at all.

It is perhaps excessive to call Heidegger a postmodern thinker. Yet it is obvious that such postmodern thinkers as Rorty, Gadamer, Derrida, Lyotard, and others have increasingly tended to eschew careful examination of knowledge claims that they merely dismiss. The early Heidegger still retains a highly systematic approach familiar in German idealism that disappears without a trace in his later thought. Gadamer, Derrida, and others influenced by Heidegger are all nonsystematic thinkers.

Hans-Georg Gadamer, in this respect a typical postmodern writer, directly eschews justification of claims to know. He straightforwardly maintains that efforts to justify one's position are unnecessary since at a certain level the denial of claims to know cannot be made in good faith. He pretends to solve what he calls the epistemological problem through phenomenology,[12] although it is unclear what he understands the problem to be or in what his solution consists. Derrida's stress on deconstruction often seems to come down to a concerted effort to show that no one, neither Heidegger, nor Husserl, nor Hegel, nor anyone else can justifiably make a claim to know, or even a definite reference in the course of making such a claim.

Developments in recent analytic philosophy and postmodernism focus on the increasingly evident failure to provide the type of rigorous justification of claims to know that are insisted on by Descartes and his followers and that are formalized in various efforts to make out the foundationalist

epistemological strategy. Analytic philosophy and postmodernism share the
common view that the idea of a seamless justification of claims to know, as
Husserl insightfully said, is a dream that is dreamed out. The difference in
the respective reactions to this result is highly interesting.

We have already noted that analytic philosophy has drawn the inference
that philosophy now has mainly a secondary role to play, since science is,
and in all likelihood will remain, the leading source of knowledge in the
foreseeable future. The obvious exceptions, here as elsewhere, are Rorty
and Hilary Putnam. The latter, who was earlier a stalwart of positivist scientism,
in a long career that has seen him take a bewildering variety of stands from
positivism to Marxism-Leninism, has now completed the process of turning
against his former self, in the result of turning his earlier position inside
out.[13] Postmodern thinkers, who to a man are uninterested and unversed in
science, draw a radically different inference that is only superficially similar
to Paul Feyerabend's famous claim that anything goes.

In advancing his methodological claim about the proper procedure in
scientific discovery, Feyerabend[14] was pointing out, against Norwood Russell
Hanson and others concerned with isolating a particular method of scientific discovery, that there is no single, specifiable algorithm. He went on to
draw anarchistic conclusions in politics[15] that have little do with his studies
in the philosophy of science, but, as Fichte would say, a lot to do with the
kind of man he was. Postmodernists and their allies make use of an apparent inability to provide an ultimate justification of knowledge claims to call
into question the idea of knowledge itself as well as political responsibility.

Derrida's theory arguably comes down to a kind of anti-Hegelianism easily understood through his own interest in Hegel and Hegel's influence in
the French context when he began to write. His vaunted deconstruction
generalizes Hegel's argument at the beginning of the *Phenomenology* stating
that language, which is intrinsically general, cannot be used to identify
particulars. In Derrida's hands, this becomes an argument against definite
reference, a form of antisemantics, in effect a claim that you cannot say
what you mean and mean what you say. A possible political consequence of
this approach is apparent in the view of Paul de Man, Derrida's close associate. He holds that since we cannot make out the distinction between
history and fiction, even the bleakest of crimes, as well, by inference, all
responsibility for them can simply be explained away.[16]

The authors represented in this collection have all previously worked,
and mostly published, on issues and problems normally connected with German
philosophy in general, and Kant and/or Husserl in particular. The papers
collected in this volume represent a series of different interpretations, written from different perspectives, either on the overall themes of transcendental philosophy, or on the intersection between transcendental philosophy

and everyday life. The contents of this book are divided into three main parts, beginning with the problematic relation between philosophy and everyday experience treated in Part 1, which is composed of four papers.

Both the relation and tension between transcendental philosophy and everyday life and experience, extending from the street and the home to the scientist's laboratory, has already been envisaged at the inception of transcendental philosophy in Kant's *Critique of Pure Reason*. Kant, who recognized that in everyday cognitive experience it is perfectly normal to act as a realist, also held that as philosophers, when we are called upon to examine the framework for all such cognitive or noncognitive acts, we cannot but think as transcendental idealists.

Kant's influential theory has provoked a steady series of attempts to revise it. Joseph Margolis presents his own kind of revision, in partial agreement with the above mentioned views of Rorty. His main point is that to retain transcendental arguments as a form of legitimative reasoning, though without reducing the latter to the former, requires that we abandon the hope for synthetic a priori judgments of any kind and that we recognize the historical and conditioned character of all such forms.

J. N. Mohanty's paper reviews the basic difference between Kant's and Husserl's forms of transcendental philosophy, and concentrates on the concept of transcendental subjectivity, in particular on the complementary relation between transcendental and empirical subjectivity. (This part of his paper is a direct response to the views of another author represented here, David Carr, and both contributions can be considered as parts on an ongoing dialogue between two of the most important, contemporary Husserl scholars.) The rest of his paper shows the relation between the concepts of life-world and praxis (meaning "practice," from German *die Praxis*), as well as the importance of the proper understanding of this relation for the constituting of transcendental subjectivity.

Erazim Kohák, another important Husserl scholar, chooses a rather unconventional approach, as the roles of transcendental philosophy and everyday experience get reversed; the former becomes familiar, the latter problematic. His detailed analysis, supported textually by references to Husserl, ends with the unexpected conclusion that "It would be more accurate to speak of transcendental experience and everyday philosophy."

Tom Rockmore's paper takes as its basis the Platonic position, and pursues its aspects through a critical analysis of Kant, Heidegger, and Habermas. Given his broad conception of transcendental philosophy, and his social interpretation of everyday life, Rockmore reaches radically different conclusions from those of Kohák.

The first part of the book is primarily problem-oriented or at least directed to a series of related problems. Papers in the second part, devoted to

Kant and neo-Kantianism, are more limited in scope and tend to concentrate on analysis of relevant issues in the works of Immanuel Kant and the main representative of the Marburg School of neo-Kantianism, Hermann Cohen.

Rudolf A. Makkreel, a leading Kant scholar, here pursues his study of Kant's concept of transcendental reflection, which was earlier presented in his recent work on *Imagination and Interpretation in Kant*. In an indirect exchange with Dieter Henrich, he develops the idea of the orientational role of transcendental reflection for the understanding of human life and its relation to the overall order in the world.

David Carr attempts to provide the reader with something that Kant nowhere systematically offered: his theory of the subject. Projecting Husserl's conception of intentionality into Kant's own philosophy, he proposes that the "empirical subject" and "transcendental subject," two ways of speaking about ourselves, must both be understood as ultimately referring to the world. However, the ahistorical character of Kant's claims may lead us to further revisions of Kant's concept of transcendental self.

Vladimir Zeman turns his attention to Hermann Cohen, a leading representative of the Marburg School of neo-Kantianism. First in his interpretative commentaries (starting in 1871) and then (after 1900) in his own systematic writings, he presented the conception of transcendental method. Zeman assumes the standard interpretation of Cohen's work as a necessary mediating link between Kant and Husserl, possibly further mediated by Paul Natorp, in order to focus on Cohen's way of interrelating Kant's theory of experience, his ethics, and the limiting role of ideas.

The papers in Part 3 present applications of transcendental philosophy to problems in areas such as literary theory, art theory, and problems of artificial intelligence. Taking as his example a well-known poem by the French modernist poet Paul Valéry, Peter McCormick studies the problem of interpretation. He points out that the model represented in analytic philosophy of language, say the early Wittgenstein, is unsuccessful in specifying the object of literary interpretation. He suggests a less restrictive account that, going beyond classical analytic views, is more helpful for literary interpretation.

Alistair Neher analyzes the focal concept of later German neo-Kantianism— the concept of symbolic form—in its development from the original formulation by the German neo-Kantian, Ernst Cassirer to its application and reinterpretation in the work of art historian Erwin Panofsky. He is especially concerned with Panofsky's well-known reinterpretation of the very idea of symbolic form as perspective.

Dagfinn Føllesdal, another well-known Husserl scholar, is concerned with the relation between transcendental phenomenology and everyday life. From this perspective, he reviews two strategies on what computers can and cannot do. The first and most common strategy focuses on the incapability of computers to imitate the various aspects of the life-world; while the second and moral radical one concentrates on the consequences of the absence of consciousness in computers.

To round out the volume, Dallas Laskey suggests that the concept of empathy, which may provide an interpretive key to some of the most pressing problems of contemporary ethics and social philosophy, can be best viewed from the standpoint of transcendental phenomenology.

NOTES

1. See, e.g. *Reading Kant: New Perspectives on Transcendental Arguments and Critical Arguments*, ed. by Eva Schaper and Wilhelm Vossenkuhl (Oxford: Oxford University Press, 1989).
2. See Karl-Otto Apel, *Charles S. Peirce: From Pragmatism to Pragmaticism*, trans. by John Michael Krois (Amherst, MA: University of Massachusetts, 1981).
3. See Mark Okrent, *Heidegger's Pragmatism: Understanding, Being, and Critique of Metaphysics* (Ithaca: Cornell University Press, 1986).
4. See Jürgen Habermas, *Faktizität und Geltung, Beiträge zur Diskurstheorie des Rechts und des demokratischen Rechtsstaats* (Frankfurt a. M.: Suhrkamp, 1994).
5. See "The End of Philosophy and the Task of Thinking," in Martin Heidegger, *On Time and Being*, trans. Joan Stambaugh (New York: Harper and Row, 1977), pp. 55–73.
6. See *Lebenswelt und Wissenschaft in der Philosophie Edmund Husserls*, ed. Elisabeth Ströker (Frankfurt a. M.: Suhrkamp, 1979).
7. See Tom Rockmore, *On Heidegger's Nazism and Philosophy* (Berkeley: University of California Press, 1992).
8. See Michael Friedman, *Kant and the Exact Sciences* (Cambridge: Harvard University Press, 1992).
9. See Jean-François Lyotard, *La condition postmoderne* (Paris: Editions de Minuit, 1979).
10. See Roderick M. Chisholm, *The Foundations of Knowing* (Minneapolis: University of Minnesota Press, 1982).
11. See *Antifoundationalism Old and New*, ed. by Tom Rockmore and Beth J. Singer (Philadelphia: Temple University Press, 1992).
12. See "The Overcoming of the Epistemological Problems through Phenomenological Research," in Hans-Georg Gadamer, *Truth and Method*, trans. by Garrett Barden and John Cumming (New York: Crossroads, 1988), pp. 214–234.
13. See, e.g., Hilary Putnam, *Renewing Philosophy* (Cambridge: Harvard University Press, 1992).
14. See Paul Feyerabend, *Against Method* (London: Verso, 1978).
15. See Feyerabend, *Erkenntnis für freie Menschen* (Frankfurt a. M.: Suhrkamp, 1980).
16. See Paul De Man, Allegories of Reading: Figural Language in Rousseau, Nietzsche, Rilke and Proust (New Haven: Yale University Press, 1979), p. 293.

Part 1

Philosophy and Everyday Experience

1

Transcendental Philosophy and Praxis

Joseph Margolis

Asked to assess the prospects of transcendental philosophy, one's natural inclination is to deny that there are any. But we ought to resist the temptation if only because it obviates by its finality the explanation it owes us and because some clever fellow may yet show us a way of recovering something like the original Kantian project. There's too much of a trap in the frontal question. A little indirection is called for.

Doubts about the viability of transcendental philosophy come in three colors: in red, because we suspect that Kant himself cheats in constructing the pertinent line of reasoning—he invokes the noumenal just where the charm of the other is supposed to escape it altogether. In blue, because every optimistic approximation of Kant's project, for instance in Jürgen Habermas and Charles Sanders Peirce, whether empirically or morally or pragmatically pursued, requires some very strong principle of charity that presupposes what we thought to have put in question—it claims quite arbitrarily that the transcendental objective is the *telos*, at the inaccessible limit of perfect rationality, of all our reflexive inquiries, all the while we congratulate ourselves on being so fortunately on the way. In white, because, as in such preposterous repudiations of transcendental reasoning as those tendered by Richard Rorty and Jean-François Lyotard, the declaration that its prospects are quite dead is itself a peculiar transcendental argument that would have us ignore that fact—it is, after all, supposed to be invisible while its effect is not.

This, of course, is itself no more than a rhetorical way of leading us to the center of the issue, a kind of knowledgeable gossip that might just be content to leave matters at that. We, however, need a firmer policy.

14

I

Allow if you can the following sketch of an argument to hover benignly over our quarrels: where successful, transcendental arguments arrive at true synthetic *a priori* findings; but the most compelling themes of late twentieth-century philosophy, possibly of the whole drift of philosophy, commit us to holding: (1) that the actual world has no invariant or timelessly fixed or exceptionless structures; (2) that any and all forms of right opinion or true knowledge are (or are therefore) addressed only to contingent or salient regularities of some sort; (3) that the very cognitive capacities of man, his powers of inquiry and reasoning and understanding, are in some important and ineliminable sense historically generated artifacts of his changing world; and (4) that there is no principled way of segregating the regularities of the world he maps and the regularities of his own comprehension, the regularities of his own mind. Hence, there *are* no transcendental arguments worth a tinker's damn. The red, white, and blue arguments are all in their own way quite valid.

The only trouble is this: the argument just sketched looks like a transcendental argument of its own. In fact, considerations (1)–(4) *are just what* a minimal notion of *praxis* would invoke in attempting either to subvert or transform what we may yet be prepared to call transcendental argument or transcendental reasoning—with only a modest nod in Kant's direction. Also, of course if, as we surely are, we are prepared to transform our conception of transcendental reasoning by way of (1)–(4)—or by similar means— then, clearly, we have already conceded that there need be no official line on what must be maintained in putting forward a transcendental argument.

The short way, then, with transcendental arguments is this: every would-be synthetic *a priori* judgment is itself determined under conditions that could never legitimate its being construed as strictly synthetic *a priori*, no matter how compelling it might seem: (1)–(4) could never support synthetic *a priori* findings in principle; and any inclination in their direction threatens to subvert any such findings. Then perhaps we should revise our sense of the logical syntax of transcendental judgments, and so recover the *function* of Kantian-like reflections without the disadvantage of Kant's own (now) quite impossible constraint. That would be a reason, for instance, for reconsidering "blue" arguments, whether of the progressivist sort Habermas and Peirce favor—or of the sort Karl Popper and Hilary Putnam, and Thomas Kuhn and Imre Lakatos and all inductivists favor—or other arguments of a similarly weakened sort (Karl-Otto Apel's, for instance).

II

Now, in Kant's own *Critique*, it may be impossible to find a single compendious rule for the use of the expression "transcendental." But there can be no question that what is at the heart of Kant's own daring use of the term is this: (a) that it concerns a distinct kind of knowledge (or philosophy or science), namely, second-order knowledge; (b) that it concerns a distinct kind of second-order knowledge, namely, legitimative knowledge, knowledge of how first-order knowledge is conceptually possible, knowledge of what is conceptually necessary for first-order knowledge; and (c) that it achieves a logically distinctive kind of legitimative knowledge, namely, its findings are synthetic *a priori*, unconditionally necessary, of a necessity that is strictly universal or exceptionless but also, being ampliative, of a deeper sort than that of mere formal or logical necessity.[1]

As soon as we grant this much, we are bound to worry that, for just these reasons, Kant never succeeded in disjoining, as he intended, the "transcendental" and the "transcendent." This is partly so (but only partly) because Kant sometimes slips, just when he confines his findings to the phenomenal world of experience, into taking some sort of noumenal stance with respect to it—as in the following well-known lapse, in the Transcendental Aesthetic, regarding the concept of space:

> Our exposition therefore establishes the *reality*, that is, the objective validity, of space in respect of whatever can be presented to us outwardly as object, but also at the same time the *ideality* of space in respect of things when they are considered in themselves through reason, that is, without regard to the constitution of our sensibility. We assert, then, the *empirical reality* of space, as regards all possible outer experience; and yet at the same time we assert its *transcendental ideality*—in other words, that it is nothing at all, immediately we withdraw the above condition, namely, its limitation to possible experience, and so look upon it as something that underlies things in themselves.[2]

This appears to signify not merely that the use of spatial distinctions is confined to experience, that we have no way of extending its use to things not conceived within the terms of possible experience, but also that we *know* space to be no more than "ideal," no more than a structuring feature of experience. If the *Critique* were systematically construed in this way, then Kant's characterization of our knowledge of the phenomenal world would be ineluctably tarred with noumenal privilege.

However, if we relent here, we cannot help worrying that if transcendental knowledge is a kind of "knowledge absolutely independent of all [possible] experience"—opposed in this respect to all *a posteriori* knowledge, "knowledge possible only . . . through experience"[3]—then how do we ever know that we have *a priori* knowledge and not some deceptive use of *a posteriori* knowledge? Certainly, in holding that transcendental knowledge is synthetic as well as *a priori*, Kant leans in the direction of supposing that *such* knowledge *is somehow connected* with noumenal things, about which (otherwise) we know nothing. Otherwise, he would fall into the trap posed by the lesson of (1)–(4) already cited. For, on that argument, why would not the apparent necessity of this or that transcendental judgment—in particular, why would not the force of a judgment extended nontrivially to "all possible outer experience"—be ultimately contingent? Indeed Kant does present his view in a troublesome way, as when he says: "though we cannot *know* these things [objects of experience] as things in themselves, we may yet be in position at least to *think* them as things in themselves; otherwise we should be landed in the absurd conclusion that there can be appearance without anything that appears";[4] or, again, distinguishing between colors and "objects of outer sense": "For these [colors] cannot rightly be regarded as properties of things, but only as changes in the subject, changes which may, indeed, be different for different men. . . . The true correlate of sensibility, the thing in itself, is not known, and cannot be known, through these representations; and in experience no question is ever asked in regard to it."[5] Furthermore, once this worry takes hold, we find that we cannot avoid the deepest worry in supposing that Kant has transcendental knowledge of the conceptual constraints of perception, understanding, and reason. He must be supposing, effectively, that he has knowledge of the invariant structure of a "mind" distributively discernible in every member of the species, perhaps even sharing common properties (in its exercise of reason at least) with the minds of the members of every other pertinently gifted species (however unknown), properties characteristically obscured by the empirical analysis of transient experience (for instance, regarding colors, as Kant himself observes).

We get an inkling of Kant's optimism here in specimen remarks like the following:

> If I remove from empirical knowledge all thought (through categories), no knowledge of any object remains. For through mere intuition nothing at all is thought, and the fact that this affection of sensibility is in me does not by itself amount to a relation of such representation to any object. But if, on the other hand, I leave aside all intuition, the form of thought still remains—that is, the mode of determining an object for the manifold of a possible intuition. The categories accordingly extend further than sensible intuition, since they think objects in general, without regard to the special mode (the sensibility) in which they may be given. But they do not thereby determine a greater sphere of objects.[6]

Kant appears to be suggesting that the categories are not constrained by their having application to sensible things or to whatever we might imagine in accord with *our* mode of sensible intuition. He even remarks, in the same passage, that not only concepts but "the concept of a *noumenon*" may—and must be called into play (consistently and coherently), because "we cannot assert of sensibility that it is the sole possible kind of intuition."[7]

III

Difficulties of these sorts are, of course, well-known. They justify the kind of worry that leads in the direction of "blue" and "white" arguments, but they do not automatically justify such arguments. In fact, the "blue" argument (that is, the argument our own critique means to examine) *is* simply the "red" argument illicitly *approximated* by some sort of empirical progressivism (or otherwise logically weakened justification) that could not pretend to reach or approach its objective without presupposing that its most verisimilitudinous line *was* transcendentally (transcendentally = transcendently) directed by some ideally necessary rule of reason. In any case, there is no self-evident argument in Kant that shows that there *must be* true synthetic *a priori* judgments or sound transcendental arguments. Kant claims only that there *are* true synthetic *a priori* judgments and that, *if* there are to be transcendental arguments, then there must be such truths.

The second leg of the transcendental stool is profoundly unsteady in its own way; and all of Kant's would-be specimens of the first (arithmetic truths, for instance) are notoriously uncompelling. Furthermore, if we subscribe to (1)–(4)—which we have dubbed, without ceremony, *praxist*—then there cannot be synthetic *a priori* truths or sound transcendental arguments of Kant's sort.

In a curious way, Peirce, as a "blue" philosopher, postpones the payoff of a Kantian-like transcendental argument so that it appears only as the asymptotic limit of all sequentially ordered self-corrective phases of the infinite inquiry of an infinite community of inquirers pursuing truth: "The opinion [Peirce declares] which is fated to be ultimately agreed to by all who investigate, is what we mean by the truth, and the object represented in this opinion is [the] real."[8] Peirce's most careful formulation maintains that "this conception essentially involves the notion of a *Community*, without definite limits, and capable of definite increase of knowledge."[9] So Peirce's transcendental argument concerns the directionality of diachronically distributed beliefs regarding truth and reality *only* at the limit of the (infinite) long run, hence, only with regard to the *general* progressive drift of belief, not with regard to any actual replacements of belief from particular to particular. It is easy to see, therefore, why such exotic American pragmatists as

Karl-Otto Apel and Jürgen Habermas—more robust Kantians than Peirce— would wish to insist that Peirce's optimism must harbor some more convincingly invariant rulelike presupposition (than he supposes) embedded in the ongoing rational structure of all inquiry and communication. As it happens, however, W.V. Quine had already reported in a devastating critique, well before Apel and Habermas proposed their own sanguine gloss on Peirce's formulation, the fatal weakness of Peirce's optimism. It would be hard to improve on its economy or force, and, we may suppose, it serves to subvert as well Apel's and Habermas's transcendental accommodations—whether by way of a progressive consensualism or by way of an allegedly invariant rule somehow presupposed in argumentative interchange. Quine says quite simply:

> Peirce was tempted to define truth outright in terms of scientific method as the ideal theory which is approached as a limit when the (supposed) canons of scientific method are used unceasingly on continuing experience. But there is a lot wrong with Peirce's notion, besides its assumption of a final organon of scientific method and its appeal to an infinite process. There is a faulty use of numerical analogy in speaking of a limit of theories, since the notion of limit depends on that of "nearer than" which is defined for numbers and not for theories. And . . . there is trouble in the imputation on uniqueness ("*the ideal* result").[10]

Quine does not pursue the matter in terms of its full ramifications. But his counterargument decisively shows that there *is* no possible way of pragmatizing Kant's would-be transcendental strategy by grounding knowledge in any formally or ethically responsible self-corrective process of inquiry. This rules out any simple cumulative inductivism or falsificationism as transcendental options. Yet Habermas sees himself as obliged to redeem something like inductivism as a transcendental "bridging principle" in order to secure the possibility of a rational, universal ethics—or, in fact, to secure any form of practical argument possessing objective standing.

Habermas's reasoning is rather tortured, but it will pay to have his statement before us:

> Normative claims to validity . . . *mediate a mutual dependence* of language and the social world that does not exist for the relation of language to the objective world. . . . We must distinguish between the social fact that a norm is intersubjectively recognized and its worthiness to be recognized . . .; rationally motivated assent will [have to] be combined with empirical *acquiescence* [however] effected [in order] to form a belief in legitimacy whose component parts are difficult to isolate.[11]

Habermas specifically construes the transcendental rationale as operating (in the long run) on the perceived validity of the acceptance (in the short run) of socially current norms:

> But if in the long run [he says] the social currency of a norm depends on its being accepted as valid in the group to which it is addressed and if this recognition is based in turn on the expectation that the corresponding claim to validity can be redeemed with reasons, it follows that there is a connection between the "existence" of norms and the anticipated justifiability of the corresponding "ought" statements, a connection for which there is no parallel in the ontic sphere [that is, no parallel wherever we suppose we can appeal directly to the structure of the real world].[12]

Apparently, the gradual increase in "the qualified assent of all who are or might be affected" by any socially promoted moral principle acquires validity just insofar as *that* sort of acceptance instantiates a universalizing "bridging principle" that is both the analogue of "some canon or other of induction" and also a "variant" of "the basic intuition contained in Kant's categorical imperative": "The moral principle [required, he says] is so conceived as to exclude as invalid any norm that could not meet with the qualified assent of all who are or might be affected by it."[13]

Habermas is concerned here with what is admittedly a very tricky problem. For one thing, he does not want to ground his cognitive claims about moral and practical matters in any realist presumption regarding the norms of human life: hence, he insists on a sharp disjunction between "assertoric" and "normative" claims.[14] Second, speaking in the Peircean spirit and against, say, John Rawls (and perhaps Kant himself), he holds that the required "bridging" principle cannot be "monologically" discerned or tested: it must be consensually and communicatively operative in some actual argumentative practice.[15] Third, the required moral or practical principle must be universalizable or at least must approach universality asymptotically.[16]

Now, what are the prospects of Habermas's "blue" argument? Unfortunately, there is a good deal of obscurity in the account, which, we may suspect, runs through all "blue" arguments (all arguments our "blue" critique addresses). Here, Habermas proceeds by what he calls "presuppositional analysis," which he borrows from Karl-Otto Apel. That is: "all transcendental-pragmatic arguments [he says] must satisfy" the presuppositional conditions of the discourse to which they are to be applied; only in this way, apparently, can the required universality be recovered, given that strict synthetic *a priori* truths cannot be independently discerned. The idea is, first, to avoid "ethical formalism" (along the lines indicated in the Hegelian critique of Kant) and, second, to concede that, although the practical principles adduced are logically "very strong" (being universalistic), their transcendental "status" is also "relatively weak"—in being presupposed in what we may explicate "as the meaning of normative claims to validity" *in* pertinent forms of practical argument.[17] That, you must admit, is a mouthful. What does it all mean?

The essential strategy Habermas favors is one of exposing "performative contradictions": that is, the presuppositions of practical communication and argumentation "are [said to be] identified by convincing a person who contests the hypothetical reconstructions offered that he is caught up in performative contradictions" *by* opposing those presuppositions.[18] Habermas offers as an example the rather uneasy case of doubting one's own existence (the Cartesian *cogito*). Be that as it may, and drawing on various authors, Habermas adduces principles of various kinds: "logical-semantic" principles ("No speaker may contradict himself"; "Different speakers may not use the same expression with different meanings"), pragmatic-procedural rules that may have or may lack ethical content ("Every speaker must assert only what he really believes"), and substantive argumentative rules suited to given sectors of inquiry ("Every subject with the competence to speak and act is allowed to take part in a discourse"; "Everyone is allowed to question any assertion whatever"; "No speaker may be prevented, by internal or external coercion, from exercising his rights as laid down [in the preceding two rules]").[19]

These rules of discourse, Habermas claims, must be shown to be "not mere conventions [but rather] inescapable presuppositions."[20] This is what he means by saying that they are logically "strong" (universalized) but "weak" in transcendental justification (pragmatic rather than strictly Kantian):

> We may no longer burden these arguments with the status of an a priori transcendental deduction along the lines of Kant's critique of reason. They ground only the fact that there is no identifiable alternative to our kind of argumentation. In this respect, discourse ethics, like other reconstructive sciences, relies solely on hypothetical reconstruction for which plausible confirmation must be sought.[21]

An entire battery of philosophic difficulties, however, stare us in the face. For one, Habermas freely admits that the pragmatic rules he adduces—or finds others adducing—"are not *constitutive* of discourses in the sense in which chess rules are constitutive of real chess games"; so we may "have to be content with approximations" only.[22] For a second, Habermas acknowledges "*a pluralism of ultimate value orientations*" (which defeats any sort of straightforward universalistic cognitivism—intuitionism for instance), and yet insists on "the existence of a bridging principle that makes [universal] consensus possible";[23] so it may yet be that any consensus regarding would-be pragmatic presuppositions is nothing but an artifact of different "ultimate value orientations." Third, Habermas nowhere examines the bearing—*on* the admittedly "weak status" of his own argument—*of* historicizing emancipative reason's competence *to* discern universal rules of argumentation; so a hermeneutic treatment of reason may well subvert Habermas's own universalistic pretensions.[24] For a fourth, Habermas pursues his argument without benefit of reflection on the actual features of the different sectors of practice to which he means to assign particular argumentive presuppositions—or, indeed, whether or in what way such different sectors may be justifiably compartmentalized with respect to one another; so it may even be that ethical discourse actually fails to support any universal rules—just as (as Habermas seems to concede) argumentation in aesthetic criticism pertinently fails.[25]

These four objections may be quite congenially linked with what we briefly called, earlier on, our praxist conditions (1)–(4). We may even clinch this part of the argument by observing that *if* argumentatively competent human persons were historically or socially constituted or constructed along Michel Foucault's lines, say, or even Marx's, *if* their rational competence were an artifact of their social formation, then a universal pragmatics would be quite impossible.[26] The trouble is that Habermas never addresses this possibility even as he discounts the radical criticism of his own position advanced by Hans-Georg Gadamer.[27] In any case, against his own concessions to Marxist, Frankfurt Critical, and hermeneutic considerations, Habermas blithely supposes that human persons *are* constrained in universally invariant ways and *are* transhistorically competent in discerning transcendental-pragmatic arguments. This is the upshot of "presuppositional analysis." But he never offers the slightest smidgen of evidence that the required competence actually holds. So the "blue" argument totters.

IV

Still, we want the details laid out in a clearer way.

Habermas is admirably explicit about what he is up to. He introduces a principle of universalization (U) for all candidate forms of practical reasoning—"a rule of argumentation in practical discourses," as he says—and then he "justifies" it (in the transcendental-pragmatic way) "in terms of the substance of the pragmatic presuppositions of argumentation as such in connection with an explanation of the meaning of normative claims to validity."[28] It all sounds perfectly straightforward.

Here, now, is principle (U), which in accord with G.H. Mead's notion of "ideal role taking," is, Habermas says, "intended to compel the *universal exchange of rules*":

> (U) All affected can accept the consequences and the side effects its *general* observance can be anticipated to have for the satisfaction of *everyone's* interests (and these consequences are preferred to those of known alternative possibilities for regulation).[29]

(U) seems to be formally self-consistent, but it is certainly not clear that its meaning *can* be separated from any candidate norm addressed to this or that sector of discourse. For instance, it cannot be separated from what Habermas calls principle (D), which he says is different in that it "already contains the distinctive idea of an ethics of discourse":

> (D) Only those norms can claim to be valid that meet (or could meet) with the approval of all affected in their capacity *as participants in a practical discourse.*[30]

Habermas claims that "every valid norm has to fulfill" (U) but not any particular (D); also, the rational advocacy of (D) "already *presupposes* that we *can* justify our choice of a norm." So (D) presupposes (U), our "bridging principle" in practical argumentation, now cast (as Habermas wishes) "in a way that precludes a monological application of the principle."[31] The specific rules associated with (D), those we have already sampled earlier are then collected dialectically by invoking the strategy of "performative contradiction."

(U) is *possible*—that is, possible to adhere to in a practical way—*in* the purely formal sense that it *is* self-consistent. But is it practically possible? Is it possible even in an approximative way for anyone to act in accord with (U) (abstractly), especially if it must be nonmonologically? It is certainly possible to *intend*, or to say one intends, monologically, to adhere to U (nonmonologically). Nevertheless, how could *the question of whether one adheres to (U) in practice* be decided without specifying what is meant, in (U), by the mention of "affected," "*everyone's* interests," "consequences," "side effects"? Also how could *that* information be secured without transforming (U) into (D) or some similar rule? How could one know what (U) means *nonmonologically*? Habermas never says. So it looks as if (U) is an abstraction from (D) and from similar principles, *not an independent, prior presupposition of it*—as required. If so, then Habermas's entire venture collapses.

Again, (U) may be trivialized, rendered utterly vacuous, if it means (it could quite easily be made to mean) no more than this: that whether construed monologically or nonmonologically—"similar cases must be similarly judged under similar circumstances." This last, of course, is the well-known trivialization that dogs R. M. Hare's universalizability principle.[32] It could, of course, also mean, as Hare also intends, that, in judging, one must judge relevant matters in terms of *its practical bearing on everyone and on everyone's being prepared to support a particular judgment, claim, recommendation, action, commitment or the like in terms of its effect on all.* But it's not in the least bit clear that *that* is pertinently manageable in the abstract or that, once fleshed out in any concrete nonmonological way, it would be at all reasonable. There's no question, for instance, that when I shop generously for food for my family, what I do bears on (U) as well as on (D); and yet I have no idea at all of how to invoke "performatory contradictions" to elucidate either the considerations in virtue of which I accept (U) as more than merely vacuous, or in virtue of which I could outfit (D) with suitably universal rules of moral argument. In fact, if practical questions implicate one's "life-world" in the way Habermas admits, it begins to be seriously problematic whether and why we should ever suppose that *practical* matters could be resolved in universalistic terms at *any* level of discourse.

Habermas himself is frank enough to treat "the actor," the human agent, the human person, as "a *product* of the traditions surrounding him, of groups whose cohesion is based on solidarity to which he belongs, and of processes in which he is reared."[33] In the same spirit, he says: "Practical discourse is not a procedure for generating justified norms but a procedure for testing the validity of norms that are being proposed and hypothetically considered for adoption"—that is, norms that are generated from within one's life-world but conceivably open to universalized rational support.[34] But then, (U) *and* (D) *are* frankly problematic, certainly not always invoked in pertinent discourse, and possibly never really or meaningfully invoked at all. It's hard to say.

There are still other difficulties. For one thing, although it is reasonably clear that, *in* entering a dispute or conversation, one surely presupposes *some* measure of sharing objectives, expectations, norms, conditions of intelligibility and the like, there is no reason to think that one presupposes (*or* reasonably presupposes or must presuppose ideally) that *whatever* is offered in a discursive exchange *is* or would be in accord, or would be or would need to be brought into accord, with some set of *universal* pragmatic presuppositions of the sort Habermas advances. Moreso that one presupposes that whatever facilitates a successful communication in *this* particular context of exchange will also work in *that* context or will be universalizable for all contexts of discourse, or may be assumed to be uniformly presupposed by every party or possible party to any discourse. Finally, that there could be a discourse in which *everyone* does participate, or could participate in such a way as to confirm any of Habermas's presuppositions.

Secondly, Habermas is characteristically quite casual about what exactly one does presuppose *modally* in entering a discourse. Do we, for instance, in interpreting a text, claim to understand what the author actually meant or must have meant or possibly meant? Consider the following passage, which pretty well captures Habermas's labile habit in these matters:

> The interpreter . . . understands the meaning of a text only insofar as he understands *why* the author *felt* [*fühlte*] justified in putting forth certain propositions as being true, in recognizing certain values and norms as being right, and in expressing certain experiences (or attributing them to others) as being authentic. The interpreter has to clarify the context that the author *must have* [*haben muss*] presupposed as being common knowl-

edge in the audience he was addressing if the difficulties the interpreter currently experiences with the text did not exist, or were not so difficult to resolve, at the time it was written. This step indicates the immanent rationality that interpreters *expect to find* in all utterances insofar as they ascribe them to a subject whose mental competence they have no reason to doubt in advance. Interpreters cannot understand the semantic content of a text if they do not make themselves aware of the reasons the author *could have* [*hätte . . . konnen*] brought forth in his own time and place if required to do so.[35]

But this is an utter jumble. For, if the interpreter has no reason to *expect* his "subject" not to be rational, that hardly means that he universalizes (or knows how to universalize) over reason. And if he can understand the meaning of a text only if he understands what the subject actually *"felt justified"* in believing true, then what he understands hardly bears directly on the universal conditions of rationality, or even on what it may be possible to believe. Also, if he cannot understand what another *could have* offered as reasons, in his own time, for what he said or wrote, then it seems quite impossible for him to pretend to grasp the universal conditions of rationality in any practical sense—that is, without understanding the actual range of beliefs of the societies involved.

None of this suggests the least plausibility of ever detaching (U) from the context of this or that life-world or of invoking more than trivial pronouncements about the presuppositions of discourse—although it is true enough that one need not be confined entirely within the boundaries of one's own life-world.

Finally, Habermas specifically distances himself from Apel's version of the method of "transcendental pragmatics." He finds Apel's belief that transcendental pragmatics may rightly claim "ultimate justification"—unconditional *a priori* standing—to be "inconsistent."[36] Habermas of course was immensely influenced by Apel in formulating (U) and (D) and the entire "transcendental-pragmatic" procedure. He also rightly backed away from Apel's formulation, since he realized that it violated the pragmatist's constraint and therefore returned us to no more than a "dialogized" analogue of Kant's transcendental claims. For his own part, however, Apel was also right, for *he* realized that he could not offer any genuinely transcendental claims unless, like Kant *or* Peirce, he was willing to advance an unconditional ampliative universal rule.

Apel's thesis, therefore, is both fascinating and preposterous, a genuinely explicit Peirceanized version of Kant's transcendental maneuver:

I should like to reconstruct [says Apel] the ethical preconditions for the possibility and validity of human argumentation and, consequently, of logic. This attempt differs, however, from Kant's classical transcendental philosophy in that it does not see the "highest power"—which transcendental reflection takes as its starting-point—in the "unity of consciousness of the object and self-consciousness" that is posited in a "methodologically solipsistic" manner, but rather in the "intersubjective unity of interpretation" *qua* understanding of meaning and *qua* consensus of truth. This unity of interpretation must, in principle, be attainable in the unlimited community of those engaged in argumentation by virtue of the experience derived from experiment and interaction, if argumentation is to have any *meaning* at all. To this extent, my attempt is conceived as a *transformation of transcendental philosophy that is critical of meaning*, one which develops from the *a priori* fact of argumentation as an irreducible, quasi-Cartesian starting-point.[37]

Apel's confidence in the infinite community—which he so extravagantly claims is the *necessary* "transcendental-pragmatic" condition on which "argumentation is to have *any meaning* at all"—is precisely what Quine, as we saw, had neatly exposed as Peirce's fatally flawed vision. Furthermore, Apel's argument, like Habermas's, has absolutely nothing to say about whatever, in this sector of inquiry or that, we may reasonably take to be the given cognitive possibilities for which transcendental reasoning should account.

Now then, to the extent that he backs away from this unconditional claim, either Habermas provides no proper basis for overcoming (on second-order grounds) the deep historical contingency and horizonal bias of particular societies, or else he must be extraordinarily more sanguine, inductively, than is either Peirce or Apel regarding the potentially vicious play of (*first-order*) universal consensus in the short run. In either case, the vacuity, regress, arbitrariness, or privilege of these two options is clear enough— which, by the way, was just the point of Hans Albert's use of the "Munchhausen trilemma" that both Apel and Habermas so futilely rail against.[38]

Apel explicitly regards his transcendental claims as "*unconditionally*" telling, that is, as he says, "regardless of empirical conditions."[39] This alone subverts his (and Habermas's) objections to the effectiveness of the "trilemma" (though it may indeed implicate the Popperians as well); it also confirms, for instance in the claim Apel makes for regarding his own reasoning as a "transcendental-pragmatic radicalization of the later Wittgenstein's work,"[40] the deep inconsistency of advocating both a universalism and a historicism.[41] For his part, Habermas cleaves more closely to praxist and historicist constraints; hence, where Apel is dogmatic, Habermas is merely arbitrary.[42]

V

What all this shows is that "blue" arguments, like "red" arguments, cannot be reconciled with anything like our conditions (1)–(4). Once you give up privileged foundations, once you admit the horizoned bias of judgment and action, the indissoluble symbiosis of word and world or subject and object, every form of strict universalism must be rejected. Kantian-transcendental arguments are out, therefore, and "transcendental-pragmatic" arguments as well. It is an easy step to extend the force of these reflections to "white" arguments also. For "white" arguments (once again: the arguments our "white" critique addresses) merely claim that all forms of second-order legitimation must be transcendental arguments in something like Kant's sense (or Husserl's, of course), Peirce's, Apel's, or Habermas's. But that is a *non sequitur*.

By this time, the *locus classicus* of "white" arguments lies in Richard Rorty's account—or, perhaps, in Jean-François Lyotard's as well—although those two thinkers are hardly of one mind. The common burden of their separate views is this: that transcendental arguments are essentially second-order legitimative arguments, *and* that legitimative arguments *are* invariably full-blooded-transcendental arguments. The slippage is plain enough. The deeper question that confronts us, however, is whether there *could be* fruitful, even indispensable, legitimative arguments that are *not* transcendental in either the "red" or "blue" senses—that "white" theories simply fail to acknowledge. One sees this, for instance, in Rorty's contrast between pragmatism and Kantian-like realism:

> [Consider] pragmatism's claim that truth is simply the most coherent and powerful theory, and that no relation of "correspondence to reality" need be invoked to clarify "true" or "knowledge." This claim, which would put out of court the traditional notion of "legitimizing knowledge claims" (and thus the traditional conception of the function of transcendental arguments), is opposed by what I shall be calling "metaphysical realism"— typified for my purposes by [Wilfrid] Sellars, [Jay] Rosenberg and [Hilary] Putnam. . . . I shall say that any transcendental argument which has as its aim to guarantee correspondence of logic, or language, or the practice of rational inquiry to the world is a "realist" argument. Such an argument has as its paradigms the arguments (those of the Transcendental Deduction and the Refutation of Idealism) which Kant used to illustrate his claim that "only the transcendental idealist can be an empirical realist."[43]

Rorty goes on at once to affirm that "Philosophy *does* depend on transcendental arguments for its existence, *if* philosophy is conceived of as a nonempirical criticism of culture. But there are [he adds] conceptions of philosophy (e.g., those of Heidegger, Dewey, and the later Wittgenstein) in which philosophy is *not* concerned with the legitimation of knowledge-claims."[44] So, first of all, Rorty does not concede that there is any positive form of legitimative argument that is not transcendental in the pejorative sense given; and, second, he insists that there are other uses of philosophy that are not legitimative (what he elsewhere calls "edifying philosophy").[45] Now, Rorty's summary of the defeat of "red" and "blue" arguments—

Kantianism in general—is extremely telling. It follows, as is well-known, the repudiation of the so-called "scheme-content distinction" offered by Donald Davidson.[46] (It needs to be borne in mind, though we cannot pursue the matter here, that Rorty falls in with Davidson's profoundly mistaken notion that there cannot be any discernibly diverging conceptual schemes—the denial of which, first of all, does not entrench the distinction between "conceptual scheme" and "conceptual content" that Davidson and Rorty oppose, and, second, does not entail the incoherence Davidson extravagantly draws from the first. It is the fatal combination of these two notions that leads Rorty to believe that philosophy cannot but be transcendental in the pejorative sense.)[47] Still, Rorty's account deserves a closer look. "To be transcendental," to have a distinctively Kantian flavor, Rorty offers, a realist argument must be such that

> (d) The scheme-content distinction is construed as a distinction between that which is better known to us (our subjectivity, roughly) and that which is less well-known to us.
> (e) our "legitimating" transcendental knowledge of the necessary truth that content will correspond to scheme, is made possible by the fact that our subjectivity (the scheme) *creates* the content.[48]

Rorty's conditions (a)–(c)—preceding these two—are more general constraints to the effect that "a distinction between scheme and content is assumed," that "legitimation" is needed beyond the "internal coherence" of any given scheme, and that legitimative arguments need not be particularly informed about the details of the claims involved. Rorty then proceeds to mount an argument to counter the Kantian argument, "by saying that 'Only the pragmatist can be an empirical realist'—that is, only if we give up the notion of legitimation can we rest content with accepting the knowledge-claims of science at face value. . . ."[49]

The counterargument to Rorty is marvelously simple: legitimation need not be transcendental in *any* sense inclined to favor *any* of Rorty's conditions (a)–(e); and yet there remains an argument that leads us to suppose that legitimation cannot be convincingly abandoned. Notice that, on Rorty's own view, science's "knowledge-claims" are to be honored in some way *detached from a Kantian-like legitimation*. Now, if that much should be granted, then it is quite reasonable (though not itself a Kantian argument) that: (i) the complexity and risk of making first-order truth-claims invite *some* form of critical legitimation of the sources of confidence about the "empirical realist" status of *such* claims; (ii) there need be no privileged or foundational distinction and no principled distinction in epistemic power between first-order and second-order claims; (iii) legitimative arguments may be conceded to obtain in a symbiotized space of subject and object, in which no viable "scheme-content distinction" is presupposed; and (iv) legitimative arguments may, in fact, obtain quite coherently within the constraints of (1)–(4) that we tallied at the very beginning of this account.

You may well ask what the function of such legitimative reflection would be. The answer once again is straightforward. If we *did* have privileged knowledge at the level of first-order claims, then legitimative (second-order) arguments would already be entailed *in* such first-order discourse: we would not need to make a special effort to formulate them; and if we had privileged transcendental knowledge, then we could not fail to have *some* privileged first-order knowledge as well. But if, in pursuing knowledge-claims within the constraints of our original tally (1)–(4), we lacked *any* cognitive privilege at either the first- or second-order level, *then we should need to make a continually revised pragmatic bet as to how best to pursue science (any rigorous inquiry) from among the proliferating alternative strategies we might other-wise pursue.*

On the argument, *Rorty's* own conditions are the ones that best show the inescapability of legitimative reasoning. We *cannot* afford to follow a mere laissez-faire policy in inquiry. For example, *if* Quine's argument against Peirce holds, then Peircean optimistic fallibilism is simply misguided; and *if it is misguided,* then, precisely because Peirce *is* so aware of the paradox of possessing infinitely many abductive possibilities within the confines of finite inquiry,[50] *we* must, acknowledging Peirce's perception, do the best we can *within* the constraints already collected. (In fact, Rorty's appeal to "coherence" and "power" pretty well admits the same point, but neglects to say so.)

We may, if we care, call such recovered arguments "transcendental" as long as the label is not misunderstood. In any case, they are legitimative— in the sense in which: (a) the distinction between first-and second-order questions is admitted without admitting cognitive privilege; (b) that very distinction is itself a second-order distinction, also without privilege; and (c) legitimative arguments offer at best candidates for universalized conditions regarding the possibility of knowledge or of *de re* necessities regarding knowledge—under the blind constraints of horizonal bias, the symbiosis of word and world, and the rest—without ever overtaking the contingencies of historical life.[51] In a word, legitimative arguments (or "transcendental" arguments, if we may reclaim the term) are as blind to privilege, as much captured by the controlling features of our form of life, as are the (our) first-order claims that they propose to monitor. They are synthetic arguments, therefore, clearly ampliative; and they are, if we care to put things this way, "*a priori*"—in the new sense that they are concerned to speculate about (on grounds *internal* to our inquiry and form of life) what we might then suppose are the necessary conditions *external* to that inquiry that first makes it possible to support particular first-order claims. However, they cannot be synthetic *a priori.*

The upshot is this. The best option against "white" arguments is to hold: first, that legitimative arguments need not be Kantian-like transcendental arguments; and, second, that truth-claims cannot arise without implicating legitimative claims. This *is* a legitimative or transcendental argument of the new-fangled sort we are proposing. Furthermore, wherever we make more profound or problematic the terms of our so-called praxist conditions (1)–(4), it will turn out that some form of relativism, of plausibilizing, of open-textedness, of contingency, of lack of categorical force, of weak universalizing are bound to obtain. Here, it pays to bear in mind that these looser features of legitimative arguments tend to arise wherever the following themes are salient: first, that persons or selves are culturally or artifactually constituted; second, that, however abstractly schematized, human thought and behavior are inseparable from the immediate context of surviving in the world; and third, that theorizing is itself a form of just such practice. These considerations form the very center of what we mean by *praxis*, by the bearing of "everyday life" on our philosophy, and especially by Marx's master contribution to understanding our original tally (1)–(4):

> even the most abstract categories, [says Marx,] despite their validity—precisely because of their abstractness—for all epochs, are nevertheless, in the specific character of this abstraction, themselves likewise a product of historical relations, and possess their full validity only for and within these relations.[52]

It is perhaps this single notion—that thought and knowledge are social *products*—that completely subverts the transcendental line of thinking ranging through "red," "white," and "blue" arguments and that brings us closer, without disallowing legitimative reflection, to the philosophical orientation that dominates the close of our century.

NOTES

1. All references to Kant are to *Immanuel Kant's Critique of Pure Reason*, corr. trans. by Norman Kemp Smith (London: Macmillan, 1953). See, here, B 3–4, pp. 13–14.
2. Ibid., A 28=B 44.
3. Ibid., B 3.
4. Ibid., B xxvi–xxvi.
5. Ibid., B 45. Cf. B xx, A 249–250. I have benefited, here, from the discussion in Jonathan Bennett's, *Kant's Analytic* (Cambridge: Cambridge University Press, 1966), §8.
6. Ibid., B 309.
7. Ibid., B 310.
8. *Collected Works of Charles Sanders Peirce*, 8 vols., eds. Charles Hartshorne, Paul Weiss, and Arthur W. Burks (Cambridge: Harvard University Press, 1951–59), 5.407.

9. Ibid., 5.311. See, for instance, Karl-Otto Apel, "From Kant to Peirce: The Semiotical Transformation of Transcendental Logic," *Towards a Transformation of Philosophy*, trans. by Glyn Adey and David Frisby (London: Routledge and Kegan Paul, 1980).
10. W. V. Quine, *Word and Object* (Cambridge: MIT Press, 1960), p. 23.
11. Jürgen Habermas, "Discourse Ethics. Notes on a Program of Philosophical Justification," *Moral Consciousness and Communicative Action*, trans. by Christian Lenhardt and Shierry Weber Nicholsen (Cambridge: MIT Press, 1990), pp. 61–62.
12. Ibid., p. 62.
13. Ibid., p. 63.
14. Ibid., pp. 57–62.
15. Ibid., pp. 57–60.
16. Ibid., p. 64.
17. Ibid., pp. 78–83; also, "Moral Consciousness and Communicative Action," *op. cit.*, p. 116. Habermas relies rather heavily on Apel, "The A priori of the Communication Community and the Foundations of Ethics: The Problem of a Rational Foundation of Ethics in the Scientific Age," *op. cit.* Cf., also, particularly, A. J. Watt, "Transcendental Arguments and Moral Principles," *Philosophical Quarterly*, XXV (1975), which Habermas cites.
18. Ibid., p. 89.
19. Ibid., pp. 87–89. These are drawn from R. Alexy, "Eine Theorie des praktischen Diskurses," in W. Oelmüller (ed.), *Normenbegründung, Normendurchsetzung* (Paderborn: 1978).
20. Ibid., p. 89.
21. Ibid., p. 116.
22. Jürgen Habermas, "Discourse Ethics," p. 91.
23. Ibid., p. 76.
24. See, for instance, Hans-Georg Gadamer, "On the Scope and Function of Hermeneutical Reflection," trans. by G. B. Hess and R. E. Palmer, *Philosophical Hermeneutics*, trans. by and ed. by David E. Linge (Berkeley: University of California Press, 1976).
25. Habermas, "Discourse Ethics," p. 105. Here, Habermas follows Albrecht Wellmer's unpublished manuscript, "Reason and the Limits of Rational Discourse," which he cites.
26. See Jürgen Habermas, "What Is Universal Pragmatics?" *Communication and the Evolution of Society*, trans. by Thomas McCarthy (Boston: Beacon Press, 1979), for the original version of his thesis—which confirms his indifference to history and the detailed context of discourse.
27. See Jürgen Habermas, *On the Logic of the Social Sciences*, trans. by Sheirry Weber Nicholsen and Jerry A. Stark (Cambridge: MIT Press, 1988), III, §8.
28. Habermas, "Moral Consciousness and Communication Action," p. 116.
29. "Discourse Ethics," p. 65. See, also, George Herbert Mead, "Fragments on Ethics," *Mind, Self, and Society* (Chicago: University of Chicago Press, 1954), pp. 379ff; cited by Habermas.
30. Ibid., p. 66.
31. Ibid.
32. See R. M. Hare, *Freedom and Reason* (Oxford: Clarendon Press, 1963), chaps. 2–3; cf., also, p. 139.
33. Habermas, "Moral Consciousness and Communicative Action," p. 135.

32JOSEPH MARGOLIS

34. "Discourse Ethics," p. 103; see all of III, §8.
35. Habermas, "Reconstruction and Interpretation in the Social Sciences," *op. cit.*, p. 50; italics added.
36. Ibid., p. 96.
37. Apel, "The Communication Community and the Foundations of Ethics," p. 267.
38. See Hans Albert, *Treatise on Critical Reason*, trans. by Mary Varney Rorty (Princeton: Princeton University Press, 1985), Preface to the American Edition and chap. 1.
39. "The Communication Community and the Foundations of Ethics," p. 270; cf., also, pp. 262–269.
40. Ibid., p. 269; cf. also, "Discourse Ethics," pp. 79–80.
41. See Joseph Margolis, *Pragmatism without Foundations; Reconciling Realism and Relativism* (Oxford: Basil Blackwell, 1986), chaps. 2, 7.
42. I may say that, in a conference sponsored by the Greater Philadelphia Philosophy Consortium, held at Bryn Mawr College, Bryn Mawr, Pennsylvania, February 19, 1983, I had occasion to draw this inconsistency to Habermas's attention—particularly but not merely because he appealed in his talk to "all possible worlds." I suggested to him that he was not "entitled" (as a historicist-and praxist-minded thinker) to invoke that or any such notion. At the time, he suggested that "we might discuss this in Germany sometime."
43. Richard Rorty, "Transcendental Arguments, Self-Reference, and Pragmatism," in Peter Bieri, Rolf-Peter Horstmann, and Lorenz Krüger (eds.), *Transcendental Arguments and Science; Essays in Epistemology* (Dordrecht: D. Reidel, 1979), pp. 77, 79.
44. Ibid., p. 78.
45. See Richard Rorty, *Philosophy and the Mirror of Nature* (Princeton: Princeton University Press, 1979), chap. 8.
46. See Donald Davidson, "On the Very Idea of a Conceptual Scheme," *Inquiries into Truth and Interpretation* (Oxford: Clarendon Press, 1984).
47. Cf. Margolis, *Pragmatism without Foundations*, pp. 79–81.
48. "Transcendental Arguments, Self-Reference, and Pragmatism," p. 79.
49. Ibid., p. 84.
50. Cf. *Collected Papers of Charles Sanders Peirce*, 5.47, 5.623.
51. I have attempted a fuller account of these features in *Pragmatism without Foundations*, chap. 11.
52. Karl Marx, *Grundrisse; Foundations of the Critique of Political Economy*, trans. by Martin Nicolaus (New York: Vintage Press, 1973), p. 105. Cf., also, Joseph Margolis, "The Novelty of Marx's Theory of Praxis," *Journal for the Theory of Social Behaviour*, XIX (1989).

2

Transcendental Philosophy and Life-World

J. N. Mohanty

A Note About the Meaning of "Transcendental"

Even after Kant and Husserl, it is surprising that it should be necessary to distinguish between "transcendent" and "transcendental". Yet many authors, and especially critics of transcendental philosophy, mistake the transcendental for the transcendent. So it would be helpful to reiterate at the beginning that the domain of the transcendental is not one which transcends the empirical, or lies beyond it, raised high above it, belonging to a Platonic realm of supersensuous realities. It is rather that which constitutes, and thereby, renders the empirical possible.

However, to this last statement, we need to add a note. While it is usual to contrast the transcendental with the empirical, *that* is *not* the fundamental contrast whether for Kant or for Husserl. Not for Kant, because for him the transcendental is the *a priori* condition of the possibility of empirical cognition as well as of synthetic *a priori* knowledge (in mathematics and in physics). Consequently, the transcendental (pertaining to the *a priori* constitution of the faculties of sensibility and understanding) explains how any cognition (empirical as well as *a priori*) is possible. In Husserl's thinking, the basic contrast is between the constitut*ing* and the constitut*ed*: to the latter belong material objects as much as cultural objects, individuals as much as essences, numbers as much as logical forms. Nothing that is constituted is transcendental. The transcendental is the life of consciousness, intrinsically intentional and temporal, meaning-conferring and synthesizing, objectivating and interpreting.

If the fundamental contrast is *not* between the transcendental and the empirical (for both Kant and Husserl), it would be mistaken from the perspective of Husserlian phenomenology to claim that the transcendental is

33

a priori. If all *a priori* is not transcendental (the mathematical *a priori*, e.g., is not), neither is the transcendental *a priori*. Thus the transcendental ego as such is not an *eidos*, although one can speak of the *eidos* "transcendental ego". A transcendental ego is an ego with its own transcendentally purified (through epoché) stream of experience, in which case the locution "transcendental experience" has an undeniable legitimacy.

Two Senses of "Subjectivity"

For the purpose of bringing out the full power of transcendental thinking, it is necessary to distinguish between a narrow and a wide sense of the constitut*ing* domain. In the narrow sense, it is the domain of consciousness; in the wider sense, it is the domain of subjectivity. Obviously, for my present purpose, "subjectivity" has a wider extension than "consciousness".[1] Consciousness is a subset of the domain of subjectivity, and—as a consequence—not all subjectivity is consciousness. Thus, e.g., bodily subjectivity—the subjectivity of "oriented" movement—is not consciousness. What characterizes the entire domain of subjectivity is intentionality, but all intentionality is not intentionality of an act. Even the unconscious which presumably inhabits and underlies consciousness is not material, but rather subjective unconscious, consisting in unconscious intentionalities. These distinctions need to be kept in mind if we are to be able to evaluate the rather too often advanced claims that the corporeality of the self as also the presence of the unconscious in the heart of consciousness militate against transcendental philosophy. They limit the power of consciousness, but do not affect the constitutive scope of subjectivity. The Kantian categories are constitutive forms of consciousness, just as the Kantian forms of intuition and schematism *via* imagination are operations of subjectivity which fall outside the limits of consciousness. The constituting, and so transcendental domain, in Husserl's philosophy, is subjectivity, and not restricted to consciousness.

Two Senses of "Esssence"

It is also necessary to be clear about the logical relation between transcendental philosophy and essentialism. More often than not, it is taken for granted that a transcendental philosophy is essentialistic. While this larger question will not be discussed in this essay; it is however a preliminary requisite for a discussion of this question that we be clear as to what "essence" could mean in the context of transcendental philosophy. There is a certain *prima facie* opposition between essentialism and transcendental philosophy inasmuch as the former lends support to a dogmatic ontology (and a dogmatic epistemology of intuition, of eidetic intuition in this case) and the latter generates the spirit of critical overcoming of any ontology and dissolution of any provisional givenness by exposing their hidden, anonymous constitution. At the same time, since a theory of transcendental constitution can only *begin* with what is already constituted, or rather with its *sense*, it cannot afford to indulge in that seemingly radical critique which begins by "suspecting" that very constituted sense. Consequently, a certain kind of essentialism is not only compatible with, but goes with transcendental philosophy. For such an essentialism, the *essence* is constituted, has had a history, and thus in Hegel's sense, has come about, "*was gewesen ist*". At the same time, being tied to the idea of meaning (*Sinn*), the essence becomes relativized to a certain perspective and hovers in between a purely *de re* and a purely *de dicto* construction. What is essential and what is accidental to an entity are thereby relativized to the perspective of the investigator, to the meaning one assigns to that entity. The two conceptions of essence I have in mind are then: the classical, which is based on separating the invariant features from the total content of a thing: and the phenomenological which results from "transforming" every content of the *what* of a thing into an essence of detaching it from its existence here and now.

TWO FORMS OF TRANSCENDENTAL PHILOSOPHY

We can now introduce the important distinction between a transcendental philosophy which, à la Kant, investigates the *a priori* conditions of the possibility of a given body of *truths* such as (in Kant's case) Euclidean geometry and Newtonian physics; and a transcendental philosophy—à la Husserl—which, not committed to any such privileged body of truths, would enquire into the constitutive conditions and origin of any such theory regarded as a *meaning*—structure (its truth-claim suspended) as well as into the constitution of the prescientific perceptual world. With this difference in the nature of the tasks undertaken, the two conceptions of transcendental subjectivity also differ. In the Kantian sort of philosophy, the transcendental constitutive source is a pure, nonempirical, also an ahistorical formal consciousness whose structure corresponds to the categorial features of Newtonian mathematical physics. In the Husserlian sort of philosophy, the constituting subjectivity is concrete, sensuous-hyletic and also intentionally meaning-bestowing, corporeal and historically developing, anonymously constituting and reflectively discovering its operations. It is this latter sort of transcendental philosophy with its idea of a concrete constituting subjectivity which is the concern of this essay. This constituting domain is transcendental in the second of the two senses of "transcendental" distinguished above; it is essential in the second of the two mentioned senses; it is subjectivity in the second of the two defined senses.

The Transcendental–Empirical Distinction

As distinguished from the Kantian philosophy, for a phenomenological transcendental philosophy, transcendental subjectivity and empirical subjectivity do not form two distinct domains, but are one and the same life of consciousness considered from two different perspectives. Considered as a part of nature, as subject to the laws (especially causal) of nature, as belonging to a natural entity (i.e., to a physical, biological, and psychic being called "man") in whom it is caused by external and internal causal conditions, it is empirical. Considered as that through which nature receives its meaning as "material", "biological", or "psychic" being, which provides the access to all that is, but for whose internal structure no world as a world (i.e., as an organized whole of objects, could be presented) subjectivity is transcendental. "Being natural" (or a part or a product of nature) is an interpretation of subjectivity of itself, but as the source of this, indeed of any such, interpretation (both of itself and of its world) it is transcendental. This way of distinguishing the two applies to every component or layer of subjectivity. The body, observed from outside and thematized by objective sciences, is a natural entity. The same body, as lived from within, as felt and experienced by itself, is transcendentally subjective inasmuch as its intentions and intentionally movements and projects confer meaning upon the surrounding world as well as upon itself.

Construed in this manner, the understanding of transcendental subjectivity as the form-giver—with the associated picture of someone (the putative transcendental ego) who legislates from above—needs to be abandoned. Conscious life is not a chaotic disarray of sensations, but always meaningful intending of objects belonging to a world, and this intending is made possible by consciousness's own inherent structures through which multiplicities are unified at every level. No absolutely rock-bottom givens and no absolutely empty forms are needed. Sensations emerge as organized into the perception of objects; perceptions of objects emerge against the background of a larger horizon; impulses and desires are organized into meaningful goal-directed actions; and actions are organized as exhibiting a character; and a character as characterizing a whole life. These organizations exhibit principles of organization and categories of meaningfulness. To say that they are unified by an ego, a self, a subject, is to say that these principles and categories constitute experience as it grows and develops. The putative ego is a unity that comes about as a result of modes of synthesis inherent in a conscious life.

Regarding the empirical-transcendental distinction, I have elsewhere advanced three claims.[2] First, I have claimed that transcendental subjectivity is *ontologically* prior to the empirical-causal order. Also I have, claimed that the life of consciousness, *in itself*, is not mundane but transcendental. More so, I have maintained that the *concept* of transcendental subjectivity has superior explanatory power. Against these three claims, David Carr has raised the following criticisms.[3] Carr first argues, that *only if* the empirical-causal order is considered as a meaning-structure (this antecedent is not his but mine) must it then be traced back to its constitutive origin in the transcendental, as all meanings must be. However, this conclusion follows a certain perspective of the empirical-causal order, not otherwise. Second, my contention that phenomenological reduction shows consciousness to be, in itself, transcendental, begs the issues, for the reduction presupposes a prior decision not to consider consciousness as mundane. Third, the physicalist and the existentialist can have a place in their schemes for intentional meaning-bestowing acts; they can explain these latter *in their own terms*, if not, to be sure, in terms of transcendental constitution. In that case, my claim that "transcendental subjectivity" has greater and more comprehensive explanatory power must be mistaken. The consequence being that the university-claim of the transcendental philosopher is as much based on his prior decision, as is the universality-claim of the physicalist.

Carr's first argument implies that the transcendental philosopher must have to show that the empirical-causal order is a meaning-structure. Since Kant and Husserl both show this, in their different ways, I need not repeat their arguments here. However, if such an argument is admitted as being reasonably plausible, it would seem one cannot stop there; one must be willing to admit that even the transcendental structures—including the transcendental subjectivity itself—is no less a meaning-structure. I have, at various places, conceded that the talk of transcendentality itself is an interpretation taken over from the history of Western thought. In that case, the truly transcendental is that which is the source even of this interpretation, the source of all interpretations—the historically developing life of the spirit (to use a Hegelian locution). Carr's second argument rests upon the question: what could possibly motivate the transcendental reduction? If reduction is to open up access to the transcendental domain, the reduction has to be motivated from within the mundane order. This question has been discussed in the literature at length, and such commentators as Eugen Fink and Ludwig Landgrebe have taken part in the discussion. Three answers are suggested. First, reduction is totally unmotivated; in exercising reduction the philosopher is exercising his freedom not to participate in the beliefs of the natural standpoint. The second answer is that reduction is motivated by one of many possible mundane motives—e.g., the idea of philosophy as first science or the idea of providing foundation for all cognition, these ideas being available from the history of human thought. The third response insists on a certain ambiguity in the entire situation: in the natural attitude, reduction appears completely unmotivated; in a philosophical attitude which seeks to understand the natural attitude, it finds sustenance in the historically available ideas of first science and foundational cognition; but the true sense of reduction emerges only at the end and not at the beginning. The charge of begging the issue has to be examined in the light of these three possibilities. But while doing so one needs to also bear in mind that the reduction is *not* a method to isolate a new domain of being—Husserl's misleading locutions to that effect notwithstanding—but to understand our experiencing-of-the-world in its inmost nature as meaning-bestowing and constitutive of the world.

At this point, Carr's third worry confronts us. Why should what reduction "lays bare" be regarded as the *inmost* nature of our experience-of-the-world? At most, this is just another way of looking at things. How does one establish the superiority of this way of observing the many others—the physicalist, the psychologistic or the existential? My point is that the physicalist, e.g., has no plausible account of the meaning—bestowing function of intentionality, whereas the transcendental philosopher has an explanation of physics. Let me, however, further elaborate upon this contention. The physicalist's explanation of intentionality would not only relegate intentionality-phenomenon to a phenomenal status, but would, in the long run, *refuse* to find a place for it in the scheme of things as envisioned in physicalism. He would refuse to do so not because he is hardheaded, and were he more liberal he could admit intentionality into his scheme, but because the scheme itself has no place for it. So his explanation of intentionality has to culminate in a rejection of the explicandum. Now, consider the other possibility: the transcendental philosopher explains physics by assigning to it a phenomenal status (as did Kant) and/or giving an account of the interpretive acts that go into the constitution of physics as a theory (which would involve an account of the constitution of logic, pure mathematics, measurement theory, and something similar to Husserl's account of Galilean physics in the *Crisis*). He may have to go beyond this, and account for what more, beyond physics, is involved in physicalism. But in no case does he need to reject them as simply false. He would have done so, if he had his own ontology, his own preferred picture of the world, e.g., a sort of pan—psychism or an idealistic metaphysics. Since he abjures all ontologies as constituted theories, he need not say that physics or physicalism is simply false. This is what I meant when I said that the transcendental point of view has superior, more comprehensive, explanatory power.

Carr states the problem in a manner which makes it appear almost insoluble: "Perhaps, they [the physicalist and the existentialist] cannot *account* for these acts in transcendental—phenomenological terms; but then that is not their job. Science provides causal accounts and existentialism provides existential accounts. To ask them to provide transcendental accounts would be like asking phenomenology to give causal or existential accounts." Carr's statement concedes that I do not want this to be so. The impossibility of phenomenology's giving a causal account or of physics's giving a constitutive account is trivial. In comparing the two points of view, I was not asking: which, of the two, can do *both* the jobs, or which (of all possible points of view) can take over the jobs of all the rest. I was asking which, of the two, can have an account of the possibility of the other's *theory* without simply rejecting it as being false?

In addition, Carr raises the question, which would seem to be unavoidable for philosophy, Which one—the transcendental subjectivity or empirical subjectivity—is the real me? Am I, my true self, an intentional, meaning-giving, nature- and world-constituting being? Am I a natural, causally conditioned being? Note that the questions, Am I embodied or not?, Am I historical or ahistorical?, are, at this level, not decisive questions, for, as I have argued elsewhere[4] and as phenomenology recognized, contrary to the philosophical tradition, transcendental subjectivity is historical and corporeal as well. More so, the decisive question here is if "transcendental" and "empirical-natural" are two ways of considering the same thing, namely, my conscious life or life of consciousness, what is this life of consciousness (within which my sense of my own "I" is constituted) in itself: is it one or the other, or is it neither?

My contention is: transcendental philosophy need not make a metaphysical assertion as to what my self is. It can show only the priority of the transcendental perspective insofar as it can critically reflect upon its other, the natural; but, one could also say, it, namely the transcendental, presupposes the natural as the *given*, already available, upon which to reflect. Furthermore, transcendental philosophy cannot answer the question "what is the mode of being of transcendental subjectivity?" (a question which was posed to Husserl by Heidegger) because the very sense of "being," of "reality," or even of really real" would have transcendental explications or constitutive origin. The transcendental, then, has to be located beyond being and nonbeing, beyond any ontology.

Alternately, if one wants to construct a metaphysics of the self on the basis of transcendental phenomenology, one may construe the transcendental as a possibility of self-reflection, self-critique, self-understanding, and self-legitimation—a possibility which defines me as a thinking, rational being. Such a possibility of rational selfhood may then be regarded as *founded upon* a *given* experiential and existential basis of facthood, in which case one can speak of "layers of selfhood" rather than of *the* real self. However, to develop such a thesis is beyond the scope of this paper.

TRANSCENDENTAL PHILOSOPHY AND THE LIFE-WORLD

One of Husserl's great achievements was to sketch the possibilities of transcendental reflection to its outermost limits in order to encompass within its scope what always resisted its domination, namely, the everyday, concrete, world or the life-world. This is in sharp contrast to the classical transcendental philosophy which was a philosophy of science, and dealt with perception (Kant's synthetic *a posteriori* judgment) only in so far as perception was incipient physics or the perceptual world was the world of physics. It should be recognized, however, that Kant, of whom the above characterization is true, went beyond the limits of philosophy of science when he thematized, in his third critique, nature as it is the object of aesthetic and teleological judgments.[5]

Husserl's thematization of the life-world should not be read as a radical departure from his earlier mode of thinking. On the contrary, its avowed aim is to overcome a naivity of classical transcendental philosophy by making explicit an unacknowledged presupposition—the presupposition of the life-world as the forgotten "foundation of sense" for physics and mathematics. Husserl's efforts in the *Crisis* consist not alone in bringing to light this forgotten foundation of modern science, but also in pushing through questions regarding the transcendental constitution of the life-world itself. First, there is the question, How do the sciences arise from the life-world? While the general answer to this is indicated by the world "idealization," a detailed execution of the solution would involve how idealization works in the case of the mathematical sciences, how idealization is involved in the application of mathematics to the experienced world, as also how idealization, in the form of empirical typification, works in the social and human sciences.

In addition to and more fundamental than this, there is the transcendental question, what sort of intentionalities operate in the constitution of the life-world itself?—a question which itself may consist in various layers of questioning, not to speak of the equivocation of the very concept of the life-world as between the perceived world and the cultural world. The latter being explicitly historical, the former containing an ahistorical core even if we grant that the way things are perceived, their perceptual meanings, are culturally and so historically conditioned.

In view of the possibility of such questionings it would be mistaken to regard the life-world as a foundation beyond and behind which it is impossible to penetrate. It is therefore ironical that many antifoundationalists would stop at the world of everyday *praxis* as the ultimate foundation for all theoretical enquiry.

PRACTICE, PRAXIS, AND TRANSCENDENTAL QUESTIONING

Life-world is a world of *practice* (of action, making and doing) and *praxis* (of social action, of the production of goods, the exchange of goods and the distribution of goods). It would however be a mistake to say that these modes of *acting* exhaust the life-world in all its dimensions. For example, there are religious, aesthetic, and ethical dimensions. By virtue of these, the world as well as things in the world are presented to subjects inhabiting that world with different sorts of values—as useful, as sacred, as beautiful or—all of which can be brought under the general heading of "cultural." It would also be a mistake to hold that the life-world is not a *cognitively* apprehended world, or that things in the life-world are not *objects* of cognition but are simply acted upon and evaluated. It is perhaps plausible to hold that the cognition that we have within the life-world is not yet the highly idealized form of cognition that is exemplified in the natural sciences or in mathematicized and philosophical disciplines. However, there is cognition—as much as practice, praxis, and valuation. There is a core of perceptual cognition at the heart of the experience of the life-world—a perceptual cognition which is inextricably linked with action and evaluation. It would be a mistake to say that such cognition and action present things, events, persons, and situations in their unique individuality, as *this-there* in their *hic-et-nunc* and then to draw the consequence that such unique individuality cannot be "reconstructed", or "retrieved" within philosophy. A rather naive example of such sceptical questioning is the well-known challenge made by one Herr Krug to Hegel asking him if he could deduce the pen with which he was writing from the categories of his *Logic*.

It is against such a scepticism, that I will make the following remarks: things are cognized, acted upon, evaluated not alone as unique individuals, but also, simultaneously, as exemplifying *types*. The this-here-now goes together with "the this-here-now ø", where "ø" stands for a type. Furthermore, there is no ground for holding a romantic theory of action, according to which action brings one into contact—unmediated contact—with brute reality (whereas cognition, especially theoretical cognition, irremediably) removes you from that immediacy. Action and praxis present the world to the agent *as having a certain meaning*; they too have their *Sinne*; they too exhibit, to reflective glance, a noetic-noematic structure. The world is interpreted as much by the purely theoretical cognizer as by the practical agent. If that be so, transcendental questioning cannot be resisted even with regard to the life-world.

One can begin with questions about the possibility of the perceptual world with its horizontal and temporal structure, its intersubjectivity and historicity. One can go on to ask, how perceptual meanings are derived from practical orientation, from the mobility of the body as well as from the cultural tradition that is taken over. One can ask how the meanings derived from a cultural tradition succeed in "overlaying" and "clothing" the world. Needless to say, transcendental questionings at this level are not as precise and clear-cut as at the level of the idealized scientific cognition, but their meshiness reflects the meshiness of the categories of the life-world. We would still be looking for the modes of subjective (even if bodily, á la Merleau-Ponty) intentionalities which constitute the life-world; we would be, in such investigations, involved in doing a transcendental philosophy of deeper levels—of levels beneath the Kantian. We may have to be in search of Freudian unconscious intentionalities, Jungian collective unconscious, even Derridean traces (freed from the manipulations by the overpowering *Difference*). We shall be pursuing the Kantian program, encapsulated in Hermann Cohen's epigram: "Nichts ist gegeben, alles ist aufgegben." I would change it slightly, to say: everything that is given opens up new tasks (*Aufgaben*) to be solved. In this sense transcendental philosophy is critical and rejects any dogmatism, including the dogmatism of the life-world. The result, on the positive side, is that we progressively retrieve a more profound picture of the constituting transcendental subjectivity.

NOTES

1. See my *The Concept of Intentionality* (St. Louis: Warren Green, 1972).
2. See my *The Possibility of Transcendental Philosophy* (The Hague: Kluwer, 1985).
3. Two of Carr's unpublished papers are referenced here.
4. Cf. *The Possibility of Transcendental Philosophy.*
5. Frank Kirkland has suggested this line relating Kant to Husserl in some of his papers.

3

Transcendental Experience, Everyday Philosophy

Erazim Kohák

In §72 of his *Krisis der europäischen Wissenschaften*, Edmund Husserl introduces the term, *die absolut fungierende Subjektivität*, telling us that it refers not to human subjectivity but to subjectivity as such which only manifests itself as human subjectivity. The task and achievement of transcendental phenomenology, he tells us, was

> ... die absolut fungierende Subjektivität zu entdecken, nicht als die menschliche sondern als die in der menschlichen, oder zunächst in der menschlichen, sich selbst objektivierende. [Hua VI:265]

Or, in David Carr's noble English translation,

> ... to discover the absolutely functioning subjectivity, not as human subjectivity but as the subjectivity which objectifies itself, (at least) at first, in human subjectivity. [Carr 1970:262]

Whether in German or in English, the passage has since become something of a *locus classicus* for all who wish to claim that transcendental philosophy is an esoteric obscurantism, hopelessly removed from everyday experience.

In the present paper, I would like to suggest that it may be our understanding of transcendental philosophy and of everyday experience rather than Husserl's text that is at a fault. If we come to understand those two terms clearly, in at least approximately the way Husserl appears to have intended them, I believe that transcendental philosophy will prove to be rather an everyday affair, not at all obscure or esoteric, while our everyday experience will turn out to have a distinctly transcendental dimension overlooked by traditional empiricism.

Unfortunately, the terms transcendental philosophy and everyday experience do not glitter with a crystal-like clarity even in our philosophical

43

usage, much less in our ordinary discourse. Both evoke such a rich cluster of associated commonplace that it is possible to use them in an appalling variety of ways—or even without any clearly specified meaning at all. Thus, our first task must be one of conceptual and experiential clarification. All of our associated commonplaces aside, how do we wish to have the two terms function in our philosophic discourse? Also, beyond that, what in our presentive experience do we wish them to evoke?

For all its lack of colloquial familiarity, the term transcendental philosophy may be the one more easily clarified. We commonly mean by it—and in our inquiry we shall mean by it—any philosophy which seeks to derive from the structure of our experiencing normative propositions which can be said to be true or false independently of any particular factual (and so contingent) content of that experience.

Were we to resort to time-honored Kantian idiom, we could call any philosophy transcendental if it considers synthetic *a priori* propositions possible. For the purposes of our inquiry, however, we would like to interpret the term synthetic *a priori* rather more broadly than is usual in Kantian discourse, to include any proposition derived from the structure—or perhaps from the *ideal possibilities*—of experiencing, whereof more anon, and applied to its factual contents or *Sachverhalt*. Bracketing prior knowledge for the sake of a convenient if inaccurate example, we would like to use as a metaphor the rather non-Kantian assertion that, "Whatever human explorers may see on Mars will be of a color between infrared and ultraviolet." That is a synthetic statement, since it asserts something about the *fact content* of experience. However, it does so not on an empirical basis but rather on the basis of the *structure* or *ideal possibilities* of human experiencing. The human eye can only register as color wave frequencies between the two limits. Admittedly, on a higher level of generalization that is itself a factual rather than an ideal possibility. Still, we can use it on its own level as an illustration of the principle of *a priori* synthetic judgments— asserting something about the content of experience on the basis of its ideal or structural possibility.

However, while our interpretation of *synthetic a priori* is purposefully broad, our interest is far more specific. We are concerned with the possibility of normative value judgments of the type, "Causing unprovoked injury is morally wrong." Within the limits of traditional empiricism, such judgments would be clearly illegitimate. Those limits would permit an empirical generalization, for instance, that humans in most or perhaps in all cases do in fact tend to regard causing unprovoked injury as wrong. A command such as, "Refrain from causing unprovoked injury," might then be legitimate as an expression of personal revulsion, an elaborate version of "ugh," or perhaps as an expression of a wish that others refrain from such acts. It would make no sense as a description of a putative "truth" that acts of unprovoked injury in some sense *are* wrong, of themselves, intrinsically, wholly independently of what this or that historical community of speakers might or might not say of them.

Normative value judgments of the order, "Causing unprovoked injury is wrong," could become possible, if at all, only on grounds other than those of empirical observation, that is, either on transcen*dent* or on transcen*dental* grounds. We might invoke transcendent grounds, claiming, for instance, that our normative judgment is justified wholly independently of observed empirical conditions by conforming to some putative higher or deeper reality said to transcend our (ordinary) experience. Such transcendent reality may then be said to be the Will of God, a Platonic realm of forms, Spinoza's *Deus sive natura* or perhaps Hegel's or Marx's history. In all cases, however, a second, transcendent (or perhaps "authentic") level of reality is said to be the basis for statements which we can apply normatively to a first, empirical or experiential level of reality.

If, however, with Kant, we were to consider any such putative transcendent reality in principle inaccessible to human cognition or if, like Auguste Comte, we were to deny it any reality whatever, then nonconventional normative judgments could be justified only on *transcendental* grounds, as being required by nothing external to the phenomenon but rather by the intrinsic "structure" or *ideal possibility* of our being in the world, independently of and prior to any contingent factual fulfillment of that possibility.

Using our earlier metaphor, whatever colors we shall encounter on Mars, we can, in virtue of the structural possibilities of our perceiving, validly assert that they *will necessarily* fall within the range between infrared and ultraviolet. Or, in what may be a less misleading illustration, the ideal possibility of *something to eat* does not derive from stuffed avocadoes or steamed asparagus. It is real as soon as there is a hungry agent in the world. Only thanks to it can the particular entities subsumed subsequently under it *be something*, not simply be. Yet that empty ideal possibility, *something to eat*, imposes definite conditions which anything that would be subsumed under it must meet.

Or perhaps a still less fanciful example is in order. Given the ideal possibilities of our being in the world as both social and vulnerable, we can claim that the very "structure" of our being in the world demands that, whatever our factual preferences may be, we condemn acts of wanton injury as in principle, intrinsically, necessarily wrong. No alleged transcendent reality, but rather the transcendental condition of our being, its *ideal possibility*, justifies and demands certain normative statements, prior to all empirical content. It is, in another idiom, an empty *intentio* waiting to be filled.

We shall yet see what such structure and such justification may be. For the moment, though, we can say that, in principle, a *transcendental philosophy* as we shall use that term shall be any philosophy that holds that some structural or ideal possibility of our being in the world makes it possible to make a priori normative judgments which will be applicable synthetically to the fact-content of our being.

For all its easy familiarity, our other term, *everyday experience*, may prove to be rather more problematic. Its reference is experiential, not merely conceptual. Thus, the question of its meaning is not simply one of how we wish to have it function in our discourse, even though that, too, requires attention. Rather, we need to also ask what experienced reality we wish to evoke by it.

Everyday experience is, presumably, something that humans have always had. Whatever else it may be, human life is something humans live day by day, even in the most dramatic periods of their lives. Interestingly, though, throughout most of philosophy's history humans appear to have experienced little need to designate their everyday experience by any special technical term. Over the centuries, philosophers have generated a whole range of terms to designate segments and types of experience which stand out of the ordinary and the everyday, such as the experience of the holy, of revelation, of inspiration, or of madness. When it comes to ordinary experience, however, such terms as we do have to designate it tend not so much to describe it, in itself, as to distinguish it from special experiences, as in the case of the term "secular," the anticlimactic counterpart of the sacred. Terms like everyday, *alltäglich or všedni* tend to be lackluster neologisms which never acquired the status of *termini technici*. Ordinary everyday experience was apparently just too everyday, too ordinary to warrant special attention or special designation.

The need for a special term designating what appeared not at all special seems to have arisen only with the positivist revolt against the implicit metaphysics of natural science and against metaphysics in general. Only when a special meta-reality came to appear inaccessible or downright nonexistent did ordinary reality acquire sufficient importance and dignity to warrant a special designation—and, as history goes, that happened rather more recently than we commonly assume. As conventional wisdom would have it, the great turning point in Western thought was the rise of modern natural sciences in the seventeenth century, in the work of Descartes, Galileo, or Newton. However, as Jan Patočka points out (Kohák 1989: 239–44), while those thinkers did transform the metaphysical commonplaces of Western thought, they did not similarly transform Western methodological commonplaces. While Western assumptions about the nature of reality changed dramatically, those concerning the nature of explanation remained remarkably constant. The representatives of the new science had a boundless scorn for the earlier, "prescientific" *scientia*, whose metaphysics they regarded as idle speculation fit only for the Platonic or the Baconian cave. Yet the science they themselves put forward remained essentially *metaphysical*.

Here, though, a terminological clarification may be in order. We are using the terms *metaphysics* and *metaphysical* in an etymologically strict sense to designate any conceptual system which seeks to explain the putatively "physical" reality of everyday experience by relating or reducing it to an allegedly deeper, usually hidden level of reality, literally a meta-reality which allegedly accounts for the superficial, overt or "phenomenal" reality. Thus claiming to explain, say, speech inhibition as the effect of archaic and unconscious mind contents is a classic instance of a metaphysical explanation in our sense. Generally, the rhetoric of *discovery*, for which natural science remained notorious well into the late nineteenth century, betrays its metaphysical cast. Scientific explanation here evidently is not regarded as a matter of formulating descriptive formulae summing up observed regularities. When we speak of a discovery, we imply the uncovering of a hitherto hidden, deeper reality, perhaps of natural forces or natural laws, said to underlie and account for the merely apparent reality of our everyday experience. While the uninitiated layman is said to live on the level of mere experience, in a world of tables, loves, chairs, resentments, and apple trees, the scientist is said to uncover a hidden, deeper world of atoms, forces, molecules, and physical laws—or perhaps of psychic mechanisms or laws of history—which govern and explain the appearances of everyday experience. For all the rhetoric of empiricism, everyday experience remains for it merely apparent, uninteresting in itself, just as it appeared from the perspective of other metaphysical realities, the holy or the mystical. Only a new kind of experience, that of the scientist, has been added, as the one true and reliable means of penetrating at last beyond everyday experience to true reality.

That is worth noting. For all the ostentatious empiricism of modern science and philosophy alike, everyday experience still remained too ordinary to warrant a special designation. Even for the empiricists, everyday experience proved interesting not for its own sake, as ordinary, but again as special, as the privileged means of access to a deeper reality. That special access might be assured by the tools of science, statistics, and mathematics. Alternately, it might be assured by the tools of hermeneutics, reaching past the contemptible *Alltäglichkeit* to the meaning of History or, later, to Being. Either way, though, experience remains interesting only as special, as revelatory. In its ordinariness, everyday experience remained inherently uninteresting to the scientist and the philosopher alike.

That everyday experience came to prominence only with the positivist revolt against the metaphysical or "transcendent" mode of explanation. Whatever its later fortunes, positivism did not initially propose a new conception of (meta)reality but rather a new conception of explanation. When Kant denied reason's claim to penetrate beyond the phenomenal to a noumenal realm, he might still have been thinking of Gottfried Leibniz and of Christian Wolff. When Comte rejected the "metaphysical stage" of human knowledge as one that should be and has been surpassed, he was referring to the implicit metaphysics of the science of his day, which assumed it was discovering a second level reality, one of laws and forces, which would explain the merely phenomenal reality of everyday experience.

In this context, the crucial point of the "positive" conception of science is that sciences do not "discover" any hidden reality but rather record and articulate the observed regularities of everyday experience—and that it is the very same reality present to and observed by the mystic, the metaphysician and the scientist. The scientist was now said to differ from the mystic and the metaphysician not in what he observed but in the way he observed it "scientifically." Positive science is said to observe everyday experience with utmost objectivity, clarity, and rigor, scrupulously avoiding all observer bias and faithfully recording observed regularities of occurrence in the unambiguous language of mathematics. It does not claim to discover hidden laws of nature, only to note observed regularities to make prediction and control possible. For classical positivism, rigorous description *is* explanation, the only explanation possible, and the everyday experience it describes *is* reality. It is not a veil of appearance which true knowledge, be it *scientia* or science, would need to penetrate. Everyday experience has come into its own at last.

It is in this sense that Edmund Husserl was entirely justified in claiming that the phenomenology he put forward in *Die Idee der Phänomenologie* and in *Ideen I* is the only authentic positivism. In the familiar passage in *Ideen I*, he tells us that

Sagt "Positivismus" soviel wie absolut vorurteilsfreie Gründung aller Wissenschaften auf das "Positive", d.i. originär zu Erfassende, dann sind wir die echten Positivisten. [Hua III:46]—If "positivism" is tantamount to an absolutely unprejudiced grounding of all sciences on the "positive," that is to say, on what can be seized upon originaliter, then we are the genuine positivists. [Kersten 1983:39]

The original program of phenomenology was simply one of clearly seeing and faithfully expressing the eidetic structures of lived experience. The attempt to treat alleged "phenomenological" experience as a privileged instance which would lead us beyond average everydayness to a deeper authentic reality misses the radical nature of Husserl's project which was genuinely positivistic in description, but fundamentally transcendental in explanation. Husserl sought to see clearly and to express faithfully the experienced reality of everyday experience, not to "discover" a putative transcendent one. However, he sought to see it and express it not in its contingent particularity or in a generalization derived from it, but rather in terms of the (empty) ideal possibilities which such particularity contingently fills.

Ironically, Husserl's idiosyncratic use of the term "positivism"—Eugen Fink, at the time innocent of any sensitivity to British terminological conventions, even spoke of "radical positivism"—led to misunderstanding because the scientific positivism of the time was not nearly positivistic enough. The everyday experience to which it turned was not the experience of human beings in their everydayness but rather experience reinterpreted and reconstructed to conform to the metaphysics of Cartesianism as Descartes's British heirs came to understand it.

The point at issue here is the place of the subject in the economy of reality. In everyday experience, as we shall note later, the subject and the subject's intentional acts are an intrinsic part of reality itself. That is what Descartes's great contemporary, John Amos Comenius, understood so well and bequeathed to his pansophist heirs and, ultimately, to Husserl. Descartes offered a different reading. For him, reality is a self-contained region of *res extendes*, entities whose sole characteristic is spatiotemporal extension and whose only relations are mathematical and causal. The subject is a reality of a wholly different and discontinuous order, the *res cogitans* for which there is no room in extensional reality. Thus any subject-related categories—the intelligible order of experience which we shall later describe as that of the categories of *the near and the dear*—represent a distortion of and an imposition upon reality itself. In cruder, later terminology, they came to be described as the *observer bias* which science must eliminate to reach reality itself. Reality then comes to be conceived as whatever there would be were there no subjects while experience comes to be reduced to accidental passive recording of such reality on the ephemeral screen of subject mind. On such a reading, the everyday experience to which positivism proposed to turn becomes the "subjective" and somehow less than real reflection of reality. In another idiom, our ideas could be said to be faded impressions. Experienced reality is once more determined not by actual experiencing but by a set of metatheoretical presuppositions.

That conception of reality may have awakened Kant from his dogmatic slumbers but it did so at the cost of generating enough philosophical problems to become a nightmare itself. For if experienced reality cannot be explained in terms of a transcendent reality—something on which Kant and David Hume fully agree—and if its immanent structure is solely extensional or mathematical, how can it be qualitatively intelligible at all? Or, in the much later idiom of the Baden School, how can it be *understood*, not merely *explained*?

In his conception of phenomenal reality, Kant makes a valiant attempt to revive a more adequate understanding of experienced reality and use it to resolve the problems generated by Hume's Cartesian bifurcation. Experienced—or "phenomenal," appearing—reality is structured by cognizing reason which introduces into it structural elements not subject to the contingency of fact. Later we shall speak of them as ideal possibilities. On the level of sensibility, it is space and time as the necessary forms of sensibility. On the level of understanding, it is the categories of judgment. On the level of reason, it is reason's necessary ideas. The crucial point is that these are ideal possibilities, structural elements and not simply characteristics of an alleged reflection of reality on the screen of *res cogitans*. They are necessarily the characteristics of any experienced reality as such. Experienced reality thus is no longer an epiphenomenal reflection. It is reality, the reality amid which we live, breathe, and have our being; a reality of which the subject is an intrinsic part, not merely its epiphenomenal observer. However, because it is structured by the subject, experienced reality can be understood in terms of the necessary structure of any experience, that is, *transcendentally*.

The brilliance of Kant's transcendental solution is impressive, but its effectiveness is contingent on a conception of our everyday experienced reality to which Kant paid little thematic attention. The problem is the conception of the structuring subject. As Kant saw it, in this respect very much an heir of the Enlightenment, only those aspects of subjectivity can qualify as transcendental which are truly universal, wholly free of any admixture of factual contingency. This stands out most clearly in his *Fundamental Principles of the Metaphysics of Morals* and in the *Critique of Practical Reason*. Only pure reason—or here, pure practical reason—in its absolute universality can be a source of valid *a priori* synthetic judgments. Or, in another terminology, only universalizable, rational subjectivity can be truly transcendental subjectivity, an intrinsic aspect of experienced reality rather than an aspect of its contingent and merely empirical fact content.

A number of commentators, Max Scheler in his *Formalismus in der Ethik* among them, have pointed out the critical weakness of this solution. Our prereflective experiential reality is not irrational. It has a "reason" of its own, as Blaise Pascal and Comenius knew. It is intelligibly structured. However, it is prerational in Kant's narrow sense of rationality as a matter of universalizable cognitive judgments. Reason in that latter sense is in fact a latecomer in our lived experience. In actual experience, that kind of rationality is a subsequent imposition which can appear as arbitrary as John

Rawls's *Gedankenexperiment* or as Kohlberg's moral dilemmas; hence, superimposed by well-meaning teachers on a schoolboy's attempt to discern between good and evil. A viable transcendental philosophy would need a more adequate conception of the intelligible structuring—"rationality" in our sense—of our everyday experience. Transcendental philosophy can be viable if its conception of the meaningful ordering of lived experience—its "transcendental subjectivity"—reaches to something more basic than Kant's conception of pure reason.

Husserl's conception of the meaningful ordering of everyday experience seeks to do just that. His proposal to see clearly and articulate faithfully the meaningful ordering of everyday experience—literally the *logos of phenomena*—is not only positivist in the original sense of that word but also, as Iso Kern points out, profoundly Kantian. It is positivist: unlike some of his more romantically inclined successors, Husserl does not seek a privileged access to some putative deeper reality but a clear view of the experienced reality of everyday experience. Also it is Kantian: Husserl seeks to see and articulate not simply the contingent factual content of that experience but is intrinsic modes of being or *Wesen*.

Translating that term as "essence," though not without some justification in Husserl's early writings, is problematic. German philosophical terminology does include the term *Essenz*, yet Husserl never uses it as an equivalent of his *Wesen*. Nor do the philosophical dictionaries of Husserl's time so define it. Eisler's *Handwörterbuch der Philosophie* describes it as the set of rules governing the conduct of any entity falling under them. Husserl himself uses only one German synonym for *Wesen*—*ideale Möglichkeit*. In English, that would be ideal possibility or, more accurately still, *possibility in principle*. His "rational intuition," *Wesenserschauung*, focuses on the structural aspect of lived experience—on the transcendental ideal possibilities which it acts out and which render it intelligible. Even at his most Kantian, as in the first volume of his *Ideen*, written at a time when he was most intensely coping with Kant, Husserl operated with a conception of reason significantly broader than Kant's. The wonder of wonders, he tells us, is *Bewußtsein*, the self-awareness of lived experience or, less awkwardly, reality as experience, *Sein as bewußt*, not simply reason. In his late works, in *Krisis* and in the third volume of his *Intersubjektivität*, that becomes clearer still. The focus now is explicitly the intrinsic intelligible structure of *Lebenswelt*, of reality as meaningfully constituted as a world by the presence of life.

The term *Lebenswelt* or "life-world" has acquired a cluster of associated commonplaces of its own and has come to cover a multitude of sins. Its genesis, though, is reasonably clear. Husserl is building on a concept he introduced in his pivotal *Ideen II*, that of experienced reality as constituting an intelligible whole or a "world" with reference to the active intentional presence of a subject. In *Ideen II* he speaks of *die Welt als Korrelat der Naturwissenschaften* (Hua IV:4). A dictionary translation would render that as "the world as a correlate of the natural sciences." A less literal but more faithful rendering might speak of "experienced reality ordered as a coherent whole with reference to the activity of the natural sciences." Analogously, we could speak of *Lebenswelt* as *die Welt als Korrelat des alltäglichen Lebens*— literally, the world as a correlate of everyday living or, more faithfully, experienced reality ordered as a coherent whole by the presence of ordinary life. The long overlooked everyday experience here comes to thematic focus at last.

At this point, the clear seeing and faithful articulation Husserl called for is much to the point. What is the overlooked reality we seek to designate by the innocuous term "everyday experience?" The point of the adjective "everyday," I presume, is to exclude any of the special qualifiers introduced by reflection, such as "religious," "objective," or even "phenomenological." We are concerned with experience as we live it, not as we categorize it in what in *Ideen II* was called *the theoretical attitude*, from the standpoint of one of our special concerns. But what is that?

At this most elementary level, let us presume further, the term experience refers to any and all of our aware transactions with the context of our being, from merely observing it to acting within it. It does not, let us stress, refer simply to the awareness of our transactions, but to the transactions themselves. An element of awareness must be present, though in much of our everyday experiencing we would be unintentionally overstating our case were we to claim that the subject is "conscious" of the act. Much of the time, we are preoccupied with something else and not conscious of what we are doing in the usual colloquial sense of that word. Yet, in Paul Ricoeur's felicitous phrase, we are *not unaware* of what we are doing. An event of which we would be wholly unaware, though it might involve us, would not be a part of our experience. A dimension of awareness is necessarily a part of everyday experience.

Yet experience, as we ordinarily use that term, is not simply a matter of awareness. It really is a transaction with the context of our being. It is not simply an interaction, with the usual mechanistic connotations of that term: John Dewey's term, "transaction," captures the sense of our organic presence which Heidegger describes rather more accurately as the existentiale, "being in." Nor would I wish to speak of it as a transaction with a "world," since it is first that transaction which constitutes what-is in the unity of "the world." Nor does the transaction need to be "external." An awareness of pain, especially if it is a pain occasioned by a memory, is not an interaction with the world. Yet it is a transaction with the context of our being. The pain presents itself as autonomous, as a reality with which I must come to terms, integrating it within the whole of my experience even though it may present itself solely as an unwelcome intruder. Thus everyday experience is neither merely an awareness nor merely an interaction with an external context of which we are aware. Rather, everyday experience is an activity constituting a whole within which, on reflection, we distinguish the dimensions of awareness itself and of the object of awareness. Everyday experience is the unity of aware transactions with the context of our being which, in colloquial usage, we designate by the words rendered technical by Heidegger, "being in the world."

Here a minor terminological excursus may be in order. In *Ideen I*, Husserl introduced the term *die natürliche Welt*, somewhat misleadingly translated as "the natural world," and subsequently confused the situation further by introducing a second term, *Lebenswelt* or life-world. In his usage, "the natural world" has nothing to do with nature. Here "world" means not a set of entities but rather the way in which our experienced reality fits together in a coherent whole. "Natural" has the colloquial sense of easy, familiar, spontaneous, much as we speak of a "natural" thing to do and mean by it simply the accustomed, familiar mode of acting which may in fact be entirely conventional, but has become so familiar that we are not even aware of it. Thus "the natural world" of *Ideen I* refers to the way we habitually, unreflectingly make sense of the manifold of our experience. It is "natural" in the sense of being effortless rather than being a self-conscious, reflective, theoretical construct. Nonetheless, Husserl points out, it is already a low-level theory, not simply the way we experience the world but the way in which we habitually, unreflectingly interpret it. This low-level theoretical construct must be set aside or "bracketed" in order to reach experience prior to interpretation, simply as experienced, the "phenomenological residuum" of *Ideen I*.

The *Lebenswelt* of *Krisis III* really is that residuum. However, by this time Husserl has become aware that the world, as experience, is not a static given but rather something that is constituted—literally, given a constitution that makes it into a coherent whole—by the presence of life, of purposive activity, entirely prior to any conscious reflection. When we become aware of our "being in the world" in a phenomenological attitude, we are becoming aware of what-is as it had been constituted as a meaningful whole by the prereflective, purposive presence of a life. We are becoming aware of "life's-world" or *Lebenswelt*. When we become aware of it from our habitual perspective (the *natürliche Einstellung* of *Ideen I*), we are interpreting that meaningful whole in terms of a series of habitual filters, in the West usually Cartesian ones. The term "everyday experience" is thus ambiguous. It can either mean being in the world in the sense of aware transaction within the life-world or the habitual interpretation thereof. The question for this inquiry presupposed the latter, our answer is presenting the former meaning.

In any case, it will be wise to pay closer attention to the unity of our experience. The point being that, as we actually live it, our everyday experience is not a buzzing, booming confusion but rather a coherent whole. It may at times lack the lofty transcendent unity we assume when we speak about "The Meaning of Life." But as William James noted clearly and persuasively, it is not discontinuous (James 1890:237–64). Its components fit together. Even its radical transitions are continuities. We can speak about it coherently because, prior to all reflection, it is already coherent—or in Husserl's terminology, it is a life-world. That typewriter is on the table, the table is next to the window, the sunstruck New Mexico landscape continuous beyond it. This morning followed last night as a page follows a page, anticipations turn to memories. Some events stand out while others recede into the background. There is an order.

For the purposes of analysis, however, it may be useful to distinguish between two kinds of order, or better, two types of relations that order our experienced reality and render it intelligible. One kind of structuring relation—or essential possibility—is that in which the subject functions simply as an observer. These are the relations which, at least in principle, could be recorded no less effectively by a measuring instrument set up by a visitor from Mars. Thus, in the context of everyday experience the bear on the shelf presents itself as standing in a definite spatial relation to the silhouette calendar on the wall. They are 2.76 meters apart. That distance, though we are aware of it, is constant and independent of our awareness. Our measuring is incidental to it. There are other such constant relations, as the regular correlation between a hammer stroke and the penetration of a nail into the wood. As long as we remain most scrupulously aware that we are using a conceptual shorthand, not "discovering" any hidden force, we can speak of such constant correlation of two events as "causality" and describe that order of our experience into which the subject enters only as an accidental observer as *spatiotemporal*, the order of interactions among extended entities in space-time.

Let us then reserve the term "objectivity" for this mode of ordering experienced reality. So used, *objectivity* is not the code name for an object or a characteristic of an object. Rather, it refers to a characteristic of our everyday experienced reality, namely, that it is spatiotemporally ordered. It is this characteristic that renders experienced reality explicable. We can account for the occurrence of any event within it in terms of the spatiotemporal, causal relations of that event to all other events, all subsumed within an observed general regularity or a "law." On this level, accounting for the occurrence of a particular event is all we mean by an explanation. Thus, when we ask about a particular event, as when asking, "Why did my child have to die?", about a child crushed by a truck, this ordering of our every-day experience—its objectivity—enables us to provide a full explanation. The compression of vital organs by a pressure exceeding X atmospheres is regularly correlated with the cessation of vital functions. So?

That example, admittedly, is emotively loaded, and for a reason—to make the point that the spatiotemporal ordering of experienced reality, its "objectivity," typically plays a rather secondary role in the ordering of our every-day experience. It is an essential aspect of it, to be sure. But the questions we normally ask and the answers we normally seek are of a different order, having to do with relations in which the subject is not merely an observer but a participant. The question about the death of the child asks about the place of that event within a no less real but a rather different ordering of our everyday experience, a subject-relative one.

For the moment, let us designate such subject-relative relations as those of *the near and the dear*. The relation of *the near* is not a spatiotemporal one, a part of the objectivity of our experience. It is subject relative: the bear on the shelf is nearer *to me* than the calendar. However, neither is that relationship "merely subjective" in the colloquial sense of being merely private and arbitrary. The bear really is nearer, and no amount of wishing other-wise will change that. Though I may get up and change it, from where I now sit, the bear is nearer to me than the calendar. Yet it is a subject-related relation, structuring lived experience with reference to a subject.

Similarly the relationship of *dearer than* is not a "merely subjective" one. The bear and the silhouette are far dearer to me than the table. Though subject-relative, that is the way it is. I might, for good and sufficient reason, wish it were otherwise. In time, it might even become otherwise, just as a few steps can change the "nearer than" relation. But, at this moment of experiencing, the table is nearer, the bear is dearer. That is how my expe-rienced reality is ordered. It is not a buzzing, booming confusion, capable only of an explanation, not of understanding, because it presents itself as ordered also with reference to a valuing subject, by relationships of *the near and the dear*.

Let us call this type of relationship a *meaning relation*, using the term meaning to designate the way an entity or an event present themselves as integrated within the unity of experience with reference to a subject. Let us then reserve the term "subjectivity" for the sum total of the meaning rela-tions ordering our everyday experience. As with objectivity, subjectivity so used is not a code name for a subject or a characteristic of a subject. Rather, it refers to a characteristic of experienced reality, that of being ordered not only in spatiotemporal terms, but also in terms of meanings, in relation to

a subject. The meaning order is not an order of the mind, imposed by mind—
or by "reason"—upon a merely spatiotemporally ordered reality. It is the
order of experienced reality itself. As we speak of the objectivity of experienced reality and mean by it its spatiotemporal ordering, so we can speak of
the subjectivity of experienced reality and mean by it its meaningful ordering with reference to a subject.

Here another marginal aside might not be amiss. When we subject our
everyday experience to more careful scrutiny, as Husserl does in *Ideen II*,
we discover that its objectivity—its spatiotemporal ordering—presents itself as one of the dimensions of its subjectivity, that is, as one mode of
meaningful ordering, with reference to the subject. Husserl speaks of it as
the constitution of objectivity within subjectivity. Objectivity is the way
our experience is structured when we assume the posture of an observer, in
the *natürliche Einstellung*, our habitual posture. It is a valid and useful way
of ordering experienced reality, though not a privileged one, somehow "more
true." It is justified by a specific purpose, and its usefulness is contingent on
that purpose, that of prediction and control. Metaphorically speaking, it is
a useful posture when we wish to know how to construct nuclear bombs,
but a wholly inappropriate one for asking whether to construct them at all.
It is equally inappropriate in the case of our earlier question, "Why did my
child have to die?" Thus, strictly speaking, it is inaccurate to speak of two
ways in which experienced reality is ordered, of objectivity and subjectivity. The basic order of experienced reality in lived experience is first, its
subjectivity, its meaningful ordering with reference to a subject. One of the
possibilities within that basic order, one subcategory, is the order in which
experienced reality assumes as a correlate of disinterested observation. Reality—what Nicolai Hartman called *die Härte des Realen*—is not created by
a subject. We encounter it as an other, in its hardness. Objectivity, however,
the particular ordering of that reality, is constituted within subjectivity and
is reducible to it. Subjectivity is the basic order of experienced reality.

Were it not for the unfortunate cluster of associated commonplaces which
tend to link the term *reason* with the ability to establish relations among
discrete individuals rather than with the ability to grasp the meaning of a
whole, we might speak of the subjectivity of experienced reality as its *rationality* rather than its subjectivity. That is certainly a time-honored usage,
reflecting the recognition that experienced reality has its *ratio*, its rhyme
and reason, its rightness. There is not only the flux of changing fact contents
but also the *logos* of their relations. It is a usage which people like Comenius
or Leibniz would have readily understood. In our time, though, the connotations of economic "rationalization" and of syllogistic reasoning render the
term *rationality* problematic. Thus there is good reason for the Husserlian
usage which designates the meaningful ordering of reality as its *subjectivity*.

To be sure, that usage presents problems of its own. For a post-Cartesian age, it calls up connotations of privacy and arbitrariness with which we need to deal. At this stage, however, the crucial point is the recognition of the intrinsic subject-relative intelligibility of experienced reality as constituted by the presence of conscious purposive activity—that is, of its *subjectivity*—and the second recognition that this term refers to nothing obscure or esoteric, but rather to something we blithely take for granted in our everyday experience: that it is meaningfully ordered by relations of the near and the dear as well as by those of space and of time. Subjectivity is simply ordinary, not esoteric.

Nor does subjectivity become esoteric when we focus on its prereflective aspect and speak of it as *transcendental* subjectivity, even though the choice of that adjective to designate it is admittedly less than fortunate. Still, all we are doing is recognizing that the meaningful ordering of experienced reality is not arbitrary or private to individual subjects but rather that at least some of it is predetermined by the fact that experienced reality is necessarily *a* subject's, *any* subject's experience.

Perhaps the most obvious and most universal transcendental dimension of subjectivity—of the meaningful ordering—of experience is that it is ordered in terms of good and bad. What constitutes experience as a meaningful whole is the presence of purposive activity. What-there-is is therefore *ab initio*, ordered as that which aids and that which hinders or is irrelevant to that activity. We can, then, recognize less general categories, for instance those of the threatening and the reassuring or, in Husserl's familiar example, of at home and alien, which are applicable only to conscious, purposive agents. Still, they represent the mold into which experience is poured, the *ideal possibilities* which it acts out. The fact content may differ— you are afraid of poisonous spiders, I am afraid of lawyers—but the possibility of fear as a mode of relating precedes any particular content. It is an ideal possibility derived from—or perhaps generated by—the fact of our being finite, vulnerable beings who wish to live but are aware of their finitude and vulnerability. Given such a being, the possibility of fear as a mode of relating follows—and as such it is not an empirical but a *transcendental* possibility.

Claiming all the possible benefit of every conceivable doubt, we might here still be said to be following a Kantian lead, though with a Husserlian difference, especially as it appears in the *Krisis* and in his posthumously published writings. The ideal possibilities which render the manifold of fact contents intelligible are transcendental in the sense of being a function of the presence of subjects. However, it is the very presence of subjects—of purposive aware agents—rather than their putative pure reason in cognitive judgments that constitutes what there is as a meaningful whole. The

constitutive element is not reflection but rather purposive activity, function. That is how I would interpret Husserl's term that puzzled us at the
start, the *fungierende Subjektivität*, or Alfred Schutz's *die wirkende Welt*. In
both cases, I take it, we are dealing with experienced reality as constituted
as a meaningful whole (or "world") by the presence of functioning subjects—a meaning, incidentally, hopelessly obscured by the usual translation, "the world of work." Whatever term we use, though, the point is that
experienced reality is intelligible in virtue of the nonarbitrary qualitative
ordering it acquires as the context of subject acts.

Those acts, incidentally, need not be something highly elaborate. It can
be something as elementary as breathing. Because we are organisms which
inhale oxygen and exhale carbon dioxide, our experienced reality is value-
ordered prior to all reflection. Fresh, airy places present themselves as pleasant
and desirable, dank dark dungeons as unpleasant and undesirable. That is a
valuation which we do not constitute, but literally discover in reflection.
Also, to be sure, in reflection, we might choose to alter or reverse that
valuation. When there is an air raid in progress, dank dark dungeons can
be distinctly comforting. The point, though, is that reflection operates in a
value-ordered world and that such value ordering is not arbitrary. It is derived from the presence of the subject and while its level of generality may
vary—something that would have been anathema to Kant—it is, as derived
from the subject, not empirical but transcendental.

That, after all, was the point all along. Though the terminology might be
unfortunate, the point is that our everyday experience, at its most everyday, necessarily contains a transcendental dimension. It is not a buzzing,
booming confusion, it is ordered, and its ordering is not only quantitative,
but also qualitative. Nor is the qualitative ordering of everyday experience—
the order of *the near and the dear*—simply arbitrary, derived from individual
preference. Some of it at least is derived from our being as subjects and so
is not empirical but transcendental. Rather than of everyday experience, we
could speak of *transcendental experience*—and mean something very everyday, wholly nonesoteric by it.

With that we can return to our initial example, that of the judgment that,
"*Causing unprovoked injury is morally wrong*," presented as synthetic *a priori*,
valid "transcendentally," independently of contingent fact contents. That,
we want to suggest, is not an empirical generalization but a transcendental
deduction from the ideal possibilities of our being in the world, from its
transcendental subjectivity. We humans are in the world as vulnerable, and
aware of our vulnerability. We are also social beings, not as a matter of
cultural accident but as a matter of structural necessity. Our young do not
become self-sufficient for some dozen years after birth, requiring a relatively

stable social support structure. Our linguistic mode of communication similarly requires a community of speakers. Language is a social product. Given the reality of our being as in principle, vulnerable and social, we are, again in principle, a priori, directly dependent on our ability to trust the others, who are awake while we sleep, to act in predictably noninjurious ways. An unprovoked and so unpredictable injurious act disrupts the very texture of trust upon which our being depends. Thus the judgment, "causing unprovoked injury is morally wrong," is not a function of individual or cultural preference, but of the *transcendental subjectivity*—the necessary meaning structure, the ideal possibilities—of our everyday experience, of the way it is structured in principle, as an eidetic possibility, in virtue of our active presence in the world as functioning subjects.

Husserl, as we noted, goes beyond Kant in his recognition that the transcendental structure of everyday experience is a function not simply of cognition but of the active incarnate presence of subjects. We in turn are pushing Husserl to the limit in speaking of any subject being whatever, rather than of human subjects. In most of his work, Husserl speaks as if transcendental subjectivity, constituted by our presence, were only a function of human subjects. In the third part of *Krisis*, he explicitly links it to the community of all actual and possible human subjects, past, present, and future, in the tradition of the Enlightenment dictum that nothing human is alien to us. Still, in the passage we cited at the start of this inquiry, Hua VI, §72:265, Husserl suggests a way of going yet a step further when he speaks of the *absolut fungierende Subjektivität* as not human but as only initially manifesting itself to us as human. The monadological texts in the third volume of his posthumously published writings, *Zur Phänomenologie der Intersubjektivität*, (Hua XV:608–10, et passim), hint at a way we might interpret it. Not only human subjects, but all subject beings, all beings intentionally active in the world, constitute what-is as the meaningful whole, "world," subsuming it within a transcendental subjectivity. Their presence necessarily entails an a priori value ordering. Even apart from human presence, the world is a correlate of purposeful life; it is a *Lebenswelt* not simply in the weak sense of the world as a correlate of our everyday life, but as *die Welt des Lebens*, life's-world. As such, it is always already value laden and meaningfully ordered, never simply a world of extended entities in merely spatiotemporal causal relations. Grass is not simply there, a *res extensa* devoid of all attributes other than extension. It is already deeply good as the woodchuck's fodder. The warmth of the sun is never simply a matter of waves and particles. It is also ordered as near and dear as it warms the sunflower and the chickadees. Our human presence does not bestow meaning upon a value-free Cartesian extended reality. We are present in life's-world, meaningfully ordered by the presence of subjects. Our subjectivity is a part of the network

'who' gives it meaning

of subjectivity as such, of the *absolut fungierende Subjektivität*.

We are going beyond Husserl in thinking of the ideal possibilities, not as eternally subsisting geometrical relations, but as possibilities, variously con-stituted at different levels of generality, in the course of subject function-ing. Even that, though, is not a direction alien to Husserl. He himself suggests it in *Ideen II* and subsequently Merleau-Ponty develops it in *La phénoménologie de la perception*. Future research might well discover a warrant for such a generative reading of Husserl's conception of ideal possibility and so of tran-scendental philosophy in his posthumous texts. In any case, transcenden-tal—*a priori* synthetic—ordering characterizes specifically our everyday experience at its most everyday.

So we return to our starting point and to the topic of this conference, *Transcendental Philosophy and Everyday Experience*. Nearly four centuries of Cartesian commonplaces about the "objective" world and its "merely sub-jective" reflection predispose us to see in that topic a matter of the relation of obscure, esoteric philosophical constructs on the one hand, and of the obvious, lucid givens of our daily life on the other. Our reflections, though, lead to a different conclusion. On closer inspection it turns out that our experience is not at all what the empiricists would have it be, a passive recording of spatiotemporal relations of extended entities, arbitrarily deco-rated with meaning relations by a "merely subjective" *res cogitans*. It has its intrinsic, meaningful, value-laden ordering, there to be seen—its "transcen-dental subjectivity"—simply in virtue of the purposive presence of agent beings. That is not at all esoteric or obscure. Nor is transcendental philoso-phy when it formulates normative judgments, both synthetic and a priori, on the basis of that structure of ideal possibilities. It is very everyday phi-losophy—because the meaning structure of everyday experience is really very transcendental.

So, I would conclude, our time-honored way of speaking of transcenden-tal philosophy and everyday experience is a bit misleading. It would be far more accurate to speak of *transcendental experience* and *everyday philosophy*.

WORKS CITED

Carr 1970   Edmund Husserl, *Crisis of the European Sciences and*
                 Transcendental Phenomenology. An English translation of *Hua*
                 VI, by David Carr (Evanston: Northwestern University Press,
                 1980).
Dewey 1929   John Dewey, *Experience and Nature* (London: George Allen and
                 Unwin, 1929).
Eisler 1903   Rudolf Eisler, *Handwörterbuch der Philosophie* (Berlin: Mittler &
                 Sohn, 1903).

Hgg 1927   Martin Heidegger, *Sein und Zeit* (Halle: Niemeyer, 1927).

Hua II   Edmund Husserl, *Die Idee der Phänomenologie*. Husserliana, vol. 2. Walter Biemel, ed. (Den Haag: Martinus Nijhoff, 1947, 1973).

Hua III   ———, *Ideen zu einer reinen Phänomenologie und phänomenologischen Philosophie*. Erstes Buch, *Allgemeine Einführung in die reine Phänomenologie*. Husserliana, vol. 3. Walter Biemel, ed. (Den Haag: Martinus Nijhoff, 1950).

Hua IV   ———, Ibid., Zweites Buch, *Phänomenologischen Untersuchungen zur Konstitution*. Marly Biemel, ed. (Den Haag: Martinus Nijhoff, 1952).

Hua VI   ———, *Die Krisis der europäischen Wissenschaften und die transcendentale Phänomenologie*. Husserliana, vol. 6. Walter Biemel, ed. (Den Haag: Martinus Nijhoff, 1962).

Hua XV   ———, *Zur Phänomenologie der Intersubjektivität: Texte aus dem Nachlaß*. Dritter Teil: 1929–35. Iso Kern, ed. (Den Haag: Martinus Nijhoff, 1973).

James 1890   William James, *The Principles of Psychology*, vol. 1 (New York: Henry Holt, 1890, reprint; New York: Dover, 1950).

Kant 1947   Immanuel Kant, *Grundlagen zur Metaphysik der Sitten* (Leipzig: Meiner, 1947).

Kant 1951   ———, *Kritik der praktischen Vernunft* (Leipzig, Meiner, 1951).

Kern 1964   Iso Kern, *Husserl und Kant* (Den Haag: Martinus Nijhoff, 1964).

Kersten 1983   Edmund Husserl, *Ideals Pertaining to a Pure Phenomenology and to a Phenomenological Philosophy: The First Book*. An English translation of *Hua III*, by Fred Kersten (The Hague: Martinus Nijhoff, 1983).

Kohák 1989   Erazim Kohák, *Jan Patočka, His Thought and Writing* (Chicago: The University of Chicago Press, 1989).

MM-P 1945   Maurice Merleau-Ponty, *La Phénoménologie de la perception* (Paris: Gallimard, 1945).

Ricoeur 1960   Paul Ricoeur, *Le volontaire et l'involontaire* (Paris: Editions du Soleil, 1960).

Scheler 1912   Max Scheler, *Formalismus in der Ethik und die materiale Wertethik* (Halle: Niemeyer, 1912, 1921).

Schutz 1932   Alfred Schutz, *Der sinnhafte Aufbau der sozialen Welt* (Wien: Springer, 1932, 1970).

4

Penelope's Web:
Reconstruction of Philosophy
and the Relevance of Reason

Tom Rockmore

Since its origins in ancient Greece, philosophy has been concerned with reason in the service of the true and the good. On one reading, philosophy is the unique source of reason which alone knows truth and enacts the good. Truth here is understood in a traditional philosophical sense as capturing the general structure of reality comprehended as a permanent, ahistorical framework that can be known through philosophy; philosophy is conceived as the highest form of reason, and knowledge following from reason leads to the good where "good" is intrinsically related to "the good life." On this reading, philosophy is intrinsically realist since when it is correctly practiced it yields statements whose truth and falsity consists in their correspondence with an independent reality.[1] That philosophy yields the good depends on the idea of philosophy as yielding the true, since truth is either the prerequisite to the good or even the good as such.

This normative view of philosophy as the custodian of the true and the good goes back a very long way in the philosophical tradition. It continues to exert its hold upon the philosophical imagination as a regulative idea that has long guided philosophical discussion. Yet in practice, persistent, widespread doubt about the success in attaining these twin philosophical goals has led to a long series of efforts to reconstruct philosophy. The problem of how to reconstruct philosophy has only become more complex through the decline of the earlier consensus in the wake of the Hegelian view. One

This chapter was earlier published as "Penelope's Web: Reconstruction of Philosophy and the Relevance of Reason," in *Journal of Speculative Philosophy*, vol. 7, no. 2 (1993): 114–136.

strategy employed in order to recover the link between philosophical reason, truth, and goodness is through a qualified return to Kant. The present paper considers the problem of the reconstruction of philosophical reason, with particular attention devoted to the reconstruction of the critical philosophy. I will argue that it is a mistake to attempt to recover philosophy as socially relevant through a reconstruction, however distant, of the critical philosophy.

I

The traditional claim for reason can be stated simply as follows. There are different levels of reason, and the highest level is philosophical reason. Reason, correctly applied, yields truth and knowledge, and philosophical reason is the unique source of truth and knowledge in an absolute sense. Also, truth and knowledge are either the good or the condition of the good, where "good" is understood here intuitively as meaning "socially useful, even socially indispensable." Examples are the Socratic view that the unexamined life is not worth living and its Platonic restatement, according to which philosophy is a necessary condition of justice in the state. Stated in this way, we have a short formulation of the traditional philosophical claim for philosophy as the final, ultimate source of truth and goodness.

This normative philosophical claim for itself that has long been integral to philosophy's self-understanding, has rarely seemed satisfying to anyone, including philosophers. The history of philosophy can fairly be regarded as a concerted effort over many centuries to make good on this claim, to be equal to the traditional, metaphilosophical, normative view that has long tended to dominate philosophical discussion. This effort is expressed in the proposed reconstruction of the philosophical view of reason, in the examination of the link between philosophy, truth, and goodness.

I am convinced that the examination of reason is a main philosophical task. This is a central topic even today. The development of the discussion in this century has been largely concerned with the nature and function of reason. On the one hand, in the efforts in analytic philosophy, following upon Frege's effort to construct a formalized language of pure thought, to provide a more rigorous language for philosophy in the work of Ludwig Wittgenstein, Bertrand Russell, and the members of the Vienna Circle, particularly Rudolf Carnap. On the other hand, from a different, less focused perspective in continental philosophy in the writings of Henri Bergson, and in those of phenomenologists such as Husserl and Heidegger. More recent developments in the continental side of the debate have only extended the examination of reason in Gadamer's proposed substitution of hermeneutics for epistemology,[2] in Foucault's genealogical analysis of the link between knowledge and power, in Derrida's sceptical, anti-Hegelian assault on reason as such,[3] in Habermas's concern to recapture the link between reason and relevance, and in Rorty's apparent conclusion that since all efforts at knowledge fail there is only edifying conversation.

Although there is agreement about the need to reconstruct philosophy, there is little agreement about how this is to be done. So far as I can see there are two main models of philosophical reconstruction in the modern portion of the philosophical tradition; although I do not want to claim that any individual theory precisely corresponds to either. Let us call them the systematic and the historico-systematic models. Of the two, it is certainly the systematic model that has garnered the most attention in the discussion since, say, Descartes. On this model, historical and systematic considerations are mutually exclusive, and philosophy is a systematic enterprise, although this view of "system" has little or nothing to do with building systems, certainly not in the sense associated with German idealism. The history of philosophy is nothing more than a vast wasteland, a conceptual swamp that we must ignore as replete with errors and only occasional insights. Individual thinkers are occasionally significant, yet prior thought is not studied as part of an ongoing dialogue, from a historical point of view.

The conviction that we had best ignore the history of philosophy, or at most discuss prior thinkers on a very selective basis, is surprisingly widespread in recent philosophy. Its acceptance has given rise to the notion, as common among continental philosophers as their analytic counterparts, that we need to begin again, on one reading finally to make an adequate beginning through breaking with our former views and through advancing a new way of going about things fully independent of what has come before. A classical illustration is provided in the "Copernican turn," a move intended to identify a new, wholly systematic approach, uninfluenced by historical considerations that must be excluded if knowledge is solely *a priori*.[4] Yet Kant's own theory clearly fails this test since it necessarily presupposes as the justification for the Copernican turn, historical knowledge of the failure of prior views of knowledge.

The other, rival model is based on the idea that philosophy and its history are not discontinuous, but necessarily continuous. Philosophy cannot start over without regard to its past efforts. Philosophy takes into account and builds upon prior philosophical views. The history of the philosophical tradition resembles a Socratic dialogue spread out through time in which later thinkers engage the views of their predecessors in the ongoing effort to formulate an increasingly satisfactory theory. Philosophy continues the ongoing discussion through winnowing the wheat from the conceptual chaff, utilizing the relative successes of previous views as material for future thought.

The two models distinguished here are obviously antithetical. If philosophy proceeds in a merely systematic fashion, then it cannot be an historical enterprise; and if it proceeds in cognizance of its history, then it is not merely systematic. Yet the obvious differences should not be allowed to obscure a residually foundational character of both models of philosophical recon-struction. The idea that we need to start over, finally to make a true begin-ning upon which to build an acceptable theory, is a powerful restatement of the classical Cartesian line, as developed in the very seminal "Discourse on Method" and elsewhere. A similarity exists in the rival view that later theories carry forward and refine the foundation laid in the earlier studies.

Hegel is frequently interpreted as an antifoundationalist thinker. Yet he, too, adopts a version of the foundationalist metaphor, according to which later theories necessarily take into account and build upon the positive as-pects of their predecessors. Although he is cognizant, in an unprecedented manner, of the entire prior philosophical discussion, his officially optimistic reading of prior thought, as leading up to and culminating in his own, is unwarranted. Inspection of the history of philosophy does not reveal steady progress; despite Hegel's optimistic view of the history of philosophy, in this respect later is not always better. It is often the case that chronologi-cally later is conceptually earlier, since insights are forgotten, lessons go unlearned, and the past is not made a constitutive part of the effort to construct new and better views. If this is correct, then a more likely meta-phor for the philosophical tradition is *Penelope's Web*, which is constantly being unraveled and rewoven in the ebb and flow of the philosophical dis-cussion.[5] A later philosophical theory is less likely to build upon its pred-ecessors in a direct or even an indirect way than to deconstruct them in order to reconstruct something else, a new theory, to put in their place.

II

Although philosophy has always been under reconstruction as it were, this task has become more difficult in recent times in the wake of the critical philosophy, roughly since Hegel. In the modern tradition, as early as Descartes, there seems to have been widespread agreement that the business of phi-losophy was to propose an adequate theory of knowledge. In simplest terms, the disagreement between the rationalists and the empiricists is about whether knowledge arises from the intellect or experience. The dispute between them does not concern the ends, but rather means to arrive at knowledge. The two movements represent ongoing efforts to work out the utility of two different, parallel approaches to knowledge as either the result of the intel-lect or experience.

The concentration on means rather than ends is, if anything, only height-ened in Kant's wake. The discussion from Kant to Hegel is largely taken up with the problem of the critical philosophy. If we except the rare thinker unconcerned with Kant, then the others can be divided into those who thought that Kant had failed to answer Hume, including skeptics such as Maimon and G. E. Schulze (also known as Aenesidemus); those who held that Kant's view of reason was intrinsically untenable, such as Hamann, Herder, and perhaps Jacobi; and those who were convinced that the critical philosophy was basically correct, but that it failed its own test of scientific system. Among those who held that the critical philosophy required a reconstruction in systematic form we can mention Reinhold, Fichte, Schelling, and Hegel.

III

The reconstruction of philosophy from Descartes roughly to Hegel is based on a large consensus about the need for philosophy as systematic or even as system, in fact as a universal system of knowledge in the full, or traditional sense, that quickly disappears in the wake of Hegel's thought.[6] The problem on the horizon at that point was less the significance of a philosophical solution to the problem of knowledge than how to provide the solution. The lack of consensus which characterizes the discussion in the post-Hegelian period has tended to make the problem of arriving at a viable reconstruction even more difficult. It is no longer simply a question of a strategy yielding a theory that is the source of truth and knowledge since the utility of philosophy has now been called into question.

The consensus about the nature and utility of philosophy is widely apparent in the modern tradition. Descartes's standard of apodicticity is applied throughout later thought, at least until Husserl,[7] as late as Heidegger's early thought,[8] and is still applied in some areas of analytic philosophy.[9] Descartes provides us with a convenient distinction between knowledge in the absolute sense as the only resource against skepticism which echoes through the later discussion.

The large consensus which existed throughout the modern tradition from Descartes to Hegel, particularly in the period from Kant to Hegel, concerns the normative conception of knowledge. During this period, with some notable exceptions for most philosophers, the main philosophical problem was to determine the strategy appropriate to realize the common goal. This consensus, which prevailed through the completion of the Hegelian system, rapidly disappears after the death of Hegel. The breakup of the Hegelian School into various fragments is important for the appreciation of Hegel's thought, as well as for an understanding of later developments. In some ways, we are still witnessing the results of the split between left wing and right wing Hegelians. Certainly, a number of post-Hegelian philosophical positions, including those of Marx, Marxism—and in this century those of

Georg Lukács, Korsch, and the Frankfurt School—including Max Horkheimer, Theodor Adorno, Herbert Marcuse, and Habermas can be directly traced to the left-wing variety of Hegelianism that emerged after Hegel died.[10] But the breakup of the Hegelian School is important for another, different reason. For it is symptomatic of a larger change in the philosophical context which goes well beyond Hegel's thought.

I see four main factors as contributing to the loss of the consensus concerning philosophy in the post-Hegelian discussion, including the divorce of science and philosophy, the emergence of history as a central concern, the decline of foundationalism, and skepticism about the limits of philosophy. The divorce between science and philosophy, subsequent to the rise of modern science, began around the turn of the nineteenth century. The two disciplines were still sufficiently connected for Schelling and Goethe to engage in scientific research under the guise of the philosophy of nature, whereas this same term means what we now understand as "philosophy of science" in Hegel's writings. The gradual emancipation of the new science from philosophy undercut the traditional philosophical view of itself as the science of sciences and the sole source of knowledge in the final sense. This view was now inverted in the claim that science is the sole source of knowledge and the role of philosophy is to concern itself with the fundamentals of science. This basic trust in science, as opposed to philosophy, is an article of faith throughout recent philosophy, in pragmatism (Peirce), in the Vienna Circle thinkers and their heirs, in analytic philosophy of science of all kinds, and in various forms of physicalism, materialism, and so on.

Second, there is the gradual emergence of the idea of history as constitutive of knowledge, above all in the writings of Vico, Hegel, and Marx. If philosophy is part of the historical process, it is no longer possible to take an ahistorical approach to knowledge. Philosophical theories, including theories of knowledge, that are ahistorical are, then, fundamentally flawed. By implication, the theory of knowledge needs to be rethought from a historical point of view.

Third, there is the decline of foundationalism, the most widely favored epistemological strategy of modern times. It has sometimes seemed as if this strategy were only discussed by analytic thinkers.[11] Yet, on certain readings, it is present very early in the philosophical tradition. Fichte and Hegel can both be read as foundationalist thinkers, but also, and I believe more perspicuously, as antifoundationalist thinkers.[12] At the present time, this strategy is still favored by a few writers, such as Apel and Chisholm.[13] But it is fair to say that the prospects for an effective defense of the foundationalist approach to epistemology have never seemed as weak and most philosophers have now simply abandoned the effort.

Finally, there is a renewed scepticism about the intrinsic limits of philosophy, either about its capacity for knowledge or its social relevance. This emerging scepticism expressed itself in various forms, including the inability of philosophy to resolve its concerns, which, for that reason, needed to be solved on an extra-philosophical, scientific plane. This view is associated since Engels with Marxism of all kinds.[14] More recently, another effort to solve the problems of philosophy on a plane beyond philosophy, in this case through a claimed relation of philosophy to poetry, has emerged in Heidegger's turn away from philosophy to so-called thinking.[15] Then there is the capacity of philosophy to know existence, which is doubted by Kierkegaard.[16] A third factor is the demotion of philosophy's claim to a neutral epistemological status, which is doubted by Nietzsche and Marx.

Another whole set of doubts was raised about the utility of philosophy. The general problem can be symbolized by Marx's famous complaint that philosophy fails to change the world, which directly denies Hegel's early confidence in the self-realizing capacity of theory. The conviction that philosophical theory at best retains only a tenuous link to social practice is echoed in this century in various ways, including Wittgenstein's view that when philosophy has finished with its problems, those of life remain untouched;[17] Russell's view, compatible with Wittgenstein's, that the interest of philosophy lies not in its answers but only in the questions it considers;[18] and Dewey's effort to show that the split between theory and practice must be overcome through a reconstruction of philosophy that will take into account the new movements in science and the change in the human condition.[19]

The difference between the early Wittgenstein and Russell on the one hand, and Dewey on the other is instructive from the angle of vision of the traditional philosophical concern with useful knowledge. The former hold to the traditional view of knowledge, while inclining to the conclusion that we can only know that philosophy is not the source of such knowledge. Both continue to conceive of philosophy as an enterprise which unfolds in its own universe, the kind of view which the later Wittgenstein is at pains to deny. Dewey, on the contrary, maintains that philosophy very much belongs to and unfolds in the world, and hence denies the concern with knowledge in any absolute sense, with the so-called quest for certainty.[20] He advocates a philosophical reconstruction that acknowledges this relation in order to recover the claim, if not to knowledge as traditionally conceived, at least to relevance, to philosophy as linked to the social good.

Recent philosophy, say since Hegel, can be understood as an effort to find its bearings after it seemed to peak, and to many to come to an end in a final grand synthesis. Yet the agreement concerning the normative Platonic idea of philosophy which prevailed as late as Hegel, and was still the model for Husserl has now disappeared; and Plato, who for so long was the "official" hero, has now become the "official" enemy. Although the Platonic

model which attracted attention for so long has now gone out of style, it retains its interest in the renewed interest in Kant's theory. None other than
Kant insisted on the link between the critical philosophy and Plato's view.[21]

After the breakdown of the informal philosophical consensus concerning
philosophy as the arbiter, the final source of the true and the good, there
were four possible strategies: (1) to begin with a denial that philosophy is
either the source of the true or the good, (2) a philosophical concern with
the true without regard to the good, (3) or a philosophical concern with
the good without regard to the true, (4) and finally the effort to recover the
idea of philosophy as the source of both the true and good. The first view
is illustrated by certain varieties of Marxism which maintain that philosophy cannot know the truth, that it is available only to science, and that
philosophy, which is mere ideology, contributes to maintaining an unequal
social condition. The second view is illustrated in the concern with traditional epistemology without regard to the social utility of the discipline. A
contemporary example might be Rorty's notion of philosophy as merely edifying
discourse. Here one gets on with the business of traditional epistemology—
for Rorty posttraditional theory of knowledge since he holds that epistemology has failed—and lets the good take care of itself, in Rorty's case
relying all the while on liberal irony, which he understands as including at
least the desire that suffering will be diminished.[22] The effect of this approach seems to be to reduce the relevance of reason to the efficacy of
pious thoughts. An example of the third approach is Dewey's theory that
denies knowledge in the traditional sense of the term, yet is intensely and
directly concerned with the social good. Finally, there is the effort to recover the true and the good within philosophy that, at least since Hegel,
has often meant a qualified return to Kant.

V

In the post-Hegelian discussion, many more thinkers were interested in
deconstructing than in reconstructing the old idea of the relevance of philosophical reason.[23] The renewed sceptical attacks on philosophy, the emergence of physicalism, the glorification of natural science are all aspects of
the deepening disagreement with the old normative conception of philosophy as the source of the true, and, hence, question its association with the
good. Yet there have also been important efforts once again to reconstruct
philosophical reason in a satisfactory form, finally to make a new beginning, a true beginning, a first beginning, to renew, or to recover, the valid
impulse of prior thought. Some of these efforts are concerned merely with
the problem of knowledge in the independence of any social utility which
might follow from it, either through disinterest or on the assumption that

the true is either good in itself or the key to another good; others are concerned with knowledge as well as with its social relevance.

In our own time, three of the more prominent thinkers who have taken
the latter route to recover the traditional, normative view of philosophy as
socially relevant include Husserl, Heidegger, and Habermas. Other than the
German language, these three very different thinkers have in common the
intention to provide a qualified reconstruction of philosophy to recapture
philosophy's traditional claim as the source of the true and the good. Each
of these thinkers defends a conception of reason as intrinsically useful. In
each case, the proposed reconstruction depends on the critical philosophy.
As an Enlightenment thinker, Kant regards reason as the highest human
possession. He understands the Enlightenment as the result of human being's emergence from its inability to think for itself and called for courage
in so doing. Since each of these thinkers is concerned to react against a
perceived crisis of reason, it is not surprising that each turns to the critical
philosophy; for in the modern tradition Kant's theory is widely perceived as
a main representative of the idea of philosophy as the custodian of the true
and the good, a view dominant in the discussion since Plato.

Husserl's relation to Kant is both direct and indirect, mediated through
his study of German neo-Kantianism, particularly Natorp.[24] There are numerous Kantian elements in Husserl's position, including the attack on
psychologism following Frege's critique of his alleged conflation of logic and
psychology in his first book on the philosophy of arithmetic, in his use of
the term "transcendental," and in the similarity between his conception of
pure phenomenology and Kant's view of pure reason. In the *Logical Investigations*, Husserl elaborates an initial, phenomenological defense of the conception of reason in quasi-Kantian fashion. The fundamental similarity lies
in the view of philosophy as a rigorously scientific and reflexive critique of
rational principles with the goal of realizing rationality and attaining an
ultimate metaphysics.[25] Husserl agreed with Natorp's assessment that the
goals of his pure logic overlapped with those of the Kantian critique of
knowledge.

Husserl's entire theory can be understood as a concerted attempt to defend the idea of reason against the crisis of reason through a distinction
between knowledge and opinion.[26] This concern is evident in his phenomenological breakthrough, in the elaborate critique of psychologism which
occupies the first volume of the *Logical Investigations*. Husserl restates approximately the same view in the programmatic text on "Philosophy as
Rigorous Science," which he associates with Descartes, Kant, and Fichte.
Here the problem is widened to include opposition to naturalism and to
historicism in order to evade sceptical relativism and defend apodicticity.
He continues this task in his study of *Formal and Transcendental Logic* as

the ultimate theory of all science. The problem is deepened in his final, incomplete study of the *Crisis of European Sciences and Transcendental Phenomenology*. Faced with the rise of Nazi barbarism, Husserl proposes to respond through the defense of the ancient distinction between *episteme* and *doxa*.[27] Even in his later work, he specifically understands transcendental phenomenology as the heir to the concern with reason in the traditional sense, more precisely as the unexpressed "presupposition" of the Kantian view identified as the life-world.[28]

VI

Heidegger's own concern to depict his thought as influenced only by the pre-Socratics tends to obscure the strongly Kantian and neo-Kantian component in his theory Heidegger's link to Kant is indirectly mediated through Husserl, the neo-Kantian Heinrich Rickert,[29] and especially Emil Lask; and directly as a result of his own extensive study of the critical philosophy.[30]

Heidegger's thought turns on an attempted renewal of metaphysics, precisely the Kantian question. Yet Heidegger and Kant understand "metaphysics" in different incompatible ways. What for Heidegger is ontology is for Kant, as for Hegel, mainly a question of epistemology. Being in Heidegger's sense presupposes an ontological distinction between beings, or entities, and Being in general, in one formulation the Being of beings. This problem has been forgotten since the early Greeks because later philosophy took an incorrect turning in the road. The long discussion since that time is useless, since it casts no further light on the problem; it is further harmful, since it tends to cover up the very problem that it is intended to illuminate. The subsequent history of ontology must be destroyed in order to reveal the original formulation of the problem.[31]

This logic of destruction in order to return to the original—according to Heidegger correct—formulation of the problem of the meaning of Being suggests that his attention is exclusively directed towards the revival of pre-Socratic insights. Yet this way of understanding his position is denied by his reading of Kant's position in *Being and Time* and in *Kant and the Problem of Metaphysics*. In the latter book, Heidegger maintains that his own thought takes up and completes the Kantian position by moving it beyond the point at which Kant left it because of his own inability to carry it further.[32] His whole project of understanding Being in general can be read as a novel type of neo-Kantian rereading of the Kantian the thing-in-itself as Being. Following others, including Hume, Kant distinguished between bad metaphysics that he rejected, and good metaphysics that he sought to found as a science.[33] Husserl similarly believed that transcendental phenomenology was the final form of metaphysics. Following the lead of Husserl,

Kant, and others, Heidegger's effort to return to the correct way of putting the question is intended to develop further and bring to an end metaphysics, not as epistemology, but as a theory of Being.

VII

Habermas's link to Kant developed only gradually, and then only as a result of his critical reading of historical materialism; a term he tends to apply indiscriminately to Marx and Marxism. At least since the essay, "Knowledge and Human Interests: A General Perspective," Habermas has been engaged in an effort to revive a version of Kant's idea of the intrinsic interest of reason. In his many writings, Habermas has stressed the link of his own position to the critical philosophy in various ways, including the suggestion of analogies between his thought and Kant's, the claim that epistemology decays into social theory after Kant,[34] the assertion that the "philosophy of identity" or the "theory of consciousness"—two synonyms for "German idealism"—cannot be further developed, but must be replaced by a critique of language,[35] the effort to revive the Enlightenment ideal in opposition to French postmodernism, particularly Lyotard,[36] and so on.

Habermas's position emerged within the critical theory of the Frankfurt School variety of neo-Marxism that it later abandoned to move closer to orthodox philosophy, particularly the critical philosophy. Marxism, in general, has never been friendly to Kantianism, although there were some early Kantian-Marxists around the turn of the century.[37] Marxists have always tended to see Kant as a traditional philosopher whose position excludes the kinds of interests they wished to develop. Since Engels, Marxists have tended to insist frequently and strongly, although not necessarily convincingly, that only Marxism is concerned with the relation of theory to practice. It has sometimes seemed to Marxists as if so-called traditional theory, as exemplified by Descartes's position, was interested in theory only, and unconcerned with practice. This idea was given canonical form in an influential essay by Horkheimer, "Traditional and Critical Theory."[38]

Habermas followed the Frankfurt School line to begin with. His position can be understood as a four-stage effort to interpret, to criticize, and to reconstruct historical materialism in order to correct its perceived defects; a theory that is finally abandoned in favor of his own substitute theory of communicative action.[39] To begin with, Habermas sought to grasp the specific difference between historical materialism and traditional philosophy. In an influential article, he opposed critical theory, understood from the Frankfurt perspective, to traditional theory, as represented mainly by Husserl's thought.[40] In a next step, he criticized Marx's theory from a more traditional, epistemological perspective as being self-reflexively inconsistent, in his terms as conflating work and interaction, or communication. In a further step, relying on Heidegger's view of reconstruction as freeing a possibility that has later been covered up, he has tried to reformulate historical materialism in order to palliate this difficulty,[41] before abandoning historical materialism in favor of his own theory of communicative action.[42]

His own position, which is frequently misunderstood, has never been formulated in satisfactory fashion within his own writings; it may be that it cannot be satisfactorily stated.[43] The efforts to state it, with which I am familiar, appear rather thin in comparison to the massive, sprawling treatise in which it is advanced.[44] Suffice it to say that Habermas's own position can be regarded as an attempt to make good on the emancipatory intent of historical materialism while correcting the problem arising through Marx's alleged conflation of work and interaction. Habermas holds that the old philosophy of consciousness, to which Marx's theory belongs, cannot be extended, since it is conceptually bankrupt and needs to be replaced by the analysis of language, finally through his own theory of communicative action. Yet he does not abandon the emancipatory goal of Marx and Marxism, that he means to realize through other means.

His discussion of the ideal of undistorted communication as yielding truth through consensus is correctly seen not as abandoning, but as reinforcing the emancipatory of Marx's position.[45] The result is a qualified return to Kant, since for Habermas, as for the author of the critical philosophy, reason is intrinsically socially relevant. Habermas means to recover a view of reason as intrinsically relevant, or the unity of theoretical knowledge and action, through the analysis of the ideal conditions of what he calls undistorted communication. For Habermas, true statements are linked to the true and the good, in his words "the intention of the good and true life."[46] The guiding assumption, which seems to rest on a misreading of Peirce, is the insight that the consensus of this type is not only what we call truth at any given moment but in fact equivalent to truth.

VIII

One ought not to deny the deep differences between the positions of Husserl, Heidegger, and Habermas. Yet there is an obvious similarity between these three recent attempts to recapture the relevance of philosophical reason through very different forms of reconstruction. Each of these three thinkers understands "philosophy"[47] as the highest form of reason; philosophical reason as productive of truth in something like the absolute sense current in philosophy approximately since Plato, and philosophical truth as socially useful, even indispensable. In each case, the approach to the Platonic model lies through the critical philosophy. Each of these thinkers strives to recover a form of the traditional view of philosophy as a guardian of the true and the good in and through philosophical reason.

It is obviously not possible to evaluate the philosophical contribution of these three thinkers in rapid compass. Suffice it to say that Husserl's contribution to our understanding of reason is perhaps greater than has commonly been recognized, in part because of the enormous stature acquired by his student, Heidegger. The situation now is likely to change in a basic way. For nearly a half century Heidegger's students have been fighting a rearguard action to contain damage to his thought and person following from his turn to National Socialism. At present, after the publication of the works by Victor Farías[48] and Hugo Ott,[49] it has become too late to put the genie back in the bottle, too late to prevent or even usefully to impede a thorough airing of the issue. It is likely that serious scrutiny of the constitutive link between Heidegger's thought and his Nazism will in time produce a substantial revision of the general comprehension of his philosophical contribution. In comparison, Habermas is a much less important thinker, whose measure it is difficult to take because of his inability to write clearly, as well as his tendency to multiply allusions to a vast literature as a strategy to hide his own inability to formulate a theoretical position.[50]

Instead of providing an evaluation of the respective philosophical contributions of these three thinkers, I will concentrate on the narrower issue of their respective efforts to make out a version of the traditional philosophical claim for the relevance of reason. In that regard, Kant's claim for the intrinsic relevance of reason can be regarded as a restatement of one of the two main arguments in Plato for the social utility of philosophy. According to Plato, philosophy is indispensable for politics, since only the philosopher can know the truth in the full sense. The argument that "philosophy grounds politics" is in turn rooted in the Platonic conception of philosophy as being the final source of truth.

Husserl apparently takes over this latter claim without further examining it. His conviction that the philosopher is the functionary of mankind, describing his deep ethical commitment, is only sufficient to establish a claim for the social utility of transcendental phenomenology if it is the case that philosophy is the final source of truth in some Platonic sense, as Husserl evidently still believes. Yet it has become increasingly more difficult to assert this claim with confidence. Moreso Husserl's own confidence in the virtues of a defense of reason, on a philosophical plane, seems a rather slender reed with which to combat the rise of Nazi barbarism.[51] We are accustomed to the philosophical claim for the intrinsic link between knowing the good and doing the good. Yet the social utility of philosophy as such is surely called into question by the disquieting examples of Heidegger's deep and lasting commitment to National Socialism and Lukács's enthusiasm for Stalinism.[52]

Heidegger's thought, as represented by him, is a gradual turning against the Platonic tradition, and finally is a twisting free to new thought located beyond philosophy. Yet Heidegger's own brief for the relevance of reason is a qualified restatement of the Platonic idea that politics must be grounded in philosophy. His early turn to Nazism in his rectorial address—given on the solemn assumption of the rectorate of the University of Freiburg in 1933 in Nazi Germany—is presented by Heidegger as an effort to lead the leaders who are incapable of leading themselves, as founding politics in philosophy, more precisely as grounding National Socialism in fundamental ontology.[53] His later insistence on his thought, even after the so-called turning [Kehre], as indispensable for the future of all mankind is a qualified restatement of his quasi-Platonic insistence on the socially indispensable character of his own insight into the nature of Being. Yet other than his own unsupported faith in the power of his insight, there is strictly no reason to accept Heidegger's claim for the social relevance of his own view of reason. Thus, if an identification with Nazism is an argument, then Heidegger's theory has been refuted in practice.

The positions of Rorty and Habermas are closely linked through the impact of Gadamerian hermeneutics from which they appear to draw opposing conclusions. Habermas's claim for the relevance of philosophical reason is an inverted form of Rorty's view of philosophy as merely edifying discussion. Whereas Rorty points to Gadamer, correctly in my opinion, to substitute edification for truth, since that is about all that hermeneutics can yield.[54] Habermas stubbornly maintains the traditional view of the expert as the source of higher knowledge; above all the philosopher is the source of the truth which originates in Plato. Following Gadamer more closely than Rorty, Habermas seems to accept Gadamer's claim to solve the problems of epistemology through hermeneutics, in Habermas's position through the identification of consensus with truth.

To the best of my knowledge there is no text in which Habermas straightforwardly claims to be restating the traditional Platonico-Kantian view of the social relevance of philosophical reason. Nonetheless, I contend that this is a reasonable interpretation of his effort, following Horkheimer, to make out the distinction between traditional and critical forms of theory not only in his celebrated inaugural lecture, but throughout his many later writings. Although Habermas modifies his view of the nature and character of the form of social-philosophical reasoning that he develops, he consistently maintains his view of its social utility.[55]

This identification is questionable for several reasons, to begin with since it obviously does not follow that if there is agreement there is truth, although this possibility cannot be excluded. If unconstrained dialogue ever occurs it might produce agreement, but there is no reason to accept such consensus as truth. Habermas's remark, with respect to Peirce, that "we must consider a well-founded and intersubjectively recognized view as true as long as its validity has not been rendered problematical by an unforeseen experience"[56] simply confuses truth with what various observers happen to agree on at the moment. To illustrate: enough people once agreed that prefrontal lobotomy was important enough for its discoverer to be awarded a Nobel prize for medicine, although most observers now think that this procedure is an unjustified form of patient mutilation. Yet on Habermas's understanding of truth as consensus, he has no way to distinguish between truth claims that are entirely independent of agreement, and the agreement on which they depend. If, for instance, I agree with Habermas about his theory, his theory is not, therefore, true since we could both be wrong.

There is an obvious tension in Habermas's position since his later theory of communicative action contradicts his own early defense of critical theory and fails to establish its claim to social relevance. His early critique of traditional theory, as illustrated by Husserlian phenomenology, the early Habermas—from a generally young Hegelian, specifically Marxist stance he later abandoned—rejects claims for the intrinsic relevance of traditional philosophical reason. His later return to the traditional philosophical fold after the collapse of the Marxist experiment answers none of the doubts that Habermas raised earlier about traditional theory. For it is entirely possible that the early Habermas is correct in opposition to the later Habermas in maintaining that traditional forms of theory, like the one that Habermas has lately been at pains to develop, are largely irrelevant to the world in which we live. Moreover, he simply has no argument at all for the social relevance of his theory of communicative action. To regard the theory of communicative action, as Habermas does, as a plausible alternative for the no longer defensible philosophy of history in order to permit studies of the modernization of capitalism[57] does not mean that his own position reaches Marx's aim, however that aim is construed.

IX

The three efforts to reconstruct the idea of the relevance of reason considered here represent recent versions of the widespread philosophical concern to argue for philosophy as the custodian of the true and the good by supposing that philosophy can deliver on its claim to truth in the traditional sense. Each is finally dependent on Kant's idea of philosophy as a *conceptus cosmicus* distinguished by its view of reason as intrinsically concerned with the *teleologia rationis humanae*.[58] This idea resurfaces with clarity in Husserl's defense of the ancient distinction between *episteme* and *doxa*, again in Habermas's idea of the interest of reason. Also in more distant fashion, in

Heidegger's view of the intuitive grasp of Being, what is in effect in Kantian terms a noumenology. The common element in the three proposed reconstructions is the effort to recover the traditional view of philosophy as a source of the traditional view of truth in order to maintain that philosophical truth is socially useful.

I have mainly talked about these three thinkers, but my point is more general. In ways consistent with their respective theories, these writers illustrate the Enlightenment idea, culminating in Kant, of an intrinsic but never demonstrated link between philosophy as the source of the true and the socially good. According to this idea, philosophical reason is the conceptual *vademecum* and the philosopher is the lawgiver of human reason, the one who sets the agenda for the entire society.[59] The Enlightenment view of the ideal of perfect reason, still widely present, subtends the idea of the philosopher to be the guide to life, from a political angle of vision in the conception of the leader's leader in Heidegger's theory.

Yet the Kantian thesis that philosophical reason is intrinsically relevant and the philosopher is its lawgiver is antiquated since the notion of perfect knowledge, on which it depends, is no longer a viable option. There is at present no viable way to make out a claim of this kind. There is good reason to think that the kind of knowledge that philosophy can yield, if indeed it can yield any at all, fails to attain the philosophical target as traditionally conceived. It may well be that Habermas is closest, among recent thinkers, to Kant's view of the positive potential of metaphysics, but the very idea of philosophical reason as the cognitively privileged source of truth and goodness is basically misguided. Philosophy can no longer defend the traditional claim to privileged access to truth and goodness; at best it is merely one source, among others, that contributes to this end.

The Enlightenment view provides a qualified restatement of the claim, as old as Plato, which peaks again in Kant, that when philosophical reason is isolated from its context, then it is supremely relevant to that context. Long ago Hegel criticized that claim, for instance in depicting the French Revolution as reason run amok that destroys that at which it aims.[60] Hegel's criticism is relevant to discern the actual and potential social dangers of a kind of abstract reason that has lost touch with the context from which it emerges. Here I am concerned with a related problem: the very idea that philosophy as such is supremely relevant to society. I am less concerned with the abuse of reason, which certainly undermines the idea that it is more intrinsically, socially relevant in Heidegger's position, than with the widespread conviction of the intrinsic social utility of philosophical reason.

In my view, for philosophy to be socially relevant it needs to recover its relation with the social, political, and historical context in which it arises to the extent that it can be recovered at all. We need, then, a reconstruction of philosophy, but one which abandons the idea of philosophy as the single source of truth in the traditional sense, since it is only in that way that philosophy can become relevant. In order to update philosophy and reestablish its link to the world in which we live, we need to abandon the old idea clearly stated in Plato's *Timaeus*, that there is an intrinsical harmony, a kind of conceptual synergy between the world and reason. This "cosmological" view is stated by Kant and in some moods by Hegel, and still advanced without any underlying metaphysics at all in the views of Husserl, Heidegger, and Habermas. At this late date, when we can no longer assume that reason is uniquely qualified to know reality, about which nothing at all can be said other than, "we can say nothing at all about it," we need to utilize a different model, closer to the one offered by Aristotle on the plane of practical theory and later by Dewey. For the former saw that theory depends on its object; and the latter knew that as society changes, theory also needs to change lest it abandon any claim to intersect with society, and for that reason, lose its claim to social relevance.[61]

If philosophy is to speak to us in a relevant way, then it needs to consider the problems of real human beings as they arise within our daily existence. A necessary prerequisite is to abandon the conceptual conceit, that as philosophers, we are in touch with reality itself. At this late date, we can no longer pretend that philosophy is socially indispensable in virtue of its unique access to the fixed nature of reality. Despite its frequently reiterated claim, philosophy has no discernable cognitive privilege; and it is unclear what it could possibly mean to claim access to reality. It is possible that there is an independent reality, and it is also possible that it has a fixed nature; but there seems to be no reason to hold that either the fixed nature of reality or reality itself can be known through philosophy or in any other way. If a theory which defends access to the way things are is representational, then a form of philosophy that abandons such claims can only be antirepresentational. Nor can philosophy be a realist, if "realism" means something like "getting it right." If that is the case, then philosophy is better advised to take an antirealist position.

The deeper question is how philosophy can be relevant to our lives. In my view, it is not at all obvious that society depends on philosophy at all. Society, to the degree that it gets along, seems to be doing fine without help from philosophers since at present nothing philosophers are up to, with the possible exception of recent work in bioethics, seems particularly relevant to social concerns. I share the general supposition that philosophy requires a reconstruction, that none of the versions so far available are satisfactory. Yet I am disinclined to believe that if only we can finally make out the claim to know, in an absolute sense, we will be able to resurrect a successful version of reason as intrinsically relevant in some broad Kantian

sense, be it through seeing essences, grasping being, or arriving at a consensus. There is not one way to establish the relevance of philosophy. But
certainly Dewey was close to the mark in his conviction that we need to
abandon the traditional philosophical idea of truth as such, namely truth
understood as a quest for certainty, in order to see philosophy as growing
out of the distinctive stresses and strains of existence, to which it responds.[62]
Philosophy which abandons its traditional claim to understand the way the
world is finds its utility in the clarification of the problems arising out of
human existence, not because philosophic reason is somehow intrinsically
relevant. Put another way, philosophy is on the way to recovery when it
sacrifices any effort to theoretical finality in order to confront the problems
of human life.

NOTES

1. For this view of realism, see Michael Dummett, *Truth and Other Enigmas* (Cambridge, MA: Harvard University Press, 1978), p. 146, cited in Richard Rorty,
   Objectivism, Relativism, and Truth (Cambridge: Cambridge University Press, 1991)
   p. 3.
2. See Hans-Georg Gadamer, *Truth and Method*, translated by Garret Barden and
   John Cumming (New York: Crossroad, 1988), "The Overcoming of the Epistemological Problem through Phenomenological Research," pp. 214–234. For a
   study of Gadamer's view, see Tom Rockmore, "Herméneutique et vérité. Gadamer
   entre Heidegger et Hegel," in *Archives de philosophie*, vol. 53, no. 4, (October–
   December 1990), pp. 547–558.
3. For an anti-Hegelian reading of Derrida's thought, see Vincent Descombes, *Le
   même et l'autre* (Paris: Éditions de Minuit, 1979).
4. For the famous Copernican Revolution, see Immanuel Kant, *Kant's Critique of
   Pure Reason*, translated by Norman Kemp Smith (London and New York:
   Macmillan and St. Martin's Press), B xiii, p. 20.
5. See G. W. F. Hegel, *Hegel's Philosophy of Right*, translated with notes by T. M.
   Knox, p. 1: "*Philosophical* manuals are perhaps not now expected to conform to
   such a pattern [i.e., to be a compendium—T. R.], for it is supposed that what
   philosophy puts together is a work as ephemeral as Penelope's web, one which
   must be begun afresh every morning."
6. For an interesting analysis of the development of the idea of total system in
   modern philosophy, see Georg Lukács, *History and Class Consciousness*, translated by Rodney Livingston (Cambridge, MA: MIT Press), pp. 111–121.
7. See Edmund Husserl, *Cartesian Meditations. An Introduction to Phenomenology*,
   translated by Dorion Cairns (The Hague: Martinus Nijhoff, 1960), pp. 15–16.
8. In spite of the famous hermeneutic circle, Heidegger continues to hold the
   transcendental view of truth in this work. See Martin Heidegger, *Being and
   Time*, translated by John Macquarrie and Edward Robinson (Evanston, IL:
   Macmillan, 1962), §7, p. 62.
9. See, e.g., Roderick M. Chisholm, *The Foundations of Knowing* (Minneapolis:
   University of Minnesota Press, 1962).

10. If Descombes is correct, a left-wing form of Husserlian is central to the appreciation of contemporary French thought. See Descombes, *Le même et l'autre*.
11. See e.g., Michael Williams, *Groundless Belief* (Oxford: Blackwells, 1977).
12. For a discussion of German idealism from this angle of vision, see my paper "Foundationalism, Hegel, and German Idealism," edited by Tom Rockmore and Beth Singer, *Foundationalism Old and New* (Philadelphia: Temple University Press, 1992), pp. 105–125. See the entire volume for various analyses of the problem of foundationalism extending backward in the tradition until Anaximander.
13. Others prefer to defend prior efforts to make out foundationalism. For a recent, but unconvincing defense of C. I. Lewis with respect to perceptual foundationalism, see Paul Moser, "Foundationalism, the Given, and C. I. Lewis," in *History of Philosophy Quarterly*, vol. 5, no. 2 (April 1988), pp. 189–204.
14. For a classic statement of this perspective, see Friedrich Engels, *Ludwig Feuerbach and the Outcome of Classical German Philosophy*, edited by C. P. Dutt (New York: International Publishers, 1941).
15. For a brief discussion of the so-called turning, see Martin Heidegger, "Letter on Humanism," in Martin Heidegger, *Basic Writings*, edited by David F. Krell (New York: Macmillan, 1977), p. 208.
16. See Søren Kierkegaard, *Concluding Unscientific Postscript*, translated by David F. Swenson and Walter Lowrie (Princeton: Princeton University Press, 1968), pp. 99–113.
17. See Ludwig Wittgenstein, *Tractatus Logico-Philosophicus*, German text and translation by D. F. Pears and B. F. McGuinness, with an Introduction by Bertrand Russell (London: Routledge and Kegan Paul, 1961), proposition 6.52, pp. 148–149.
18. See Bertrand Russell, *The Problems of Philosophy* (New York: Oxford University Pres, 1959), chap. XV, pp. 152–161.
19. See John Dewey, *Reconstruction in Philosophy* (Boston: Beacon Press, 1960).
20. See John Dewey, *The Quest for Certainty* (New York: Capricorn Books, 1969).
21. See Kant, *Critique of Pure Reason*, B 370, p. 310.
22. See Richard Rorty, *Contingency, Irony, and Solidarity* (Cambridge: Cambridge University Press, 1989).
23. For a recent discussion of the views of Derrida, Foucault, Habermas, and Rorty from a Habermasian, and closely Kantian angle of vision, see Thomas McCarthy, *Ideals and Illusions on Reconstruction and Deconstruction in Contemporary Critical Theory* (Cambridge, MA: MIT Press, 1991).
24. See Iso Kern, *Husserl and Kant* (The Hague: Martinus Nijhoff, 1964).
25. In his last, unfinished work Husserl goes so far as to claim that skepticism about metaphysics is equivalent to skepticism about reason. See *The Crisis of European Sciences and Transcendental Phenomenology*, translated by David Carr (Evanston: Northwestern University Press, 1970), p. 12.
26. For discussion of this point, see Tom Rockmore, "The Concept of Crisis and the Unity of Husserl's Position, in *Phenomenology and the Human Sciences*, edited by J. N. Mohanty (Dordrecht: Martinus Nijhoff, 1985), pp. 5–21.
27. See Edmund Husserl, *The Crisis of European Sciences and Transcendental Phenomenology*, p. 12.
28. See *The Crisis of European Sciences and Transcendental Phenomenology*, §28: "Kant's unexpressed 'presupposition': the surrounding world of life, taken for granted as valid," pp. 103–114.
29. Heidegger's *Habilitationsschrift* is dedicated to Heinrich Rickert. See Martin Heidegger, "Die Kategorien- und Beudeutungslehre des Duns Scotus," in Martin

Heidegger, Gesamtausgabe, Band 1, *Frühe Schriften*, edited by Friedrich-Wilhelm von Hermann (Frankfurt a. M.: Vittorio Klostermann, 1978), p. 133.

30. See, especially, Martin Heidegger, *Kant and the Problem of Metaphysics*, translated with an Introduction by James S. Churchill (Bloomington: Indiana University Press, 1962). See also Ernst Cassirer and Martin Heidegger, *Débat sur le Kantisme et la Philosophie* (*Davos, mars 1929*) *et autres textes de 1929–1931*, présentés par Pierre Aubenque (Paris: Beauchesne, 1972).

31. See Heidegger, *Being and Time*, §6: "The Task of Destroying the History of Ontology," pp. 41–49.

32. For Heidegger's reading of Kant as engaged in the same project, see *Kant and the Problem of Metaphysics*, p. 3: "The task of the following investigation is to explicate Kant's *Critique of Pure Reason* as a laying of the foundation [*Grundlegung*] of metaphysics in order thus to present the problem of metaphysics as the problem of a fundamental ontology."

33. See Immanuel Kant, *Prolegomena to Any Future Metaphysics*, with an Introduction by Lewis White Beck (Indianapolis: Library of Liberal Arts, 1950).

34. See Jürgen Habermas, *Knowledge and Human Interests*, translated by Jeremy J. Schapiro (Boston: Beacon, 1968), pp. 3–5.

35. See Jürgen Habermas, *Zur Logik der Sozialwissenschaften* (Frankfurt a. M.: Suhrkamp, 1973), p. 220. See also Jürgen Habermas, *Der philosophische Diskurs der Moderne* (Frankfurt a. M.: Suhrkamp, 1985), p. 346.

36. See "Die Moderne—ein unvollendetes Projekt," in Jürgen Habermas, *Kleine Politische Schriften I–IV* (Frankfurt a. M.: Suhrkamp, 1981), pp. 444–466.

37. These included Bauer, Adler, and Hilferding. For a discussion, see Leszek Kolakowski, *Main Currents of Marxism* "Austro-Marxists, Kantians in the Marxist Movement, Ethical Socialism," translated by P. S. Falla (Oxford: Oxford University Press, 1978), vol. 2, chap. xii, pp. 240–304.

38. See Max Horkheimer, "Traditional and Critical Theory," in *Critical Theory. Selected Essays*, translated by Matthew J. O'Connell and others (New York: Herder and Herder, 1972), pp. 188–253.

39. For a critical discussion, infrequent in the adulatory literature concerning Habermas, see Tom Rockmore, *Habermas on Historical Materialism* (Bloomington, IN: Indiana University Press, 1989).

40. See "Knowledge and Human Interests: A General Perspective," in Jürgen Habermas, *Knowledge and Human Interests*, translated by Jeremy J. Schapiro (Boston: Beacon, 1968), pp. 301–315.

41. See "Towards a Reconstruction of Historical Materialism," in Jürgen Habermas, *Communication and the Evolution of Society*, translated by Thomas McCarthy (Boston: Beacon Press, 1979), pp. 130–177.

42. See Jürgen Habermas, *Theorie des kommunikativen Handelns* (Frankfurt a. M.: Suhrkamp, 1981), 2 vols.

43. For an important recent effort, see Jürgen Habermas, *Faktizität und Geltung* (Frankfurt a. M.: Suhrkamp, 1994).

44. Habermas himself identifies four separate themes, including an attempt at a theory of rationality, a theory of communicative action, a dialectic of social rationalization, and a concept of society bringing together systems and action theory. See Habermas. *Autonomy and Solidarity: Interviews with Jürgen Habermas*, edited by Peter Dews (London: Verso, 1986), pp. 103–105.

45. See David Held, *Introduction to Critical Theory* (Berkeley and Los Angeles: The University of California Press, 1980), p. 353.

46. Habermas, *Knowledge and Human Interests*, p. 317.
47. It is worth pointing out that Husserl did not regard his phenomenology as a theory at all, that Heidegger later abandoned transcendental philosophy for so-called new thought, allegedly located beyond philosophy, and that Habermas has frequently called himself a social theorist in order to avoid the label of philosopher.
48. See Victor Farías, *Heidegger and Nazism*, edited by Joseph Margolis and Tom Rockmore (Philadelphia: Temple University Press, 1989).
49. See Hugo Ott, *Martin Heidegger: Unterwegs zu seiner Biographie* (Frankfurt and New York: Campus Verlag, 1988).
50. For discussion, see Tom Rockmore's review of Habermas, *Theorie des kommunikativen Handelns*, *Archives de philosophie*, vol. 46, no. 4, (1983) pp. 668–673.
51. See Husserl, *The Crisis of European Sciences*, p. 6.
52. For a detailed studies, see Tom Rockmore, *On Heidegger's Nazism and Philosophy* (Berkeley and Los Angeles: The University of California Press, 1992). See also, Tom Rockmore, *Irrationalism: Lukács and the Marxist View of Reason* (Philadelphia: Temple University Press, 1991).
53. See "The Self-Assertion of the German University," in *Martin Heidegger and National Socialism. Questions and Answers*, edited by Gunther Neske and Emil Kettering, Introduction by Karsten Harries (New York: Paragon, 1990), pp. 5–14.
54. For discussion of the relation between hermeneutics and epistemology, see Tom Rockmore, "Hermeneutics as Epistemology," in *The Monist* vol. 73, no. 2 (April 1990), pp. 115–133.
55. For a recent example depicting his departure from his original neo-Marxist roots in critical theory, see his statement that philosophy needs "to help set in motion the interplay between" [Jürgen Habermas, *Moral Consciousness and Communicative Action*, translated by Christian Lenhardt and Shierry Weber Nicholsen (Cambridge: MIT Press, 1990), p. 18] compartmentalized branches of culture, and his further statement that "the issue philosophy will face when it stops playing the part of the arbiter that inspects culture and instead starts playing the part of a mediating interpreter . . . is how to overcome the isolation of science, morals, and art and their respective expert cultures." Ibid., p. 19.
56. Habermas, *Knowledge and Human Interests*, p. 93.
57. See Habermas, *Theorie des kommunikativen Handelns*, vol. II, p. 583.
58. See Kant, *Critique of Pure Reason*, B 866–867, pp. 657–658.
59. See Kant, *Critique of Pure Reason*, B 867, pp. 657–658.
60. See G. W. F. Hegel, *The Phenomenology of Spirit*, translated by A. V. Miller (Oxford: Oxford University Press, 1979), "Absolute Freedom and Terror," pp. 354–363.
61. "There are periods in history when a whole community . . . finds itself in the presence of new issues which its old custom do not adequately meet. The habits and beliefs which were formed in the past do not fit into the opportunities and requirements of contemporary life." John Dewey, *Theory of the Moral Life* (New York: Holt, Rinehart and Winston, 1932), p. 7. See also, ibid., p. 29, where he argues that "vast social changes" have made previous conceptions of morality and politics inadequate.
62. See John Dewey, *Reconstruction in Philosophy* (Boston: Beacon Press, 1960), p. v.

Part 2

Kant and Neo-Kantianism

5

The Role of Reflection in Kant's Transcendental Philosophy

Rudolf A. Makkreel

Since Kant tends to collapse our current distinction between everyday and scientific experience, his account of the transcendental conditions of Newtonian science is also meant to apply to our ordinary experience of things. What sense can Kant then give to everyday experience of a pre- or nonscientific kind? By considering the full scope of Kant's appeal to transcendental conditions and by referring them to a broader understanding of his theory of judgment, as found in his lectures on logic, I will attempt to apply certain transcendental considerations to something like what we today call everyday or prescientific experience. This will be done by relating Kant's theory of reflection to his account of preliminary judgments.

Kant uses the adjective "transcendental" in a wide variety of contexts. Thus, he speaks of the "transcendental" in relation to concepts, ideas, judgments, principles, laws, even freedom, and purposiveness. One way to circumscribe the possible meanings of the transcendental is to focus on the actual philosophical operations that are assigned this label. In the *Critique of Pure Reason*, we find three such philosophical operations: transcendental exposition, transcendental deduction, and transcendental reflection. The focus of this essay will be on transcendental reflection and how it diverges from the other two transcendental operations. Whereas the transcendental operations of exposition and deduction conform to the standard foundational sense of the transcendental, transcendental reflection will be shown to have a quite different orientational sense.

Standard accounts of the transcendental deduction of the categories have been challenged by Dieter Henrich, who claims that such a deduction must be "built upon a reflective knowledge."[1] His aim is to show that the "rigidity" of the investigative goals of the deduction must be tempered by the "loose generality of reflection."[2] According to Henrich, the results of reflection must be incorporated into the project of the deduction to make experience possible. As I see it, reflection is not itself a mode of knowledge and therefore is not necessarily part of the *constitution* of our experience. Having elsewhere related reflection to Kant's theory of reflective judgments, which I regard as concerned with the *interpretation* of the overall coherence of our experience,[3] I now also want to relate reflection back to Kant's discussions of preliminary judgments, which again do not count as knowledge and are at best *orientational*. Using a threefold distinction between (1) preliminary, (2) determinant, and (3) reflective judgments, we will see that reflection relates directly to (1) and (3) and only indirectly to the knowledge claims associated with (2).

THE TRANSCENDENTAL AS EXPLANATIVE AND ONTOLOGICAL

In the Transcendental Aesthetic of the *Critique of Pure Reason*, Kant provides a transcendental exposition of the two *a priori* forms of sensibility, space, and time. Their transcendental exposition is contrasted with a metaphysical exposition, the difference being that one focuses on possibility, the other on givenness. Kant first introduces the metaphysical exposition of space when he writes: "By *exposition* (*expositio*) I mean the clear, though not necessarily exhaustive representation of that which belongs to a concept: the exposition is *metaphysical* when it contains that which exhibits the concept *as given a priori*."[4] The metaphysical exposition of space shows it to be given as an *a priori* intuition, but since it is not exhaustive it is supplemented with a *transcendental* exposition. Kant defines the latter as "the explanation of a concept, as a principle from which the possibility of other *a priori* synthetic knowledge can be understood" (*C1*, B 40). Thus, the transcendental exposition of space serves to explain the possibility of geometrical knowledge. It can explain this possibility only by showing that the *a priori* form of space derives from the subject's power to intuit.

Whereas space and time as forms of our sensibility, require a metaphysical and transcendental exposition, the categories of the understanding are said to require a metaphysical and transcendental *deduction*. Kant's *metaphysical* deduction of the categories consists of proving their *a priori* origin "through their complete agreement with the general logical functions of thought" (*C1*, B 159). Thus in Sections 2 and 3 of "The Transcendental Clue to the Discovery of All Pure Concepts of the Understanding," Kant attempts to prove the *a priori* status of the table of twelve categories by correlating them with the twelve-fold logical table of judgment. The metaphysical deduction clarifies the categories by showing their agreement with traditionally accepted forms of logical judgment. The *transcendental* deduction

of the categories goes beyond this doctrinal, even question-begging, procedure, by showing "their possibility as *a priori* modes of knowledge of objects
of an intuition in general" (*C1*, B 159). Here again the move from the
metaphysical to the transcendental is one from clarifying what is given, to
explaining its possibility. Thus, Kant continues by saying, "We have now to
explain the possibility of knowing *a priori*, by means of *categories*, whatever
objects may *present themselves to our senses*, not indeed in respect of the
form of their intuitions, but in respect of the laws of their combination,
and so, as it were, of prescribing laws to nature, and even of making nature
possible" (*C1*, B 159, 160).

Dieter Henrich has reminded us that Kant's notion of deduction has a
legal background. Deductions were used in the Holy Roman Empire to justify claims "about the legitimacy of a possession or a usage."[5] To decide
whether or not a claim is justified it is necessary to take it back to its
origin, which is some *"factum*, meaning both 'fact' and 'action',"[6] whereby
the right is acquired. Here Henrich notes that origin is not just a matter of
factual genesis (*quid facti*), but also of legitimacy (*quid juris*). He refers to
the distinction that Kant makes between Locke's *empirical deduction* of our
knowledge, which concerns the physiological derivation of our knowledge,
and a transcendental deduction. However, if the idea of the nondevelopmental
origin involved in the transcendental deduction is to make any sense, it
must be related to what Kant calls the metaphysical deduction. Qua transcendental project, the deduction is an explanation of the indispensability
of the categories, not of their origin. We have seen that the metaphysical
exposition of the forms of sensibility and the metaphysical deduction of the
categories point to an a priori origin. Thus, if there is, as Henrich claims, a
historical, finite aspect to Kant's deduction of the categories that makes it
much more complex than a mere syllogistic deduction or proof on the one
hand, or a mere empirical deduction or derivation on the other, then we
need to admit an integral relation between the metaphysical and transcendental deductions. But Henrich never mentions the metaphysical deduction.

Another way of formulating the difference between a metaphysical and a
transcendental deduction is suggested by Kant's distinction in the *Critique
of Judgment* of the difference between a metaphysical and a transcendental
principle of purposiveness. A principle is transcendental if it articulates the
sole universal a priori conditions whereby things can become objects of our
cognition in general. But a principle is metaphysical "if it represents the
a priori condition under which alone objects, whose concept must be empirically given, can be further determined *a priori*."[7] Kant gives the following examples of the difference when speaking of bodies as changeable
substances: a transcendental principle of bodily change merely requires a
cause, a metaphysical principle of such change seeks an external cause. A

transcendental principle uses only "ontological predicates" according to Kant (C3, Intro., 17); a metaphysical principle introduces some empirical content, although its determinations about it are *a priori*. The principle of purposiveness of the *Critique of Judgment* is transcendental or purely ontological because it only refers to objects of possible empirical cognition in general and contains nothing empirical. However, the principle of practical purposiveness is metaphysical because it involves the determination of a free will, which as the faculty of desire "must be given empirically" (C3, Intro., 18).

If we go back to Kant's own discussion of the Second Analogy in the *Critique of Pure Reason*, one may wonder whether he lives up to this purely ontological definition of transcendental philosophizing. At A 195/B 240 for instance, he writes: "If then we experience that something happens, we in so doing always presuppose that *something precedes it* on which it follows according to a rule" (emphasis added). Causality in the Second Analogy already seems to have built into it the notion of a prior and external source. Later in the same paragraph Kant speaks of causality as a determination by a preceding state, which could be that of the same object. A prior state would not necessarily involve spatial externality, but it still requires a temporal distinctness that cannot be fully disassociated from the notion of externality. Thus, it may be that the ontological category of causality cannot be disassociated from metaphysical concepts, just as time cannot be fully separated from space. In the B Deduction, Kant admits that we can represent time only by attending to the succession involved in the act of synthesis that produces an imaginary time line. This awareness of succession presupposes motion qua act of a subject, as distinct from the empirical motion of empirical objects. However, even pure motion involves "the describing of a space" and a reference to "outer intuition in general" (C1, B 155n.). If this reference to the externality of spatial relations is allowed to enter the transcendental considerations of the B Deduction, then it becomes unclear why Kant would have said in the *Critique of Judgment*, that the concept of an external cause is already metaphysical. It seems legitimate to conceive of externality on a transcendental level without reference to specific empirical content.

Although it seems to be the case that the *transcendental concept* of causality already has externality built into it, it is possible to argue that we also have a *transcendental idea* of causality that overcomes this externality, namely, the thought of freedom as a spontaneous cause which begins of itself (see C1, A 446/B 474, A 448/B 476). This would be a pure ontological idea of causality. To then distinguish a *metaphysical concept* of causality from the two mentioned modes of causality would require it to contain something more than externality—it must have some reference to empirical content in a general way. One could conceive this along the lines that Kant, in the *Critique of Judgment*, specifies nature into different regions such as the organic and the inorganic, each with its own mode of causality. Metaphysical causality would accordingly specify a particular kind of natural causality, such as a mechanistic conception of causality.

TRANSCENDENTAL REFLECTION AND PRELIMINARY JUDGMENTS

We turn now to the third transcendental operation discussed by Kant, namely, transcendental reflection. In an appendix to the Analytic of the *Critique of Pure Reason* entitled "The Amphiboly of Concepts of Reflection," Kant defines reflection (*Überlegung* [*reflexio*]) as "that state of mind in which we first set ourselves to discover the subjective conditions under which [alone] we are able to arrive at concepts" (*C1*, A 260/B 361). Kant then distinguishes between logical reflection, which considers concepts purely in terms of their form, and transcendental reflection which also considers their content. Here the distinction between transcendental and metaphysical operations is replaced by that between transcendental and logical operations. Logically, all concepts belong to the understanding, so that *logical reflection* is a mere comparative activity that distinguishes them according to identity and difference, agreement and opposition.

"*Transcendental reflection*, on the other hand, since it bears on the objects themselves, contains the ground of the possibility of the objective comparison of representations with each other" (*C1*, A 262/B 319). Here the objective content of concepts is considered according to its relation to the two basic cognitive faculties, namely, sensibility and understanding. In addition to the comparative concepts of identity and difference, agreement and opposition, transcendental reflection also considers the comparative concepts "of the *inner* and the *outer*, and finally of the *determinable* and the *determination* (matter and form)" (*C1*, A 261/B 317). It is crucial to locate the source of a concept in either sensibility or understanding, for each of these pairs of concepts will then be applied differently. If a concept derives from the pure understanding, then its matter is prior to its form, but if it derives from sense, then form will precede matter. Similarly, if a concept singles out an object of pure understanding, it will always be identical, but if it singles out an object of sensibility then difference will prevail. Arguing against Leibniz's principle of the identity of indiscernibles, Kant writes: "even if there is no difference whatever as regards the concepts, difference of spatial positions at one and the same time is still an adequate ground for the *numerical difference* of the object, that is, of the object of the senses" (*C1*, A 263/B 319).

Henrich points out that "Kant's theory of reflection . . . is utterly different from the meaning of 'reflection' that became current in post-Kantian philosophy."[8] For one thing, he says that reflection is not introspective, but accompanies operations as "an awareness of what is specific to them."[9] I agree with these claims, but disagree with the further one that the deduction of the first *Critique* is "built upon a reflective knowledge."[10] Henrich's account of reflective knowledge appeals to Kant's theory of "preliminary judgments," which deals with judgments that are made when there is not enough evidence to arrive at a determinant judgment. In order to decide whether preliminary judgments have the transcendental function of being presupposed by the deduction of the categories, we will have to examine the lectures on logic that Kant gave throughout his life.

In the *Logik Blomberg* Kant discusses both preliminary (*vorläufige*) judgments and prejudices (*Vorurtheile*) under the common heading of prejudgment (*Präjudicium*).[11] In the *Logic* that Jäsche published in 1800, preliminary judgments are described as maxims for investigating a subject-matter. One could also, Kant continues, "call them anticipations because one already anticipates one's judgment about a matter prior to having a determinate judgment" (Ak 9:75). A prejudice is like a preliminary judgment in anticipating more than the evidence warrants, but instead of being a maxim which is recognized as subjective, it is assumed to be a principle which is also objective. Whereas a preliminary judgment is indeterminate and subjective, a prejudice could be said to be pseudo-determinate and pseudo-objective. Prejudices arise in everyday life when "subjective reasons are falsely held to be objective because of a lack of the kind of reflection (*Überlegung*) that should precede all judging" (Ak 9:76).

Thus, we can conclude that preliminary judgments may be considered as good prejudgments and prejudices as bad prejudgments. This complicates the picture painted by Hans-Georg Gadamer, namely, that the Enlightenment was blind to the wisdom embodied in the prejudgments of traditions. All the more striking is the fact that in the *Logik Blomberg*, Kant is quoted as saying that one should not immediately reject each and every prejudice! Instead one should "test them and inquire whether something good may yet be found in them." Then, anticipating Gadamer's well-known claim that an outright discreditation of prejudice is itself a prejudice,[12] Kant says: "It is possible to encounter a kind of prejudice against prejudice, namely, when one rejects virtually everything which has arisen by means of prejudices" (Ak 24.1:169). A prejudice may thus be true in content, although it will always be false according to its form in that the truth is arrived at inadequately, i.e., without reflection.

There is, as Henrich suggests, reflection involved in preliminary judgments and it is this reflection that keeps them from becoming prejudices. But reflection does not define the content of the preliminary judgment.

Instead, it defines the relation of the judgment back to its sources, for to reflect is to "see to which power of cognition a cognition belongs" (*Ak* 9:73). When reflection indicates that the source of a preliminary judgment is merely subjective, then we are put on notice that it cannot become a determinant judgment without further objective investigation. However, the content of the preliminary judgment is already directed at the object to be further investigated—this content is indeterminate, but it is on the way to becoming a determinate judgment. There is, therefore, no special "reflective knowledge" involved in a preliminary judgment. The reflection involved in it holds us back from making a final judgment about an object. Since we will later speak of reflective judgments, we should also point out that reflection here is not to be confused with the content of a reflective judgment. Whereas reflection will hold me back from prematurely deciding whether the flower I see is a lily or an iris, I can already make the reflective judgment that the flower is beautiful before concluding what kind of flower it really is.

Given the informal, everyday nature of reflection as discussed in the *Logic*, I cannot agree with Henrich's claim that preliminary judgments provide a "reflective knowledge" on which the transcendental deduction of the *Critique of Pure Reason* is to be "built."[13] A preliminary judgment is an indeterminate, empirical judgment that temporally precedes a determinate empirical judgment, but it has no a priori status that is of any relevance to the question of how knowledge of objects in general is possible. Preliminary judgments may be involved in our everyday prescientific experience, but they have no foundational role for Kant's theory of science.

Although we must refrain from objectifying the results of reflection into a kind of reflective knowledge, we should still consider whether any of Kant's formal claims about reflection in the *Critique of Pure Reason* are presupposed by the investigative question of how knowledge of objects is possible. For instance, what Kant attributes to *reflection in general*, namely, the process of discovering the subjective conditions necessary for arriving at concepts, may also be foundational for a deduction of the a priori concepts necessary for the constitution of objects of experience. The specifically *transcendental* concepts of reflection—inner versus outer, matter versus form— are used prominently as early as in the Transcendental Aesthetic, and could thus be said to be part of a transcendental exposition and presupposed by the transcendental deduction. Yet, much of what Kant goes on to say about *transcendental reflection* seems to assume that we already have knowledge of objects, i.e., representations that have been acquired of objects are referred back to the faculties of the knowing subject. In the final analysis, Kant indicates that transcendental reflection considers whether the concept of an object refers to "something or nothing" (*C1*, A 290/B 346). By then specifying the various senses of nothingness—that is, the noumenal, privative, imaginary, and logical senses—Kant is clearly moving beyond the sphere of the transcendental deduction.

Another point to consider in evaluating Henrich's claim is that the comparative concepts of transcendental reflection are very different from the synthetic categories of the transcendental deduction that make knowledge of objects possible. Reflective concepts do not contribute to the process of synthesizing representations necessary for the constitution of objective unities. They merely orient us to the types of things that we have already come to know or think about. That is why Kant speaks of reflection as instituting a transcendental topology. Could it be that transcendental reflection allows us to make the transition from a purely ontological transcendental deduction of objects in general to a topological projection of the various regions of being?

This relation between transcendental reflection and a topological framework can be developed by also considering what Kant says about the human subject orienting itself in his essay "What Is Orientation in Thinking" (1786) and about reflective judgment in his *Critique of Judgment*. Doing so will allow us to distinguish preliminary aspects of reflection that precede the constitutive claims of the deduction of the *Critique of Pure Reason* from some ultimate investigative aspects of reflection that Kant assigns to reflective judgment. As a consequence we can see that a transcendental concept of reflection (*Reflexion*) stands midway between the original reflection (*Überlegung*) presupposed by the deduction and the final reflective (*reflektierende*) judgments about the systematic ordering of our experience in the *Critique of Judgment*. More importantly, I will show that all these modes of reflection are concerned with orientation.

ORIENTATION AND REFLECTIVE JUDGMENT

Before explicating reflective orientation, it is necessary to consider what Kant means by spatial orientation. He describes spatial orientation as a process whereby I proceed from one quadrant of my field of vision to the other three that make up my horizon. I relate what I see in front of me to the other quadrants by means of a "feeling of a distinction concerning my own subject, namely, that of my right and left hand."[14] This distinction between right and left relates to my own hands, but is not based simply on empirical intuitive evidence. In terms of empirical content my left and right hands are indiscernible. According to Kant, I rely on a feeling to make the "*a priori* determination" (Ak 8:135) that my left and right hands are oriented differently, and I apply this feeling to also relate the quadrants of my spatial field into a coherent perspective on the world of everyday experience. The feeling of orientation involved is subjective, but not in any private sense, for it is already aimed at bodies in an objective environment.

After characterizing orientation in spatial terms, Kant proceeds to apply it to thought as it transcends the bounds of my experience of nature. To orient myself in thought is to allow myself to be guided by a subjective principle of reason when objective principles are not available. Accordingly, Kant traces the rational idea of God back to a subjectively "felt need of reason" (Ak 8:139). He claims that Moses Mendelssohn's appeal to the idea of God on the basis of a so-called sound (gesunde) or common (gemeine) reason is really an appeal to a feeling rooted in a subjective maxim of reason or a natural faith (Vernunftglauben).

Kant's essay "What Is Orientation in Thinking?" thus distinguishes two feelings of orientation: the one makes possible the bodily orientation of the perceiving self to a natural realm, and the other the mental orientation of the thinking self to the supernatural realm. There is something preliminary about an orientation, especially the mental mode, but Kant never explicitly expresses orientations in terms of preliminary judgments. In the Critique of Judgment, however, Kant speaks also of judgment orienting itself, which suggests the possibility of a specifically judgmental mode of orientation. He points out that the reflective principle of purposiveness provides us "with concepts amid the immense variety of nature (so that judgment can orient itself [orientiren zu können]" (C3, Intro.; Ak 5:193). The concepts of purposiveness used to orient reflective judgment concerning a possible order in nature's immense variety can be either aesthetic or teleological. On the level of judgment, it is therefore possible to introduce two reflective counterparts to orientation in space and thought: an aesthetic orientation based on our response to beauty and sublimity, and a teleological orientation based on a recognition of natural and cultural purposes. Kant defined the positive pleasure found in beauty as the simple feeling of the enhancement of our life. The sublime involves a negative pleasure that is described as a complex feeling of both a restriction and release of the vital powers. These aesthetically charged feelings of life can be said to orient us as we judge the things around us as either adding to or detracting from the value of our existence, thus allowing us to estimate the place of the self in the world. Hermeneutically, this constitutes the basis for contextual understanding.

To arrive at what I propose as the second or teleological mode of reflective orientation, we can relate what Kant says about the sensus communis in §40 of the Critique of Judgment to his reflections on what it is in human beings that makes them the ultimate purpose of nature. "In order to find out," says Kant, "we must seek out what nature can supply to prepare [man] for what he must himself do in order to be a final purpose" (C3, §83, 281; emphasis added). The answer lies in culture rather than happiness, communal goals rather than private ends. And in the process of furthering human culture, the sensus communis is indispensable, for it allows the judgment of the individual to be oriented to the larger perspective of the community. As I have shown elsewhere, the *sensus communis* provides the basis for what Kant calls the enlarged modes of thought and interpretation necessary for an understanding of human culture.[15] Kant defines the *sensus communis* as an a priori sense: "a sense *common to all*, i.e., a faculty of judgment which, in its reflection takes account (*a priori*) of the mode of representation of all other men in thought, in order, as it were, to compare its judgment with the collective reason of humanity, and thus to escape the illusion arising from the private conditions that could be so easily taken for objective" (C3, §40, 136). The *sensus communis* orients reflective or interpretive judgments about the views and values of others in the community by means of a feeling that is "universally communicable. . . . without the mediation of concepts" (C3, §40, 135; Ak 5:293). This reflective feeling of orientation can be said to estimate the relative positions of self and other in the public cosmos.

Having characterized the *sensus communis* as an a priori mode of feeling, we must also clarify the status of the rationally felt need to which it is the reflective counterpart. Although Kant speaks of a "felt need of reason" that can orient thought, he adds in a footnote that, strictly speaking, "reason does not feel; it recognizes a lack and produces the feeling of a need through the cognitive impulse. In this regard it is akin to moral feeling" (Ak 8: 139–40n). Both the feeling of a need and the feeling of respect for the moral law are effects of reason. Just as the moral feeling of respect is pure in not being pathologically induced, so can a felt need of reason be said to be pure. But unlike the *sensus communis*, it cannot be considered a priori, since it is an effect, albeit of reason.

Earlier we claimed that only some of what Kant said about reflection in the *Critique of Pure Reason* is presupposed by the transcendental deduction. Now we must consider what, if anything, that has been claimed about orientation and reflective judgment can also be regarded as presupposed by the deduction of the categories. Spatial orientation might be because it is necessary for our geometrical intuitive knowledge. Since mental orientation involves claims that transcend experiential knowledge, it clearly is not presupposed. The feeling of life that allows us to discriminate beauty and sublimity, and the *sensus communis* that allows us to broaden our mode of thought by considering the point of view of others, both seem to transcend the concern to demonstrate that knowledge of experiential objects is possible. They both orient us to a more systematic world order, whether it be natural or cultural. Only to the extent that the *sensus communis* is also appealed to "as the necessary condition of the universal communicability of our knowledge" (C3, §21, 76), can it be relevant to Kant's transcendental deduction of the categories.

The transcendental deduction is supposed to explain the ontological possibility of experiencing objects. But transcendental reflection, whether it involves the reflective concepts of inner and outer, of matter and form—from the first *Critique* or the principle of purposiveness from the third *Critique*—seems to open up larger systematic or interpretive questions. The metaphysical exposition of space and time took these forms to be subjectively given (*gegeben*). Similarly, the metaphysical deduction of the categories used the logical table of judgments as a given guide. When transcendental reflection orients us to the overall order of what is given, its comprehension is still an unfinished task (*aufgegeben*).

CONCLUSION

Concerning the transcendental exposition of space and time and the transcendental deduction of the categories, we can say that the term "transcendental" refers to the explanation of the possibility of something by means of some indispensable condition. Thus, in relation to the problems of determinant judgment about objects of experience, transcendental philosophy is explanative in what we have called an ontological sense. Here the transcendental grounds the possibility of the scientific knowledge of *nature*. Transcendental reflection, by contrast, makes no explanative claims. When applied back to the aesthetic conditions of sensibility it establishes space and time as the *a priori* forms for intuiting a *world* in either the everyday or the mathematical sense. So applied, the transcendental is orientational in a way that points back to prereflective conditions. However, when transcendental reflection is applied forward to the systematic concerns of reflective judgment, orientation becomes interpretive. It projects not just a world, but a *cosmos* or overall cosmopolitan world-order in which I can locate my place. More specifically, the reflective feelings of orientation enable us to respond to the order of the cosmos and assent to or dissent from the consensus of the community.

From the standpoint of determinant judgment, the ego actively projects the a priori structures that constitute objects of experience and more or less passively *receives* their sense content as given. The feeling of life, as I have shown elsewhere, allows the ego to *respond* reflectively to these same givens.[16] Responsiveness goes beyond receptivity in that it expresses human attitudes. In reflective judgment, human subjects can affirm that which furthers their life and expands their cultural horizon and can reject that which restricts and constricts. The orientational, transcendental conditions of reflection thus become the basis of reflective judgments about—or interpretive responses to—the human cosmos.

NOTES

1. Dieter Henrich, "Kant's Notion of a Deduction and the Methodological Background of the First Critique," in *Kant's Transcendental Deductions*, ed. by Eckart Förster (Stanford: Stanford University Press, 1989), p. 43.
2. Henrich, "Kant's Notion of a Deduction," p. 46.
3. See Rudolf A. Makkreel, *Imagination and Interpretation in Kant: the Hermeneutical Import of the "Critique of Judgment"* (Chicago: The University of Chicago Press, 1990), pp. 1–6, 33–37, 111–171.
4. Kant, *Critique of Pure Reason* (hereafter *C1*), trans. Norman Kemp Smith (New York: St. Martin's Press, 1965), A 23/B 38.
5. Henrich, "Kant's Notion of a Deduction," p. 34.
6. Henrich, "Kant's Notion of a Deduction," p. 35.
7. Kant, *Critique of Judgment* (hereafter *C3*), trans. J. H. Bernard (New York: Hafner Press, 1984), Introduction, p. 17.
8. Henrich, "Kant's Notion of a Deduction," p. 42.
9. Henrich, pp. 42–43. In *Imagination and Interpretation in Kant*, I also relate reflection to specification. See chap. 3.
10. Henrich, "Kant's Notion of a Deduction," p. 43.
11. Kant, *Gesammelte Schriften, herausgegeben von der Preussischen Akademie der Wissenschaften zu Berlin* (hereafter *Ak*), (Berlin: Walter de Gruyter, 1902–83), 24.1:161.
12. See Hans-Georg Gadamer, *Truth and Method*, 2nd rev. ed. (New York: Crossroad Publishing Corporation, 1989), p. 276.
13. Henrich, "Kant's Notion of a Deduction," p. 43.
14. Kant, "What Is Orientation in Thinking?", trans. by L. W. Beck, in *Kant's "Critique of Practical Reason" and Other Writings on Moral Philosophy*, ed. by L. W. Beck (Chicago: University of Chicago Press, 1949), p. 295; *Ak* 8:134.
15. Makkreel, *Imagination and Interpretation in Kant*, chap. 8.
16. Makkreel, *Imagination and Interpretation in Kant*, pp. 105–107.

6

Kant's Theory of the Subject

David Carr

Is Kant's philosophy a metaphysics of the subject? Certainly not, if we take him at his word in the *Critique of Pure Reason*. That work is indeed *about* metaphysics, but it is not a work *of* metaphysics. In fact its central question is whether metaphysics, as conceived by the philosophical tradition, is even possible; and Kant concludes that it is not. But this interpretation turns on Kant's very narrow definition of metaphysics. Moreso if others attribute to him a metaphysics of the subject, it might seem that there are good reasons for doing so. The subject is, after all, not merely one topic among others in Kant's major work. Kant's celebrated "Copernican turn," his great innovation, has it that "objects must conform to our knowledge" (B xvii), rather than the other way around—i.e., our understanding determines *a priori* what is to count as objects and how they may be related. Kant goes so far as to say that human understanding has the function of "prescribing laws to nature, and even of making nature possible" (B 159f). Since the understanding in turn is conceived by Kant as the spontaneous synthetic activity of the subject, it is no wonder that Kant was taken by many of his successors to be the initiator of a radical form of idealism, a theory which can be called "metaphysical," if not in Kant's own sense then in most traditionally accepted senses of the term, and which is centered on the subject in a way that surpasses all previous idealisms. Furthermore, in Kant's moral philosophy the self is distinguished by its *autonomy*, its prescribing laws to itself. A self which legislates both to itself *and* to nature is a sovereign self in an almost blasphemously extreme sense, seemingly subjected to no power, natural or moral, beyond itself. If this is not a metaphysics of the subject, it might be asked, what is?

This picture of Kant's thought is painted in very broad strokes and ignores the context from which his views emerge and the manner in which they are put forward. If we are to understand these we must look at the

96

"theory of the subject" as it is found in the *Critique of Pure Reason* in light of the general problem to which that work addresses itself.

TRANSCENDENTAL SELF-CONSCIOUSNESS

Any understanding of what Kant has to say about the subject must begin at that place in the *Critique* where his views on this topic are most explicitly put forward, namely in the second edition of the Transcendental Deduction. What is generally noticed here is the emergence of the notion of a "transcendental" subject and its companion concept, the empirical subject. But the status of these notions, and of the distinction between them, is as much in dispute as are other aspects of this notoriously difficult section of the *Critique*. Everyone seems to agree that the Transcendental Deduction is the heart of Kant's doctrine; in light of this it is all the more significant that there is little agreement on what it accomplishes, or even on what it is meant to accomplish, what its structure is, what, if any, arguments it contains, etc.[1]

We can take it (though even this is controversial) that Kant's assumption in the *Critique* generally is that "we are in possession" of synthetic *a priori* knowledge, and that "even the common understanding is never without it" (B 3). In the Transcendental Deduction, Kant often speaks of "empirical knowledge," also called "experience" (B 147, B 166), as if *this* were the assumption on which his argument turns. In any case, in some sense we have genuine knowledge, Kant believes, and it is knowledge of the sensible world.

It is in answer to the question: *How* is this knowledge of the sensible world possible?, that Kant begins the Transcendental Deduction by speaking of the subject (*Subjekt*) of knowledge and its "self-activity" (*Selbsttätigkeit*) or action (*Handlung*) of combining the manifold of representations (B 130). Also it is here that Kant asserts that "it must be possible for the 'I think' to accompany all my representations" (B 131). Kant calls this "*pure apperception*, to distinguish it from empirical apperception." He also calls it "*original apperception*," and again " the *transcendental* unity of self-consciousness, in order to indicate the possibility of *a priori* knowledge arising from it" (B 132).

There is a certain shift of focus which occurs in these first two sections of the Deduction. In the first (§15) Kant seems to be asserting that experience requires "combination" and combination in turn requires an active subject that combines. The manifold of representations is given through the senses, but its combination or synthesis is not. Thus, the supreme condition of the possibility of experience is that there *be* a subject that acts in this way. In this sense one could speak of a "transcendental subject"—though Kant does not do so here.[2]

However, in §16, with its notion of pure apperception, while seeming simply to elaborate on what went before, actually changes its sense. From the context, it is clear that Kant uses "apperception" to mean "self-consciousness." It is this "unity of self-consciousness" that is now called "transcendental," i.e., a condition of the possibility of *a priori* knowledge. There is a shift of focus here because up to now Kant has been speaking of a consciousness of the sensible world, and now he is speaking of a consciousness of self. Thus the supreme condition is not that there *be* a subject that acts in a certain way, but rather that we be *conscious of ourselves* in a certain way.

If Kant were simply affirming a link between consciousness and self-consciousness, his assertion might seem uncontroversial; and while it would help us understand his view of consciousness it would not necessarily be equivalent to a theory of the subject. But clearly Kant is saying something much more complicated than this. His distinction between pure and empirical apperception tells us as much. It is the former, and not the latter, that constitutes the supreme condition of our knowledge of the sensible world. It is not just a matter of self-consciousness, but of a certain *kind* of self-consciousness. Kant is saying that the possibility of experience requires that I be conscious of myself in a special way.

In order to get at Kant's theory of the subject we must figure out what this distinctive mode of self-consciousness is. There are two sides to figuring out what is distinctive about it. The first concerns the self *of which* I am conscious. How, i.e., *as what* or *under what description*, is the self represented in pure apperception? The second has to do with the nature of the *consciousness* in which the self is thus represented. Kant has answers to both kinds of questions, in each case usually in contrast to empirical apperception, but it is not always easy to sort them out. It will help if we pursue these questions separately.

THE SELF OF WHICH I AM CONSCIOUS

When Kant speaks of the "I think" which must be able to accompany all my representations, he is indicating that in this "pure" self-consciousness I represent myself as *thinking*, not as walking, breathing, digesting, or in any of the other ways I might think of myself. But in German as in English, grammatically and conceptually, thinking requires an object: To think is to think *of* or *about* something or *that* something is the case.[3] In the terminology of a later period, thinking is *intentional*. Though Kant does not speak in these terms, it turns out that this feature of thinking is absolutely crucial to his project.

Of course, all thinking is intentional, but here Kant is interested in something quite specific, namely our knowledge of the sensible world. Such knowledge requires that our thinking be linked with sense-representations or intuitions. But *how* are they linked? One might expect that, since thought requires an object, it is sense-representations that serve this function. It is they that our thought is *about*.

However, this is precisely *not* what Kant is saying. In fact, his rejection of such a notion is a decisive aspect of his own doctrine and its relation to its predecessors.

Kant rejects the so-called "way of ideas" expressed notoriously by Locke when he said that the term "idea" "serves best to stand for whatsoever is the *object* of the understanding when a man thinks."[4] Kant indeed uses the term *Vorstellung*— usually rendered "representation" in English—in a way that corresponds roughly to the term "idea" in English and its cognates in other languages, as used by Locke and other modern philosophers. He believes that such representations, in the form of sensations or impressions (*Eindrücke*, A 50/B 74), are necessarily involved in our knowledge of the sensible world. But these representations are "a mere determination of the mind" (Ibid., cf. also, A 147/B 242). Also our knowledge of the sensible world is not *about* our mind or its contents or determinations, but precisely *about* the sensible world. More precisely, it is about *objects* in the sensible world. "An *object* is that in the concept of which the manifold of a given intuition is *united*" (B 134). Our knowledge of the sensible world requires that we *have* such representations, indeed that they be given. But it also requires that, by their means, objects be thought. It requires, in other words, that a manifold of sense-intuition be taken to be united, *not* in the subject that has or receives them, but in an *object*.

These considerations explain why Kant goes on to say (§18) that the transcendental unity of apperception is to be "entitled *objective*, and must be distinguished from the *subjective* unity of consciousness" (B 139). The point is that transcendental apperception represents not merely the I in relation to its representations, but the I *thinking* objects *through* those representations. The obvious question here is: What does Kant mean by "through?" The answer is supposedly provided by the *categories*, which Kant has introduced earlier, and which can be described as the *a priori* rules for combining sense-representations in such a way as to relate them to objects. Kant's insistence on the "objective" character of this self-consciousness indicates that in it, *what* is represented is not just the I, and not just the I in relation to the sense-representations it has, but the I in a thinking (or intentional) relation to the *objects* (and the relations among them) that make up the sensible world. It is the categories of substance (inherence and subsistance), causality and community that are particularly important here. Through them, we stand in relation to the regulated and ordered realm which we call nature, of which our experience constitutes empirical knowledge. Now there can be no empirical knowledge without the *a priori* knowledge embodied in the categories. Empirical knowledge would always involve the application of the categories to particular manifolds in order to produce grounded judgments about the world. These in turn require a consciousness of myself as making these judgments and through them knowing the world.

This is the place to contrast transcendental apperception with empirical apperception, with respect to how (i.e., *as what*) the self is represented in self-consciousness. Here intuition (inner sense) provides material for "determining" the self of which I am conscious. Thus what is given to me here is presumably the manifold of sense-representations that belong *to me*, and perhaps the various thoughts I have and judgments I make as well. These are all predicates or properties of me, arranged in temporal sequence, through which I acquire the status of a full-fledged object of knowledge, albeit only empirical knowledge, and only of myself as an appearance.

By contrast to the self of empirical apperception, which in this way becomes rich in content, the self of transcendental apperception may appear empty or bare. Some of Kant's language suggests this, as when he speaks of a "mere form of consciousness" (A 382) or a mere "logical subject" (A 350). He also describes transcendental apperception as being not even "a representation distinguishing a particular object, but a form of representation in general . . ." (A 346/B 404). But these declarations are misleading in several respects. Kant is concerned to insist that no intuition is involved in transcendental apperception, and hence none of the predicates that derive from intuition for characterizing the self. Moreso, it is not as if the self of transcendental apperception had no characteristics, no description at all. On the contrary, up to now we have been working out just what that description is, starting with the notion of *thinking*. Thinking has been further characterized in terms of acts of spontaneity through which combination occurs. Since Kant is dealing here with knowledge of the sensible world, that thinking has been further qualified: it is thought about objects in the world, thanks to the categories, and *not* about its own representations or intuitions.[5]

Thus in the two forms of self-consciousness, it is hardly the case that the one presents the self as full, the other as entirely empty, of content or qualification. Instead we should speak of two senses of content, which correspond approximately to Husserl's distinction between the real (*reell*) or descriptive content and the intentional content of a conscious experience.[6] This distinction is roughly that between what an experience *is* and what it is *of*. Husserl believes that experiences cannot even be described or identified apart from their intentional content. We can also think of experiences in terms of mental predicates (sensations, feelings, thoughts) we attribute to the subject, thus characterizing the *subject* by their means; as opposed to construing them *qua* intentional with reference to their intentional content.

This, I think, is the distinction Kant had in mind. In the one case (the empirical subject) I am conscious of myself as an object with certain mental properties; in the other case (the transcendental subject) I am conscious of myself *as* thinking, and thus in terms of *what it is* I am thinking—in this case the objects of the sensible world. In thinking of myself as thinking, I am of course attributing to myself what thinking is, namely the spontaneous activity of combining. I construe myself strictly in terms of the activity of thinking—specifically, thinking about the sensible world. The only sense in which I am empty or contentless is that, under this description, the only kind of content that counts is intentional content. And the intentional content of my thought is not in me or part of me but is "out there"—in the world.

This gives us an answer to our question: How, i.e., *as what* or *under what description*, is the self represented in pure apperception? The answer is articulated by contrast to empirical apperception. In the former the self is active, spontaneous, thinking, intentionally related to its objects (*not* its representations); in the latter the self is but a bearer of its representations, sensations, and thoughts (these being given through inner sense).

Granted that these two descriptions are very different from each other, are we entitled to speak of two different selves, a "transcendental" and an "empirical" self? Kant himself says they are "the same subject" (B 155), but admits to great difficulty in reconciling the two descriptions. The real question is not whether there are two descriptions, of course, but whether they are incompatible descriptions. Only this would threaten or call into question the identity of the subject(s) being described. Are the two descriptions incompatible?

There are good reasons for saying that they are. In transcendental self-consciousness I represent myself as the spontaneous activity of thinking. This means that I take myself to be following rules or reasons, not to be causally determined in my activity. As one commentator has put it, "taking something as a reason for belief, like adopting an end or deciding on a course of action, is not something that we can consider ourselves caused to do . . . For Kant . . ., the reasons for one's belief cannot be regarded as a set of causes producing it."[7] Spontaneity, in this sense, is of course a property that no natural object can have. Anything that can be given in intuition, and thus become an object of empirical knowledge, must be subject to the category of causality, i.e., it is not just an isolated object, but belongs in a regulated way to the other objects and events that make up nature. This is how the self is represented in *empirical* apperception. It is given in inner sense, it is an object of knowledge, and thus it must belong to nature, that is, be a part of it subject to its laws.

Indeed this incompatibility is insignificant compared to that which emerges when we consider not the spontaneity but the *intentionality* of the thinking subject. In pure apperception, I represent myself as intentionally related to objects of thought—in the present case, objects of empirical knowledge. But these objects are such, thanks to the categories, as to make up a whole realm or system of lawful interconnections, which we have been calling the sensible world and which Kant calls nature.[8] Implicitly it is not just individual objects, but all of nature, which constitutes the intentional object of empirical knowledge. Now if there is a conceptual requirement belonging to the concept of intentionality, that we distinguish consciousness *from* its object, or in this case knowledge from the object known, then conceptually the subject of knowledge is distinct from nature. In other words the knowledge of nature requires, as a condition of its possibility, that we distinguish ourselves from nature.

Thus the incompatibility of the two descriptions is complete. It is not even a question of two incompatible descriptions of a putative *object*. Only empirical apperception gives us a description of an object in the world together with other objects. Transcendental apperception, by contrast, represents an I which is not part of the (sensible) world at all, by virtue of standing conceptually (i.e., intentionally) over against or distinct from it, and by virtue of possessing a feature (spontaneity) that rules out its inclusion in the world.

This is not, however, to say that the "transcendental" subject could be described without reference to the world, or even simply as being excluded from the world. For both subjects can be correctly described only "with reference" to the sensible world. Rather, it is a question of two incompatible sorts of relations to the world—if we are prepared to use the word "relation" loosely enough: The empirical self stands in a relation of inclusion and thus a part-whole relation to the world; the transcendental self stands in an intentional or subject-object relation to the world.

Thus we see that "the self of which I am conscious" in transcendental apperception is radically different from the self of which I am conscious in empirical apperception. One is part of, and the other is *not* part of, the sensible world: How could they be more different than that? Is talk of a "transcendental ego" and an "empirical ego" then justified? In order to answer this we must pass to the second part of our question, concerning the nature of the consciousness in which the self represents itself under the descriptions we have been discussing.

THE CONSCIOUSNESS OF SELF

As we have seen, it is a peculiar kind of self-consciousness, not simply a peculiar kind of self, which, according to Kant, is the supreme condition of our knowledge of the sensible world. Transcendental apperception is peculiar in that it characterizes or describes the self in a quite distinctive way, as we have seen. It is also peculiar in how it does this. What sort of consciousness is this consciousness of self? Many of Kant's most difficult remarks in the Transcendental Deduction are designed to answer *this* question—again, often in contrast to the kind of consciousness present in empirical apperception.

We have seen that transcendental self-consciousness is not an intuition of self. We do indeed have an intuition of self, in the form of inner sense. Here the self can become an object of knowledge, subject of course to the categories, and accordingly given as an appearance, not as a thing in itself. But this self-consciousness is empirical, not *a priori*; it is a bit of experience, not a condition of the possibility of experience and hence not transcendental. It represents the self with its mental properties as part of the world.

Describing this form of self-consciousness and self-knowledge is not without its problems, as Kant admits. He calls it a paradox (B 152), and goes to some lengths to make sense of the idea that the self could be inwardly affected by, and thus in a relation of passive reception to, its own activity (B 153–156).

Indeed the description of transcendental self-consciousness is no less difficult. Here I am conscious of myself "not as I appear to myself, nor as I am in myself, but only that I am. This *representation* is a *thought*, not an *intuition*" (B 157). I have inner sense, which permits me to "determine" (*bestimmen*) my existence, i.e., apply predicates to it through judgments, so that it becomes a determined or determinate object. But

> "since I do not have another self-intuition which gives the *determining* (*das Bestimmende*) in me (I am *merely conscious* [my alteration, my emphasis:DC] of the spontaneity of it) . . . I cannot determine my existence as that of a self-active being; all that I can do is represent to myself the spontaneity of my thought . . . But it is owing to this spontaneity that I entitle myself intelligence" (B 157n.)

Thus we have a self-consciousness in which the self is indeed represented, even thought, as spontaneous, but not intuited, since spontaneity cannot be intuited. In the Paralogisms, Kant first speaks of the "I think" as a "judgment" involving a "concept"—indeed a concept that ought to be counted among the categories (A 341/B 399). Then a few pages later he says of the representation "I," "that we cannot even say that it is a concept, but merely that it is a bare consciousness [*ein bloßes Bewußtsein*] that accompanies all concepts" (A 346/B 404).

These remarks suggest that the transcendental unity of apperception is not only not intuitive, it is not even conceptual. Here Kant is doubtless

thinking of the "normal" employment of concepts, namely to make judgments about objects. Any such judgment, even if it attempts to be *about*
the I, would presuppose, rather than simply express, the transcendental "I
think." Here we could "only revolve in a perpetual circle, since any judgment upon [the "I"] has always already made use of its representation" (A
346/B 404). But this is just a way of saying that transcendental self-consciousness is not a direct, face-to-face awareness of myself, but a secondary
or oblique reference that is always parasitic on a first-order judgment. *Empirical* self-consciousness is direct awareness. Here Kant is speaking of another sort of self-consciousness that I have when making judgments about
anything at all: God, the world, or even myself. This is the "accompanying"
role of the "I think." And this is also another way of noting the *intentional*
character of this representation of the "I think:", I am aware of it only
through its intentional content, i.e., what it is of or about.

Thus transcendental apperception is hardly nonconceptual or preconceptual;
it is directly tied to the conceptual as the condition of the possibility of all
employment of concepts, including any employment which might refer to
the self. It takes the form of a judgment ("I think") and even employs
concepts, but it occurs only as a concomitant feature of some other judgment or judgments. It can be described as a judgment of indirect discourse
(I think that *p*).[9]

IS THERE A TRANSCENDENTAL SELF?

We have now said enough about "the self of which I am conscious" and
"the consciousness of self," in transcendental apperception, to be able to
answer the main questions with which we started and which have arisen in
the course of our inquiry.

We began by asking whether Kant's philosophy is a metaphysics of the
subject. This question is closely tied to that of whether Kant is claiming
that there are not one but two subjects, an empirical subject and a transcendental subject. We have seen that there are good reasons for saying
that he is, since he proposes two radically different, indeed incompatible
descriptions of the self. But we must remember that while Kant at first
seems to say that experience (empirical knowledge) requires that there *be* a
subject of a certain sort, the "transcendental" subject, instead he actually
says that experience requires that we be *conscious of* ourselves in a certain
way, namely *as* spontaneous, as intelligence, as intentional, and so on.

We have, then, a transcendental *description* of the self— or, perhaps, a
description of the transcendental self. However, *is* there such a self?

Kant says, in a passage already quoted, in transcendental apperception I
am conscious *that* I am (B 157), in the "I think" "existence is already given

thereby" (B 157n.). But when it comes to "determining" my existence, i.e., giving it a description as an object to be known, I can know myself only under the description provided by inner sense, and this is very different from the description attaching to transcendental apperception. Hence, in empirical self-consciousness, I not only *describe* myself in a certain way (as subject of mental predicates, as part of the world, as causally determined); I also *know* myself *as* such or *to be* such, thanks to inner sense. In transcendental apperception, by contrast, I cannot *know* myself to *be* as I am described (spontaneous, and so on) but only *take* myself to be such.

This is decisive to our question of whether there *is* a transcendental self. If the condition of the possibility of experience were that I *know* myself as spontaneous, intentional, and so on, then we would be justified in saying that the fact there is experience proves that I *am* such. But the possibility of experience requires only that I *take* myself to be such, not that I know myself as such.

If this is so we can hardly speak of two subjects. We may have two self-descriptions, but only one of them can acquire ontological status, thanks to inner sense. Lacking this ontological status, what is the other description, that of the "transcendental subject," but a *fiction?* Just as I can describe myself, in imagination, as free of gravity, so that I can soar with the birds, so can I describe myself as free of worldly causality, generally. But it does not follow that I really am so. "Fiction" is of course the word favored by Hume to describe "the notion of a *soul,* and *self* and *substance*" lying behind our changing perceptions.[10] Kant is notoriously opposed to Hume's fictionalism, both in this context and others. How, in the end, can he avoid such a conclusion, especially as regards the "transcendental self"?

The first thing to be said is that, if the transcendental subject is a fiction, it is a *necessary* fiction. The word "fiction" is closely linked, in use and in etymology, with feigning or pretending, and is thus associated with the freedom of our imagination or fantasy. Even Hume admits that his "fictions" are not mere whimsy, but the most he will allow is that they are useful or convenient. Kant's claim about the transcendental subject is much stronger. Empirical knowledge *requires* that we represent ourselves in this way, namely as distinct from and not subject to the causal order of the sensible world we know. Insofar as we have knowledge of the sensible world (and we do), we are not free *not* to consider ourselves in this way—though of course, we are equally constrained to think of ourselves in the incompatible role of object in the sensible world.

Thus while the two descriptions differ in epistemic status—one is knowledge, the other is not—and in the ontological status that seems to follow, they do not differ with respect to constraint. Both are required, though in different ways, by the same thing: empirical knowledge.

Another sense attached to the word "fiction" is that it refers to something we consciously take to be nonexistent, and in doing so we implicitly contrast it with what does exist. Fictional characters in plays and novels have the most elaborate descriptions, and we can become acquainted with their personalities as if they lived lives of their own; we do not for a moment think that they exist or ever existed. Kant says, by contrast, that in transcendental apperception I am conscious of my own existence; there is no suggestion that the self I take myself to be, in this form of self-consciousness, is a self I take *not* to exist.

To be sure, if we identified "what exists" with the sensible world, we would find it hard to avoid this conclusion, since the transcendental self has been explicitly described as *not belonging* to that world, as part to the whole, but as being distinct from it, as subject to intentional object, and as not being subject to its laws. This identification of what exists with the sensible world is one that Kant refuses to make. His notorious concept of the thing in itself, enters in. To exist as a natural object in the sensible world is to exist as what Kant calls an "appearance." Existing in this way entails being subject to the categories and the laws they prescribe. Existing in this way is not, or may not be, the only way of existing. While I cannot know myself to exist as a transcendental subject, I may yet exist in this way, not as an appearance but as thing in itself.

We have now entered the domain of the Transcendental Dialectic, particularly the Paralogisms of Pure Reason and the Third Antinomy. The former is addressed to those who would derive an *a priori* metaphysics of the subject (or "rational psychology") from the "sole text" of transcendental apperception: "I think" (A 343/B 401), and draw conclusions about the immortality of the soul. The Third Antinomy, by contrast, is addressed to those who would draw the conclusion directly opposed to that of the rational psychologists. Since I can *know* myself only as worldly, i.e., as part of the sensible world and hence as subject to its universal causality, I must conclude that I am not or cannot be nonworldly in the sense of the spontaneous, intentional, and *free* subject that I take myself to be. Now Kant is saying that although I can *know* myself only as causally determined, I may yet exist (as thing in itself) as transcendental subject. Kant believes that his doctrine of transcendental idealism, with its distinction between appearances and things in themselves, permits us to conclude that "freedom is at least not *incompatible with* nature" (A 558/B 586).

Many readers, even some of Kant's admirers, find him at best unpersuasive here. Not least among the difficulties attached to the doctrine of transcendental idealism and that of the thing in itself, is that it loosens one of our most sacred conceptual bonds, which are between knowing and being, and thus threatens a kind of conceptual anarchy. Kant insists that we have empirical knowledge, yet it is knowledge only of appearances. This implication is especially abhorrent to those who see Kant as an opponent of skepticism, since this doctrine seems to land him squarely among the skeptics. It is not our intention here to enter into a general debate about transcendental idealism, much less to defend Kant on this point. It does seem possible, however, to present a plausible reading of his views, as least as they affect his theory of the subject.

One commentator who has argued persuasively against the view that Kant is defending science against skepticism, R. C. S. Walker, writes: "Strawson and others like him start out with the expectation that [Kant's] transcendental arguments can be used to establish something about what the world must be like, and not just about what we must take it to be like, if we are to have experience of it." Walker believes that "the conclusions most [Kantian] arguments can be expected to establish are about ourselves and our beliefs, not about the world."[11] Suppose we take Kant's theory of the categories, causality in particular, as a theory of what we must *take* the world to be like, *if* we are to have experience (i.e., empirical knowledge) of it. This makes universal causality something like an assumption about the world, permitting us to subsume empirical regularities under it, or if you will, a rule for interpreting empirical regularities, namely *as* instances of universal causality. We can "know" these regularities in the sense that, in line with our assumption, we attribute them to the world, not to our own subjective impressions. But universal causality is not itself something we *know* in this way, it is only something we assume. (Of course, this would not square with Kant's claim that "every alteration has a cause" as being one of the items of synthetic *a priori knowledge* we possess.)

This would accord, at least in part, with Hume's important discovery, with which Kant heartily agreed, that causality, in the sense of necessary connection, is not something we encounter in experience. For Hume it thus acquires, like the concept of the self, the status of one of those useful and convenient *fictions*. Again Kant would object to this terminology, and for the same reasons as before: the belief in universal causality is necessary— this is probably why Kant would call it not merely a belief but knowledge— and is hence certainly not the consciousness of something we implicitly believe *not* to exist. However, Kant would probably agree that if the transcendental self is a fiction, then universal causality is *no less* a fiction, and for similar reasons: both are required for experience to be possible. If universal causality has this status—let us revert to our term "assumption"— what are the consequences for our "knowledge" of objects in the sensible world? It is true that they are given in sensation, but what we know *about* them turns out to be either an *a priori* assumption—they are objects in space and time that are strictly regulated causally—or empirical claims dependent on this assumption—this regularity we observe is an instance of that strict regularity we *assume* to be there. Thus our "knowledge" of the sensible world depends heavily on such assumptions, and the supposed conceptual connection between knowing and being can only mean that the world *is* as we take it to be, *granted* these assumptions. It is not quite correct to say, with Walker, that Kant's arguments are in the end only about "ourselves and our beliefs." They are indeed about the world; but they are about the world *qua* intentional object, the world as we (must) take or assume it to be. But of course *we make* these assumptions, and there is no sense in which they can be justified. The transcendental deduction only shows how the categories work.

This interpretation of Kant's transcendental idealism has the effect of rectifying the "ontological imbalance" we thought we had discovered earlier between the "transcendental self" and the "empirical self," and of placing them on the same or very similar footing.

We are left with the following situation: As H. Allison says, on the one side, "just as we can act only under the idea of freedom, so we can think only under the idea of spontaneity."[12] That is, in order to have empirical knowledge at all, I must *take myself* to be spontaneous, intentional, and thus distinct from the sensible world I know. In order to have empirical knowledge of myself, on the other hand, I must *take myself* to be part of that sensible world and be subject to its laws.

Is Kant saying, then, that there *are* two selves, a transcendental self and an empirical self? No, manifestly not; he is merely saying that there are two equally necessary and incompatible descriptions that we give to ourselves. If he were making the assertion that there are two selves, or for that matter only one, then he would be advancing a metaphysics of the subject (or subjects). But if Kant has not made a metaphysical assertion, he may be thought to have left us with a metaphysical *question*: namely, which description corresponds to the way I *really* am?

This has led many readers of Kant to think that his theory of the subject involves us in speaking not just of *two* selves but of *three*: the transcendental self, the empirical self, and the self in itself. It is perfectly legitimate to use this *façon de parler*, as long as one takes it to mean not three distinct selves but three possible descriptions. So I would like to suggest that, if it is legitimate to speak of three subjects, then we must also add a *fourth*. To repeat our formula: In order to have empirical knowledge I must take *myself* to be a transcendental subject and I must take *myself* to be an empirical subject. Here we have the two descriptions we have discussed, both applied to *myself*. If we consider the latter to be the "self in itself," this is of course not so much a third description as it is a placeholder to which we would apply one of the other two descriptions if we were justified in doing so.

What of the *I* that "takes itself" in these various ways? Is this yet another ego, or just an empty placeholder as well? Or can we say more about it (or me, or him)? We said: In order to have empirical knowledge I must take myself to be a transcendental subject. But what does "in order to" mean here? Does it mean *as long as* or *when* I have empirical knowledge? Kant's idea of the empirical knowledge we possess is closely identified with natural science. However, most of us are not scientists, and many people have no idea what goes on in science. Is it only scientists who have this knowledge, and thus only they who must take themselves to be transcendental subjects? Are they only subjects when they are doing science or thinking scientifically?

Kant says "we" are in possession of such knowledge, "and even the common understanding [*der gemeine Verstand*] is never without" it (B 3). Who are "we?" The unrestricted use suggests all human beings, of course, and the reference to common understanding (or better: common sense) tells us that, according to Kant, we do not have to be scientists to have such knowledge. Furthermore, the knowledge in question is knowledge of the sensible world or nature. We are all always in this world. Experience of it is something we are never without (unless we are asleep or unconscious). Thus there would seem to be no restriction on the requirement that we take ourselves to be transcendental subjects. The I that "takes itself" in this way is just all of us, all the time.

Should we accept this link between scientific knowledge and common sense? It is a familiar view that science is just an extension and refinement of the rough and ready knowledge of the world that we always already have. Many philosophers and historians of science have argued that, on the contrary, science has succeeded only to the extent that it has freed itself of common sense; that this was true already of the Newtonian science Kant so much admired, in relation to its Aristotelian precursor; and that this is even more evident in the post-Newtonian science of more recent times. On this view, "common sense" would correspond either to an unchanging pre-scientific life-world, or it would be the historical sediment of the science of a previous age. In any case, Kant is often criticized for having enshrined and frozen for all time in his categories what is in fact a passing historical conception of the world; and for having mistakenly attributed this conception to common sense, as if we all conducted our everyday lives as if we were Newtonian scientists.

If we follow this sort of criticism we might say: I must take myself to be a transcendental subject only, *insofar, as* I take the world to be a Newtonian world—something that I may never in fact do. Thus the "necessity" of transcendental apperception, and the requirement that I take myself to be a transcendental subject, would again be considerably restricted. It would, in fact, describe a self-conception tied very closely to a particular historical age.

NOTES

1. See Karl Ameriks's discussion of the various alternatives, at the beginning of his "Kant's Transcendental Deduction as a Regressive Argument," (*Kant-Studien*, 69 [1978], 273ff.) and in the second part of his "Recent Work on Kant's Theoretical Philosophy" (*American Philosophical Quarterly*, 19 [1982]).

2. Kant uses the expression "transcendental subject" at A 346/B 404.

3. Cf. Joseph Claude Evans Jr.: *The Metaphysics of Transcendental Subjectivity: Descartes, Kant and W. Sellars* (Amsterdam: B. R. Grüner, 1984), pp. 73f.

4. John Locke, *An Essay Concerning Human Understanding* (Chicago: Henry Regnery Co., 1956), p. 17.

5. The passages quoted in this paragraph are at their most misleading when they suggest that the transcendental/empirical self distinction is a concept/instance or type/token distinction, a view held by surprisingly many and sophisticated, but hasty readers of Kant. Since Kant's doctrine echoes the Averroistic distinction between active and passive intellect, some draw the conclusion that the "Transcendental Ego" is *one* while all the empirical egos are *many*. But this interpretation is untenable, since it is evident that Kant is giving us two different (and, as we shall see, incompatible) *descriptions* of the subject, and hence *two* types or concepts, not one. Whether this means that there must be two tokens, two selves, is a question we take up later on.

6. *Logical Investigations*, trans. J. N. Findlay (Atlantic Highlands: Humanities Press, 1970), vol. 2, p. 576. The word content (*Inhalt*) seems ill-chosen for Husserl's purposes, when used in its intentional sense, but this use of it is already found in Brentano before him. Unfortunately it has also been perpetuated by such contemporary philosophers as D. Dennett. Cf. *Content and Consciousness* (London: Routledge and Kegan Paul, 1969).

7. H. Allison, "Kant's Refutation of Materialism," in *The Monist*, vol. 72, no. 2, 1989, p. 202.

8. See A 216/B 263, A 418/B 446 and n. In the latter passage Kant also uses the term "world."

9. Cf. Evans, *op. cit.* p. 74.

10. *A Treatise of Human Nature* (New York: Dolphin Books, 1961), p. 230.

11. R. C. S. Walker, *Kant* (London: Routledge and Kegan Paul, 1978), p. 122.

12. Henry Allison, *op. cit.*, p. 190.

7

Hermann Cohen's Concept of the Transcendental Method

Vladimir Zeman

What will follow is an attempt to fill a gap, certainly at least in the historical sense, within the problem area of transcendental philosophy. It is usual to understand Husserl in contrast to Kant, while paying only lip service to Husserl's relationship to Cohen's closest philosophical collaborator, Paul Natorp. It is standard wisdom that Heidegger started from, and rebelled against, the Marburg School of philosophy, whose main representatives were precisely Cohen and Natorp. What we need to explore in greater depth are the consequences of the fact that, prior to the World War I, neo-Kantianism was undoubtedly the most representative philosophical orientation in Germany. Here it is important to note that among the different German neo-Kantian schools, which, depending on the classification, can number as many as seven, the Marburg School is one of the oldest and certainly the most established among its numerous schools.

It is worth noting that scholarship in the area of neo-Kantianism is rather unevenly spread. It is lively and growing primarily in Europe, especially in German-speaking countries, though enough is available in French, Italian, and Spanish. In English language circles, John Michael Krois deserves credit for renewing interest in Cassirer.[1] A similar trend in a longer tradition can be traced in French publications as well.[2] In the latter case, a somewhat broader historical approach with a focus on Cohen's philosophy is represented primarily by two senior scholars, Jules Vuillemin[3] and Alexis Philonenko.[4]

Naturally, there are still many unexplored areas of this rich field. It will not be possible here to consider more than a single issue. I will concentrate on a topic, which not only historically happened to be pivotal for the establishment of Marburg School, but which also represents an attempt to

111

reconstruct the link between philosophy and the broader world of experience. In this case, "experience" is not understood in the more usual sense of "everyday experience," but rather more technically as "scientific experience." For Cohen, "scientific experience" points to what he understands as the Kantian method, reinterpreted under the heading of transcendental method.[5]

INTRODUCTION

From a methodological point of view, the problem of transcendental method, for a contemporary scholar, is a problem of interpretation. It is a concept which appeared in, and became characteristic for, the Marburg School of neo-Kantianism. When in 1871, Hermann Cohen published his book, *Kants Theorie of Erfahrung* (*Kant's Theory of Experience*, hereafter referred to as *KTE* 1),[6] his aim was threefold:

a. historical,

b. systematico-reconstructive,

c. originative and constructive.

In a historical sense, the task was "to go back to Kant," a return for which Otto Liebmann had famously already called for in 1865. That meant, first of all, to overcome the established interpretation, or rather misinterpretation, of Kant's philosophy by the three generations of post-Kantians. Misinterpretation is always a problem in the interpretation of any important theory. Yet in this case, the problem was even more serious than usual. For the misinterpretations in question were due to those who were the most influential among the representatives of so-called German classical philosophy. "I was concerned to present once more the historical Kant, to affirm him in his own manner, as much as this was comprehensible, against his opponents" (*KTE* 1, p. iv). But Cohen was well aware that on its own, such a purely historical approach would be unsatisfactory, purely one-sided, piecemeal, and we may add, arbitrary. "I saw how systematic contradiction and historical error implied each other." (*KTE* 1, p. iv).

Moreover, without declaring the purpose behind the whole enterprise, the result might be misleading or even dishonest. "What should be determined are not the external literary facts but the cohesion of complete thoughts, the meaning of which the historical research has to clarify against the background of conceptions and interpretations, flowing nevertheless from the overall worldview of those who judge. It is impossible to evaluate Kant without betraying what type of world one carries in ones own head." (*KTE* 1, p. v).

From a systematico-reconstructive angle, Cohen's project can be understood as a form of Kant's famous claim that he could understand Plato better than the latter had done.[7] Accordingly, Cohen saw his task as an extension or reconstruction of Kant's philosophy, though *in agreement* not only with its spirit but with its letter as well. This type of approach explains both the title of his work and the claim made in the very first sentence of the Preface: ". . . to provide a new foundation for Kant's theory of a priori" (*KTE* 1, p. iii). The method to achieve it was to be a *systematic* reconstruction. "To understand Kant through his own text, it is indispensable to take diverse conceptions made possible by Kant himself and check their value for the theory of knowledge itself; the systematic partisanship cannot be avoided" (*KTE* 1, p. v).

Cohen himself returned to Kant's *Critique of Pure Reason* again in 1907, after the two first two volumes of his *System of Philosophy* appeared in 1902 and 1904. This return took the form of a commentary through which the mature Cohen projected his own philosophy back into a detailed reading of the *Critique*.[8]

Finally, Cohen's own angle for the reconstruction of the theory, at least during the time between the first (1871) and the second (1885) editions of *Kants Theorie der Erfahrung* [1871, 1885], as well as in *Das Prinzip der Infinitesimalmethode und seine Geschichte* [1883], was to reestablish and redefine in more concrete terms the relation between philosophy and science that was so typical for Kant.[9]

> Idealism generally breaks the things down into appearances and ideas, whereas the critique of knowledge [Erkenntniskritik] dissects science into *assumptions* and *fundamentals*, considered in its laws and on their own. Epistemological idealism has as its objects neither things and events, *nor even the conscious ones*, but the *scientific facts* . . . thus the epistemological idealism is the *scientific form of idealism*, attained through the concept of *transcendental*.

It should by now already have become obvious that to explain the origin of the concept of transcendental method and the role it played in Cohen's own philosophy (while not denying its importance for other representatives of the same school), it is necessary to deal with all three mentioned aspects. As we shall see, it is the last one that holds the key to the understanding of the overall *development* of Cohen's own philosophy.

HISTORICAL ORIGINS OF COHEN'S EXPOSITION OF KANT

In general, Cohen and his school believed that they followed Kant in their exploration of the unity between logic on one hand, and the world in its multiple expressions on the other hand. While "the facts" of science, morality, etc. were to be accepted, they had to be philosophically justified. For this logical process of generating the multiple forms of objectivation, Cohen used the term "transcendental method." In a preliminary way, we may characterize this term as referring to a method used by philosophy to identify, as well as to justify, the categories necessary if the above mentioned, undoubtedly existing, dimensions of our world are to be possible.

Historically, Cohen's first major work, *Kants Theorie der Erfahrung* (*Kant's Theory of Experience*) appeared in 1871. This was followed six years later, in 1877, by *Kants Begruendung der Ethik* (*Kant's Foundation of Ethics*). The second edition of Cohen's study of Kant's view of experience, which was more than twice as long as the original, followed in 1885. As already mentioned, *Das Prizip der Infinitesimalmethode und seine Geschichte* was published in 1883, thus breaking the intended sequence of expository works. In between, Cohen published a lesser work, entitled *Kants Begruendung der Aesthetik*. In the process, what had been originally planned as an explanatory series gained an important, new dimension.

To explain Cohen's original intentions as well as the general reception of his interpretative exposition of Kant, it is advisable to start with some preliminary historical remarks. When, in 1865, Liebmann sounded his battle call "Back to Kant," he did not intend to deny completely the achievements of such other well-known Kant interpreters as, say, Kuno Fischer (a Hegelian) or Adolf Trendelenburg (an Aristotelian). His intention was rather to highlight the limits of their primarily historical and philological pursuits. More importantly, Liebmann called for a reassessment of German philosophy of his day against the background of what at the time appeared to be the half-forgotten and, to a considerable degree, misinterpreted philosophy of Kant. For in his view, Kant provided the foundation stone of German philosophy. Hence, when in 1866 F. A. Lange published his *Geschichte des Materialismus* (*History of Materialism*), which almost immediately became, and remained, one of the most popular German philosophical works of the period before World War I, the pivotal point of his work was exactly the same—his view of Kant's philosophy. The importance of Kant was seen above all in his critique of theoretical reason. For without Kant's famous *Vernunftkritik*, what later came in its wake to be called *epistemology*, the second part of Kant's system, his ethics, would simply not have been possible.[10]

Cohen's own series of books, which included a monograph specifically devoted to each of Kant's critiques, is a conscious answer to this widely perceived need for a completely systematic presentation of Kant's philosophy as a living philosophy, not surpassed by the thinkers of ensuing generations. Among the older German philosophers, F. A. Lange, who himself interpreted the Kantian a priori in physiological terms, was probably the first to recognize the importance of Cohen's review and "revision of the whole of Kant's system." Lange even went so far as to change the Kant chapter in the second edition of his *History of Materialism* (1873) to reflect his appreciation of the importance of Cohen's work.[11] Among the scholars of the younger generations, the impetus to Cassirer's own path to Marburg is not atypical. It was initiated by the following remark Georg Simmel made in one of his lectures in the 1890s: "The best books on Kant were without any doubt written by Hermann Cohen, though I have to admit that I do not understand them."[12]

Nevertheless, Cohen's interpretation of Kant's *CPR* in the first edition of his *KTE* shows only the direction of his interpretative turn, without actually carrying it out to its full extent. Cohen starts with Kant's own directive to consider his *CPR* as a treatise on method, more precisely as a critique of the methods used by Kant's predecessors and as a delineation of the manner in which his own critical philosophy, or transcendental idealism, should proceed. Viewed in this way, the *Critique* is neither an ontological treatise, nor an epistemological one, but rather, as Cohen clearly saw, a theory of experience. In establishing the framework of possible experience, Kant's focus was not a metaphysical, but rather a transcendental, exposition and deduction. In this sense, perception and the concepts of the understanding can be treated separately through abstraction and for expository purposes only.

From a historical point of view, Cohen had another, more particular, reason to attempt a complete, highly-focused reinterpretation of the *Critique of Pure Reason*. *KTE* was Cohen's second and final attempt to close one of the most famous and unfortunately also rather vicious polemics of the day. This was a controversy between Fischer and Trendelenburg concerning their respective interpretations of Kant's philosophy, which appeared to be mutually exclusive. In this context, it may be useful to remember that the young Kant attempted, in the same way, to mediate between the two leading conceptions of nature and science of the eighteenth century, respectively due to Leibniz and to Newton. Though not without analogies in the twentieth century, the polemic itself appears today to be of a historical interest only. However, it worked as a catalyst for Cohen's own philosophical beginnings, since, as mentioned, *KTE* started as an apologetic work. Cohen's original intention was to take Kant's philosophy for granted while analyzing erroneous interpretations of it. In particular, Kant's original doctrine of space and time was to be presented in response to Trendelenburg's supposed misinterpretation of these doctrines.[13]

At least from a historical point of view, to understand the role of transcendental method in Cohen's interpretation of Kant's philosophy, it seems desirable to review at some length the basic features first of the position of Cohen's teacher, Trendelenburg, then of Cohen, and finally of the dispute itself. While the controversy itself took place in the late 1860s, coinciding with Cohen's public entry into philosophy, Trendelenburg developed his own interpretation between the late 1820s and 1840.[14] Among the points that were to prove influential, at least the following should be mentioned:

a. Trendelenburg attempted to overcome various dualities in Kant's position—such as those concerning the differences between subject and object, reason and intuition, things in themselves and phenomena—by conceiving them all as the elements of universal motion.

b. Trendelenburg tried to overcome Fichte's and Hegel's stress on the priority and the independence of logic, in respect to science, by postulating the relation between the two as one of mutual support.[15] His term "science" referred to *scientific activity as practiced* in various scientific disciplines rather than to some *a priori* and generic concept of science. The goal was truly to reconnect what previously had been simply seen as a given unity, with an arrogantly oblivious attitude towards the existing scientific enterprise. It is in this context that, in 1862, for the first time appears the concept of the theory of science (*Theorie der Wissenschaft*). In passing, we can note that, as with many of Trendelenburg's direct or indirect disciples, this understanding of the relation between science and philosophy naturally leads to strong positivistic inclinations, even where their orientation was basically in a Kantian direction, as was the case for Hans Vaihinger.

c. The first chapter of *Logische Untersuchungen*, specifically rewritten for the second edition, was entitled "Logic and Metaphysics as the Foundational Science."[16] Here, Trendelenburg tried to understand the complex series of relations between logic and the methods of the various scientific disciplines:

> When the way to generate necessity or the way to bring the knowledge closer to necessity and to measure the degree of this approximation to necessity is called method, then it is the method which makes the science a science. And when these methods appear against the object of sciences without being given in it, having their general ground in the thought working through the object—then this leads to the task to search for their origin [*Ursprung*] in the essence of thought.[17]

This search for the character and origin of method in the essence of thought—the so-called problem of the origin of "*Ursprung*"—was later to become the central developing element of Cohen's own philosophy.

d. Finally, another crucial element of Trendelenburg's philosophical activity was that which led to the above mentioned controversy, namely his claim that there is a "loophole" in Kant's argumentation concerning the status of space and time as pure forms of intuition. Trendelenburg believed that Kant only presented the subjective side of space and time. Were it indeed impossible to ascribe to them an objective character as well, Kant's one-sided position would necessarily lead to scepticism. To counter this danger, Trendelenburg followed Fichte's attempt to establish the origin of pure forms of intuition, which he found in the creative activity (*erzeugende Thaetigkeit*) allegedly common both to thinking and things.[18] Trendelenburg's claim that, without a return to some minimal sort of metaphysical realism, the application of purely subjective forms of intuition could lead to the falsification of knowledge, appears to be based on his own inability to follow Kant through the latter's transcendental turn. In Trendelenburg's writing, the term "subjective" appears in its classical, pre-Kantian interpretation.

Kuno Fischer's attack on Trendelenburg's position was launched in 1852[19] and continued until 1870,[20] practically only ceasing in 1872 with Trendelenburg's death. Fischer's particular point in the discussion with Trendelenburg[21] was that while all concepts could be considered classificatory concepts (*Gattungsbegriffe*), since space and time were not classificatory they could not be considered as concepts at all. Rather, they needed to be taken as wholes instead. If this line of reasoning were correct, space and time would have to be understood as pure intuitions. This in turn would make mathematics possible as general and necessary knowledge. For only in this way could pure forms be applied to objects.

This seemingly minor dispute led to potentially crucial consequences. If indeed, as Trendelenburg claimed,

> ... everybody who applies himself to philosophical studies attempts first to ponder Kant and to acquaint himself with Kant, then this question is not of great importance just for history of philosophy but also for contemporary philosophical studies. If Kant rigorously proved the exclusive subjectivity of space and time, then the path leads to (transcendental) idealism; if he did not prove it and in his proofs left the possibility open that the pure image [Vorstellung] of space and time is valid for the exterior things as well, then the path is open for securing the ideal in the real.[22]

The young Cohen should be given full credit for recognizing the importance of the problem as well as trying to solve it, without regard to his general allegiance to his teacher.

> The dispute on the meaning of *space* and *time* in *Kant* concerns all efforts of philosophical research. It is because the question: what did *Kant* teach on space and time? coincides with the question: does the nature of things depend on the conditions of our spirit? or must and *can* the law of nature confirm to our thought?[23]

Cohen obviously clearly recognized that what was at stake was not just the choice between either a realistic v. a transcendental interpretation of Kant, and subsequently the orientation of philosophy in general, since the whole concept of transcendental philosophy required both a deeper historical analysis as well as a considerable constructive effort.

In the final analysis, Cohen appears to agree with Fischer that Trendelenburg indeed misinterpreted Kant, although he identifies the latter's false turn differently. In his view, time and space have to be considered as already incorporated within the context of experience. Kant, after all, saw his transcendental philosophy as a discipline dealing with the necessary and universal conditions of all experience. But he could not have meant material conditions (*Bedingungen*), since those would lead him back to things in themselves. The German term he used was "*Bestimmungen*" ("zu bestimmen" translates as "to identify", or "to recognize as"). The neo-Aristotelian philosopher, Trendelenburg, failed to appreciate this subtle difference.[24]

Cohen's criticism identifies the basis for this misinterpretation in Trendelenburg's broader misconception of Kant's view of space and time as pure forms of intuition. His identification of Trendelenburg's mistake, and of what he consequently saw as a proof that there was no such "loophole" in Kants's philosophy, was not only one of the main reasons for his own attempt at systematic presentation of Kant's philosophy. It further marked both positively and negatively the whole development of his own philosophy as well (something which is obviously outside the scope of this paper).

COHEN'S RECONSTRUCTIVE EFFORT

In the first sentence of his Preface to KTE, Cohen claims that his aim is to[25] "develop a new foundation for Kant's theory of the *a priori*." While in his Introduction to the central aspect of his approach he writes: "*Kant discovered a new concept of experience. The critique of pure reason is the critique of experience.*"[26] It is against this latter background that the true turn from apologetic exegesis to Cohen's own interpretation of Kant's philosophy develops.

Slightly later, while composing his *Foundation of Kant's Ethics*, Cohen came up against the need to clarify the precise sense in which the method of Kant's philosophizing in CPR could be considered to be the same as the method of philosophizing in the ethical writings. In general terms, Cohen still considers Kant's philosophy to be ". . . nothing else than philosophy as a science. . . . Science is an ideal of a system built on the basis of continuous methodic work."[27] For this reason, what Cohen tries to achieve in this particular work ". . . is to present, defend, and represent the epistemological foundation of ethics."[28] The latter point stresses what Cohen identifies as the systematic problem of ethics, or the problem of "*the relation between the experiential reality and that type of validity which is appropriate for the supersensual.*"[29] Hence, this second type of validity is tied up with the second type of reality. Still, when ethics teaches "what ought to be, it must teach what is not"[30] as well.

Kant himself did not speak about transcendental method, but about transcendental philosophy, or a transcendental approach. For Kant, this meant dealing with the framework of possible experience, the framework which is not only itself *a priori*, namely, necessary and universal, but without which no necessity and universality in the world of experience would be possible. In the CPR, Kant always shows first that the pure elements of knowledge are indeed independent of experience, though found in it (a metaphysical procedure), and only then proceeds to explain their constitutive role in the production of experiential knowledge.

Cohen identifies Kant's method of critical philosophy primarily with its transcendental rather than with its metaphysical aspect, though with a "twist." At least initially, he takes Kant's general results for granted and concentrates on the problem of their validity. In the case of ethics, even after the first edition of KTE there are still at least two questions awaiting Cohen's attention: (1) How can we connect ethics or the teaching on what ought to be to the theory of experience, or the teaching on what is?; (2) Can the transcendental approach be sufficiently broadened to operate not only with the "fact of knowledge (or science)," but also with "the fact of morality?"

To make the first point, Cohen (quite correctly, I believe) stresses that the problem of "giving a foundation" to something, anything at all, "is exclusively an epistemological problem." This founding process already starts when it can be shown that "the theory of experience does not make impossible the theory of mortals."[31] Up to this point, Cohen is in agreement with the standard interpretation of the so-called "causality of freedom" in the Transcendental Dialectic. However, Cohen takes a stronger stand, since his "intention is to show, . . . *that the theory of experience not only does not negate and does not leave open the possibility of ethics, but requires it.*"[32] The world of ideas represents, at the same time, both the limits and the necessary supplement to the experiential reality.[33]

This stress on the transcendental nature of the critical philosophy allows Cohen to found the unity of his interpretation in the universal role of a method, in his case in the transcendental method. Returning once more with Cohen to the question of transcendental method as ". . . a teaching on the conditions of experience . . ."[34] we can ask, how does this method proceed? What is its content?

> . . . the experience is given—we have to discover the conditions on which depends its possibility. Once we have found the conditions which *made possible* the given experience, made it possible in a way that we may consider it as a priori valid and recognize it as strictly necessary and as general in an unlimited sense, then we can characterize those conditions as the constitutive features of the concept of experience; from this concept is afterwards to deduce whatever claims the epistemological valence of *objective reality*. That is the whole business of transcendental philosophy.[35]

From the second, considerably enlarged edition of *KTE*, and the third, still slightly more extended standard edition (1918), I have selected for our discussion some additional relevant ideas. They are to be found, in particular, in the final part of the Introduction, entitled "The Transcendental Method" and in the sixteenth (and final) chapter, entitled "The System of Critical Idealism."

In the Introduction, Cohen expressly claims the dependence of the concept of transcendental method on the way in which Newton systematized physics.

> As a systematizer of his science Newton is no more and no less than a philosopher. The concepts he assumes are philosophical concepts. [. . .] The transcendental method developed through reflection on *Philosophiae naturalis principia mathematica*. [. . .] the principle and norm of transcendental method is a simple thought that those elements of consciousness are the elements of the apprehending consciousness, which are sufficient and necessary to provide a basis and consolidation for the fact of science. . . . The elements of consciousness have to be operative as the fundamentals of science and the assumptions of science are validated as the basic features of the apprehending consciousness. The metaphysical *a priori* must become the transcendental *a priori*.[36]

Cohen's concluding chapter stresses and analyzes the systematic, or scientific, character of transcendental philosophy. Cohen here reformulates Kant's famous statement, which can be paraphrased as the claim that, while all elements of our knowledge can be found in experience, not all of them originate in it. Cohen writes that "the transcendental idealist . . . starts from scientific experience. His first word is: knowledge does not need to originate from that with which it starts."[37] However, Cohen believes himself to be in agreement with science as well, when he reiterates that in his conception the *a priori* elements of the system (e.g., pure forms of intuition and of understanding) are conceived of as methods.[38] "When the forms are conceived of as methods they make possible the unity of the system . . ." However, in post-operationalist times it is important to understand that Cohen's concept of method is a broad one. It follows that when he speaks about scientific methods, he does not mean simply scientific operations.

Cohen's conception of transcendental method could not help but create considerable attention. In general, the idea that Kant's *CPR* presents a theory of experience was accepted positively, both at the time of its appearance (e.g., by A. Riehl in his review of the work)[39] and in the contemporary Kant literature. Between the wars, Heidegger repeatedly refused to admit that *CPR* had anything to do with theory of knowledge and therefore with the theory of experience. On the other hand, G. Martin does not view Heidegger's interpretation of Kant as incompatible with the direction taken by Cohen and his followers.[40] As far as the concept of transcendental method is concerned, the critical discussion started already with F. A. Lange,[41] the otherwise sympathetic supporter of the then still young Cohen.

COHEN'S *ERKENNTNISKRITIK*

The standard exposition of Cohen's philosophy breaks it down into two phases, including the critique of knowledge (*Erkenntniskritik*) and the logic of knowledge (*Erkenntnislogik*).[42] Whether this separation can or cannot be supported cannot be further studied here.[43] Nevertheless, if we are to understand Cohen's concept of transcendental method, it must be dealt with together with Cohen's conception of the critique of knowledge.

When Husserl attacked Galileo for reneging on a true sense of science, although his criticism is perhaps one-sided, he at least put his finger on what could be understood as the very foundation of modern science. In Galileo's own words

> Philosophy is written in that great book which ever lies before our eyes— I mean the universe—but we cannot understand it if we do not first learn the language and grasp the symbols in which it is written. This book is written in the mathematical language, and the symbols are triangles, circles, and other geometrical figures, without whose help it is impossible to comprehend a single word of it; without which one wanders in vain through a dark labyrinth.[44]

One of the central issues in Cohen's early philosophy was to identify more precisely that method of mathematics which, lying at the basis of Newton's physics, further provides the basis of our general understanding of the world. He properly understood that Newtonian physics would not have been possible without the differential and integral calculus, or in more philosophical terms, without the method of the infinitesimal.[45]

While in his later stages of his thought, Cohen still retains the concept of transcendental method, the center of his attention moves from the mathematical method to the method of conceptual production, namely to a logic of origin.

CONCLUSION

Neo-Kantianism, in general, followed the same route as all neo-isms: It analyzes the original position (in this case Kant's critical philosophy), while trying to identify its foci, and (if we stay with the same metaphor) verifying whether only one ellipse could be drawn on this basis. To the degree to which we deal with philosophical *systems*, this is an absolutely necessary procedure. This is certainly the case if, following Kant's own view, it is mandatory to understand the theory better than its author. However, Kant would have made this task easier, if, instead of claiming that he could understand Plato better than the latter had understood himself, he had simply claimed that he could understand him "differently and equally well."

Probably the single most crucial point in discussions about Kant's philosophy has always been whether it must be identified with the expression it received in Kant's works and that depended on the state of philosophy *and* science of the day. While some parts of the work seem to support this claim, which have the result in turn of making Kant's philosophy a closed system, others do not. S. Körner even tried to prove that, from a logical point of view, no uniqueness claim can be supported at all. In opposition to more orthodox Kantians and to the so-called Kantian philologists, neo-Kantians consciously transgressed such limits. They treated Kant's philosophy as an open system, or as a generic structure. Their mutual disagreements were not so much focused on the point concerning who among them was truest to Kant's own codification of his theory, but rather on the very different problem of which of the alternative reconstructions was closest to the general intentions of the transcendental approach. Representatives of both the Marburg and the Baden Schools shared an interest in the role that methods play in various areas of culture, and they studied what these methods had in common and how they differed.

> Marburgers have often been characterized as philosophers who shared the common vision of the development of science, morality, art, and religion as providing the basis for the potential development of humanity. Each of these dimensions of human being rested on the stable yet dynamic logical foundations of consciousness.[46]

While such an approach, in general, surpassed the scope of Cohen's own interpretive turn towards the concept of transcendental method, the latter can nevertheless be viewed as a junction leading toward the recognition of the multiplicity of structure-giving forms, called rather appropriately symbolic forms by Cassirer, Cohen's disciple.

To describe all the activities of the Marburgers, from Cohen to Cassirer, including even the socialist politician, Karl Vorlaender, the characteristics given would appear be too general. Nevertheless, these thinkers not only actively pursued philosophical research beyond the face and scope of Kant's own writings, but also, *actively* participated in various applied or more practical spheres of our human existence. Still, their primary interest and importance had a theoretical dimension. Their attempts not to impose philosophy on science and other areas of culture, but rather to search for forms of cross-fertilization, have been always positively regarded. In their own ways, each agreed with Kant that a philosophy worthy of the name must now be critical, transcendental, and scientific. They all, however, agreed that the *a priori* would have to be of formal character only.[47]

NOTES

1. See, e.g., John Michael Krois, *Cassirer, Symbolic Forms and History* (New Haven: Yale University Press, 1987).
2. Jean Seidengart (ed.), *Ernst Cassirer: De Marbourg à New York, L'itinéraire philosophique* (Paris: Les Editions du Cerf, 1990).
3. His book, *L'Héritage kantien* (Paris: Presses universitaires de France, 1954) is usually regarded as a standard work in the field.
4. See, most recently Alexis Philonenko, *L'école de Marbourg* (Paris: Vrin, 1989).
5. For some historical aspects of this "Cohenian turn" see my paper "Leibniz's Influence on the Marburg School, in particular on Hermann Cohen's *Conception of Reality* and of the 'Infinitesimalmethode'", in *Theoria cum Praxis*, "Studia Leibniziana" Supplementa, vol. 21 (Steiner Verlag, Wiesbaden, 1980). See, for a more detailed analysis, Massimo Ferrari, *Il giovane Cassirer e la scuola di Marburgo* (Milano: Franco Angeli, 1988).
6. All further quotations will be from the recent reedition: Hermann Cohen, Werke. Band 1, *Kants Theorie der Erfahrung*, Teil 1.3 Erste Auflage (Hildesheim: Georg Olms Verlag, 1987).
7. See Kant, *Kritik der reinen Vernunft*, B 370.
8. Hermann Cohen, *Kommentar zu Immanuel Kants Kritik der reinen Vernunft*. Orig. publ. 1907, I have consulted the 5th ed. (Hildesheim/NY: Georg Olms Verlag, 1978).
9. Hermann Cohen, *Das Prinzip der Infinitesimal-Methode und seine Geschichte. Eine Kapitel zur Grundlegung der Erkenntniskritik* (Frankfurt a. M.: Suhrkamp, 1968), p. 49.
10. See F. A. Lange, *Geschichte des Materialismus*, vol. 2 (Frankfurt a. M.: Suhrkamp, 1974), p. 454.
11. Lange, *Geschichte des Materialismus*, p. 561.
12. Since Cassirer mentioned this event on various occasions, this remark appears in many works on Cassirer's philosophy. It is here cited from A. Philonenko, *L'école de Marbourg* (Paris: J. Vrin, 1989), p. 11.
13. See the two letters on his friend and future father-in-law, H. Lewandovsky from August 2 and September 28, 1870. Both are cited in G. Edel, *Von der Vernunftskritik zur Erkenntnislogik*, p. 26.
14. A. Trendelenburg, *Logische Untersuchungen*, 2 vols., 3rd enlarged ed. (Leipzig, 1870).
15. A. Trendelenburg, *Die logische Frage in Hegel's System. Zwei Streitschriften* (Leipzig, 1843), p. 50; here quoted from Koehnke, *op. cit.*, p. 37.
16. Trendelenburg, *Die logische Frage in Hegel's System. Zwei Streitschriften*, p. 36.
17. A. Trendelenburg, *Logische Untersuchungen*, 2nd ed.; here cited from Koehnke, *op. cit.* p. 36.
18. A. Trendelenburg, *Historische Beitrage zur Philosophie*. Werke. 3 Band, *Vermischte Abhandlungen* (Berlin: Bethge, 1867), p. 218.
19. K. Fischer, *Logik und Metaphysik oder Wissenschaftslehre. Lehrbuch fuer akademische Vorlesungen* (Stuttgart, 1852).
20. K. Fischer, *Anti-Trendelenburg. Eine Gegenschrift* (Jena, 1870).
21. Fischer, *Anti-Trendelenburg. Eine Gegenschrift*, p. 30–31, 48–49.
22. A. Trendelenburg, *Kuno Fischer und sein Kant. Eine Entgegnung.* (Leipzig, 1869), p. 2. Quoted in Koehnke, *op. cit.*, p. 260.
23. H. Cohen, "Zur Kontroverse zwischen Adolf Trendelenburg und Kuno Fischer.

Zeitschrift fuer Voelkerpsychologie und Sprachwissenschaft 7 (1871); see H. Cohen, *Schriften zur Philosophie und Zeitgeschichte.* Werke. Band 1. Berlin (Akademie, 1928), p. 229.

24. H. Cohen, *Schriften zur Philosophie und Sprachwissenschaft*, p. iii.
25. *KTE* 1, p. iii.
26. *KTE* 1, p. 3. Though I do not owe this point to Eder (p. 28), I found his book extremely thought inspiring, not only where I agree with him, but even more where I disagree. However, my exchange with him would start primarily at the point of Cohen's philosophical development, where this paper finishes.
27. H. Cohen, *Kants Begruendung der Ethik* (Berlin: Duemmler, 1877), p. iii.
28. Cohen, *Kants Begruendung der Ethik*, p. vi.
29. Cohen, *Kants Begruendung der Ethik*, p. 2.
30. Cohen, *Kants Begruendung der Ethik*, p. 12.
31. Cohen, *Kants Begruendung der Ethik*, p. 12.
32. Cohen, *Kants Begruendung der Ethik*, p. 15.
33. Cohen, *Kants Begruendung der Ethik*, p. 16.
34. Cohen, *Kants Begruendung der Ethik*, p. 18.
35. Cohen, *Kants Begruendung der Ethik*, p. 24
36. *KTE* 5, p. 95, 94, 108.
37. *KTE* 2, p. 605.
38. *KTE* ‥, p. 589.
39. *Philosophische Monatshefte* 8, p. 212.
40. G. Eder, *op. cit.*, p. 19, n. 5.
41. See *KBE*, p. 25. Here the problem was to clarify the distance between Cohen and Leibniz.
42. This was presented already at the time of Cohen's death by his closest associate, Paul Natorp, in his famous résumé, *Hermann Cohens philosophische Leistung unter dem Gesichtspunkt des Systems* (Berlin, 1918).
43. See Geert Eder, *Von der Vernunftkritik zur Erkenntnislogik* (Freiburg: Albert, 1988).
44. *Opere Complete di Galileo Galilei*, Firenze, 1842, ff., vol. 4, p. 171; here quoted from E. A. Burtt, *The Metaphysical Foundations of Modern Science* (Garden City, NY: Doubleday & Co., 1954), p. 75.
45. See n. no. 5.
46. Wayne Cristaudo, "Heidegger and Cassirer: Being, Knowing and Politics." *Kant-Studien*, vol. 82/4 (1991), p. 472.
47. In his conception of metaphysics, Schwart gives preference to what he calls negative theories that attempt to solve metaphysical problems with the help of the conceptual means that metaphysics shares with science. He views metaphysics and science as two different aspects of the same discipline. See Norman Schwartz's *Beyond Experience: Metaphysical Theories and Philosophical Constraints* (Toronto: University of Toronto Press, 1995).

Part 3

Applications of
Transcendental Philosophy

8

Interpretation and Worlds

Peter McCormick

The totality of existing states of affairs also determines which states of affairs do not exist.

—Ludwig Wittgenstein

What we call "possible worlds" are not really worlds but properties the one world might have, states it might be in, or ways it might be.

—Robert Stalnaker

Where now are the singular souls or the dead,
Their personal ways, the traits of speech they had?

—Paul Valéry

In this chapter I take up one basic problem in transcendental philosophy and everyday experience, that of rational interpretation.

Recall several memorable stanzas, with their surrealistic modulations on romantic themes in Hugo and Lamartine, in one of the many poetic masterpieces that help to define the modernist period and its still manifold challenges to our understandings of interpretation today.

Can you tell, sham prisoner of the leaves,
Gulf devouring these flimsy rails,
On my closed eyes, dazzling secrecy,
What body drags me to its lazy end,
What brow attracts it to this bony ground?
A spark within thee thinks of absent ones,
They have melted into a dense unbeing,
The red clay has drained the paler kind,

The gift of living has passed into flowers!
Where now are the singular souls of the dead,
Their personal ways, the tricks of speech they had?
The worm channels its way where tears formed.[1]

Writing in the *Nouvelle revue française* some years after first publishing "Le cimetière marin" in his 1922 collection, *Charmes*, Paul Valéry recalled his "strong sensation" in listening one morning at the Sorbonne, in the Amphitheatre Richelieu, to a celebrated professor interpreting this poem.[2] "Reading what has been written about you," Valéry observed, "is as nothing to the peculiar sensation of hearing yourself commented on at the university in front of the blackboard, just like a dead author.... I felt as though I were my own shadow.... I felt like a shadow taken captive."[3]

In his published commentary, the professorial interpreter has divided Valéry's poem into four major sections. The first section deals with midday and the immobility of an eternal and unconscious nonbeing or nothingness, the second section addresses the sea and the movements of ephemeral and conscious being or existence. The third section deals with the question of death and the possibility of immortality, and the final section treats of the triumph of the spontaneous, of change, and of poetic creation.[4]

The stanzas are from the third and largest section of the poem. There, the interpreter comments on the importance of the theme of death in Valéry's poem, the sense of a vast emptiness, and the "absence épaisse" as "the sign of a consciousness forever disappeared."[5]

We do not know what the interpreter had actually said during those morning classes at the Sorbonne, dedicated to the explication of Valéry's poem. But what Valéry himself heard, and what provoked the "peculiar sensation" of being as it were a "dead author," his own shadow, was presumably something very close to the remarks published later. Thus the key to that general interpretation of the poem lies in the question about the possibility of immortality in the immense awareness of death.

This question arises out of Valéry's opposition in the poem between two worlds—the unconscious immobility of the sky world at the cloudless moment of the noonday sun, and the movement of the sea incessant like consciousness itself. Coming to understand more fully Valéry's complex and difficult masterpiece of course requires, as so many studies continue to show, attention to a great number of related issues. However, without a grasp of Valéry's responses to the radical opposition, he figures here between these two symbolic worlds of the poem, the eternal immobility of the midday sun's world of nonbeing and the incessant movement of the oceanic world of being; the poem's great and moving title and summary reference to Pindar cannot be adequately appreciated. "The Graveyard by the Sea," runs the title in its questioning opposition of death and life, and the deeply puzzling citation from Pindar with its gestures towards Valéry's long meditated response runs, "My soul, do not seek immortal life, / but exhaust the realm of the possible."

How then are we to grasp Valéry's sense here of these two worlds united into such a complicated whole? In what senses and to what degree can we take Valéry's complicated whole as the proper object of interpretation? First, however, we must try to appreciate more fully Valéry's own sense of the world as a whole.

THE WORLD AND THE WHOLE

Consider briefly the peculiar constellation Valéry calls "the whole"—world, body, and mind. The most general term appears in one of the more philosophical essays, "Au sujet Eureka," included in a one volume edition Valéry himself made from his voluminous works. There Valéry settles on a word for his most general view of what there is. ". . . il nous faut principalement l'idée de tout que nous appelons univers, et que nous désirons de voir commencer. . . . Nous constituons une idole de la totalité, et une idole de son origine, et nous ne pouvons nous empêcher de conclure à la réalité d'un certain corps de la nature, dont l'unité répond à la nôtre même, de laquelle nous sentons assurés."[6]

Valéry immediately sets to work on trying to retrieve some context for misleading abstractions. The words "whole" and "universe" finally give way to a trinity of terms to which Valéry returns continually.[7] "Notez," Valéry summarizes in the 1939 Zaharoff lecture at Oxford, "que tout ce que j'ai dit ou cru dire se passe entre ce que nous appelons le *Monde extérieur*, ce que nous appelons *Notre Corps*, et ce que nous appelons *Notre Esprit*—et demande une certaine collaboration confuse de ces trois grandes puissances" (*Oeuvres* I: 1323). This constellation is at the center of Valéry's work.

Other elements also require some consideration. The notion of l'Autrui, for example, is important both in connection with Valéry's reflections on language and with his speculation about readers' roles in the performances of literary artworks. But these other elements remain secondary. The central terms themselves, while indeed abstract, take on a concrete fullness in their uses thanks to Valéry's repeated attempts at fresh description.

Before recalling these descriptions, we do well to note the crucial context here. Valéry located that context in the early years of his poetic work, roughly between 1892 and 1895. With the sole exception of some psychoanalytic critics, virtually all of Valéry's interpreters agree that the key events are crystallized in the expression, "la nuit de Gênes."[8]

In her long and revealing biographical chronology at the beginning of the Pléiade edition of Valéry's works, Valéry's daughter, Agathe Rouart-Valéry, puts this complicated matter with admirable discretion. On September 14, 1892, after finishing his law studies at Montpellier, Valéry left with his family for a vacation at his maternal grandmother's home in Genoa, not far from where, years later, Eugenio Montale would pass his summers. "Il a quitté Montpellier après avoir traversé une crise sentimentale aigue, et se trouve alors en proie au doute et à un grand découragement. Il est prêt à renoncer à poursuivre une carrière littéraire" (*Oeuvres* I: 19–20).

This passage alludes to two separate matters. The first was Valéry's experience of no longer being master of his own affectivity. A woman whom he had chanced to see several times in Montpellier, but only from afar, troubled him, upset him emotionally. Despite all his efforts, he could not rid himself of her disturbing effects.[9] The second and closely related matter was his realization, on reading the poetry of Stéphane Mallarmé, that even being the master of his own intellect was insufficient. For despite Valéry's precocious intellectual successes, the quality of Mallarme's work seemed so superior to his own capacities that Valéry thought working anymore at literature simply futile.

Thus, as a young man with many achievements already behind him, Valéry is caught up short by an experience of his own limits. The world, so to speak, breaking in on him, emotion overwhelming him with unwanted feelings and the belief in Mallarme's superb artistic achievement subverting the confidence in his own artistic capacities. Finding limits forced irresistibly upon him, Valéry doubts his control over both his sensibility and his intellect. From this time on a radical doubt, reinforced by his predilection for Descartes, marks Valéry's work indelibly.

Deeply rooted in the normative events of Valéry's maturation, this double experience of radical limitation leads to his sense of "the whole" as a conjunction of world, body, and mind. The experience is that of one of Valéry's personae, M. Teste.[10] "L'expérience de Teste," one of Valéry's critics has suggested, "l'expérience valérienne—fait éclater toute présence du sujet: il faut que l'absence jaillisse de la présence même pour que la conscience apparaisse. Mais cette conscience, et le sujet, sont faits incessament d'une brisure, d'un décollement, étant l'étant, sans particularité, absorbant toute sensation dans la répétition, en un mouvement d'échappement insaisissable puisque c'est un regard en surplomb, un regard en trop sans repère fixe qui vient à chaque instant figurer une nouvelle origine du regard."[11]

If something like this description represents Valéry's understanding of the whole, how then does Valéry understand "the world"? Speaking of his "maître" Valéry writes: "J'ai vue pour la dernière fois Stéphane Mallarmé le 14 juillet 1898 à Valrins. Le déjeuner achevé, il me conduisit à son 'cabinet de travail.' Quatre pas de long, deux de large; la fenêtre ouverte à la Seine et à la forêt au travers d'un feuillage tout déchire de lumière, et les moindres frémissements de la rivière éblouissante faiblement redits par les murs" (*Oeuvres* I: 633).

The conjunction of work and world in this passage is less important than the suggestion of a collaboration between the two. "Redits," says Valéry. As if the world is speaking a language of its own. As if a language of the world were echoing in the human milieu, in the work room, in the poet's study, in his listening, in his repetitions.

Toward the end of the same privileged text where Valéry celebrates both the master poet Mallarmé and poetry itself, "le jeu suprême de la transmutation des idées," these initial metaphorical suggestions of the speaking of the world's vitality are filled out at length. "Nous sommes allés dans la campagne," Valéry writes. "Le poète 'artificielle' cueillait des fleurs les plus variés. Bleuets et coquelicots chargeaient nos bras. L'air était feu; la splendeur absolue; le silence plein de vertiges et d'échanges; la mort impossible ou indifférente; tout formidablement beau, brûlant et dormant; et les images du sol tremblaient. Au soleil, dans l'immense forme du ciel pur, je rêvais d'une enceinte incandescente ou rien de distinct ne subsiste, ou rien ne dure, mais ou rien ne cesse; comme si la destruction elle-meme se détruisit à peine accomplie. Je perdais le sentiment de la différence de l'être et du non-être" (Oeuvres I: 633).

The "exchanges" which fill the silence of this extraordinary scene are ambiguous. They refer to a communion between two poets, like that between a father and a son. They also refer to the resonances between each of the poet's struggles with language and with the scintillating sollicitations of the physical world. This second set of exchanges is reinforced once again by the suggestion of slight movements in the air, the shimmering phenomena of a country day irradiated and finally iridescent with a burning, a blazing sunlight.

The physical world then for Valéry is not just a world full of movement. Rather, these movements themselves—the light on the river and the light on the meadow—may seem at times to speak, their occasional sounds addressing the poet as if the rustling of flowers and movement of water were voices.

The picture of course is impressionistic in the painterly sense.[12] But the impressionism here—with the intimations of death, of indetermination, of eternal return, of transmutation, of silence—this impressionism is a postimpressionism. The naivety of catching the physical world in the play of a new optics and a fuller understanding of perception is already too self-conscious. Moreso, the "Dernière Visite à Mallarme" both anticipates a leave-taking from a Newtonian world already questioned in Valéry's readings of Clerk Maxwell, of Michael F. Faraday, soon of Georg C. Cantor, and later of Albert Einstein, and prepares from afar the extraordinary achievements many years later of "Le cimitière marin."[13]

This vibrant, resonant, almost speaking image of the physical world recurs throughout Valéry's work. The sea in Italy in 1877: ". . . ces impressions de soleil et d'eau mordante, de vie consumée à demi nu, de temps ardument perdu—longtemps sont demeurées en moi à l'état de ressource et d'idéal" (Letter to Valéry Larbaud, 1887). Recall the ecstatic passages in the *Dialogues*, especially in "Eupalinos" when Socrates is speaking; or the quick, unstudied jottings in the personal notes, for example in Spain in 1924 near the Escorial: "Vue magnifique à l'aurore. C'est d'un vaste! Beauté du granit et du nu. Couleur extraordinaire, formidable, un peu sulfureuse, et le tout est plat comme la belle peinture" (*Éphémérides*; cited in A. Rouart-Valéry). Here, to close the circle and to echo the cliche, world imitates art.

Valéry rarely tried to move beyond these metaphorical descriptions of world. Though at times he speculates on the fullness and superabundance of the world, its density, its resistance to order, its irregularities, its resistance to any understanding of physical laws as more than conventions, Valéry is consistently skeptical about the value of theories in this domain. He nourishes his interest in the physical world with careful but finally amateur studies in the mathematics and the new sciences of his time. Later in life he frequents a number of laboratories. Valéry listens patiently and with genuine interest to the explanation of experiments. He concerns himself with the scientific details not just of sensation, but of physiology as a whole. But throughout these persistent enthusiasms Valéry remains faithful to his initial doubts, which he now extends beyond abstract matters to empirical matters as well.

This resistance to theory, to which we will return later on in this chapter, accounts for Valéry's refusal to think "the world" in philosophical terms such as "real" or "existence" or "being." Valéry criticizes these terms in several places, especially in the *Cahiers*. "Les mots *exister*, ou *être*, sont vagues," he writes, "'je suis' sans attribut n'a aucun sens" (19: 538). In another text much earlier, he writes: "déification du verbe *être*, voila la moitié de la philosophie" (11: 810). Valéry entertains the same suspicions about the word "réel." The word makes sense only when used in definite contexts but never when used alone. ". . . le mot 'réel' est défini chaque fois par le contexte," he writes (11: 403). And elsewhere: ". . . le réel n'a point de signification" (9: 553). The consequence is that such an abstract idea is useless. ". . . nous n'avons aucun besoin d'une notion générale du 'réel,' etc.—laquelle ne répond qu'à une demande scolaire, dialectique" (20: 16).

When such terms are used concretely, however, Valéry construes the referent as a peculiar inexhaustibility in the world. This excess both saturates sensation and overflows the perceptive processes. The world, in this guise, is always something other; it is more than we can sense and perceive. "L'idée cachée ou le vouloir caché dans la notion de réalité," Valéry writes, "est celle-ci: il y a quelque chose de plus dans toute chose réelle que la perception la plus nette et la plus complète n'en fait voir. Et donc, le quid est inaltérable par les vicissitudes de la perception. Nulle perception ne l'épuise" (11: 188).

Thus, Valéry construes the world largely by contrast with what can be known. The world is an inexhaustible and fugitive fullness of movement and sollicitation.[14] Whatever we can come to know of this world is always incomplete. "À l'aurore," Valéry writes, in 1927, at Grasse, "le cyprès *offre*. Cette maison dorée apparaît—que *fait*-elle? Elle se *construit à chaque instant*" (12: 189).

Given the centrality of Valéry's reflections on world, his structuring one of his several masterpieces in terms of a figurative, yet fundamental, opposition between two kinds of world, and yet his repeated criticisms of mere philosophical reflection on such general terms as "world," how are we to interpret Valéry's talk in "Le cimitière marin" of the radical tensions between presence and absence, fullness and emptiness, existence and nothingness, death and immortality? "Where now," we remember the poet asking, "are the singular souls of the dead?" Have they "melted into a dense unbeing"? Is the poet's "immensity" of life indeed the deep sense of an "absence"? Such questions seem all too vague.

More specifically then, when we set out to interpret Valéry's poetry, what exactly is the object of such interpretation? In the interests of trying to articulate more clearly just what understandings of interpretation might allow us a less inadequate purchase on Valéry's lived sense of being his own shadow and his poetry's repeated testimony to the centrality of the whole and the world in his book, I want now to look at another high modernist notion of "the world," this time in a philosophical text.

ATOMISTIC NOTIONS OF WORLD

Looking critically at a speculative notion of the world as the putative object of interpretation in works like Valéry's, "The Graveyard by the Sea" requires attending, at least briefly, to the most influential understandings of this notion in the modern era. This notion is that of the early Wittgenstein.

Wittgenstein propounds this view in the opening sections only of the *Tractatus* as well as in the *Notebooks 1914–1916*. In both instances, Wittgenstein presents his views in his highly elliptical, early manner. And, with many small qualifications, this difficult notion of "world" stands behind the movement of English language philosophy from Frege through Russell, and then, with major changes, into Moritz S. Schlick's Vienna Circle, through Carnap and Reichenbach, and into much of the early work of Nelson Goodman, Quine, and Putnam. Although unfashionable, and difficult, this extensive speculation on world remains, even today, in its still unfathomed modal versions a powerful and persuasive, realistic vision that continues to inspire much work in logic, philosophy of language, and philosophy of science together with their respective impacts on artificial intelligence, cognitive psychology, and both linguistic and epistemological naturalisms. What are the initial elements in this speculative notion of world, what we may call somewhat misleadingly the atomistic notion of the world, and what is its structure?

In some of his most puzzling statements at the beginning of the *Tractatus*, before ever coming to his famously controversial "picture theory" of the structure of language, Wittgenstein writes:

1.1   The world is all that is the case.
1.10   The world is the totality of facts, not of things.
1.11   The world is determined by facts, and by their being *all* the facts.
1.12   For the totality of facts determines what is the case, and also whatever is not the case.
1.13   The facts in logical space are the world.
1.2   The world divides into facts.
1.21   Each item can be the case or not the case while everything else remains the same.
2.   What is the case—a fact—is the existence of states of affairs.
2.01   A state of affairs (a state of things) is a combination of objects (things).
2.011   It is essential to things that they should be possible constituents of states of affairs.[15]

This series of ten propositions, strongly articulated and meticulously subordinated in terms of their logical importance, already contains the major elements in the atomistic notion of world—facts, states of affairs, and objects.

Skipping ahead to the end of the initial discussion of world at 2.1 where the picture theory is introduced, we can highlight these major elements before turning briefly to some details. Thus, after continuing to qualify 2.01 with five further comments, Wittgenstein continues (with my ellipses):

2.02   Objects are simple.
2.022   It is obvious that an imagined world, however different it may be from the real one, must have *something*—form—in common with it.
2.023   Objects are just what constitute this unalterable form.
. . . [seventeen propositions omitted.]
2.03   In a state of affairs objects fit into one another like the links of a chain.
. . . [four propositions omitted.]
2.04   The totality of existing states of affairs is the world.
2.05   The totality of existing states of affairs also determines which states of affairs do not exist.
2.06   The existence and non-existence of states of affairs is reality. (We also call the existence of states of affairs a positive fact, and their nonexistence a negative fact).
. . . [two propositions omitted]
2.063   The sum total of reality is the world.[16]

The result of these additional remarks is further elucidation of the basic
elements, their interrelations, and the introduction of the difficult ideas of
unalterable form and reality. Wittgenstein proposes still more propositions
about the world in other important parts of the *Tractatus* and the *Notebooks
1914–1916*, but I want to restrict my comments to his initial remarks here
at the beginning of the *Tractatus*.

How then are we to understand these initial elements of the atomistic
notion of world? One way to make some further sense of the elements and
elementary structure of the world is to view them with the help of their
reflections in the correlated elements and elementary structures Wittgenstein
believed he had found in language. At successively finer levels, the structure of world is said to correlate with that of language.

At the first level, we may say rather roughly, we find a correlation between what Wittgenstein calls facts and propositions, at the second and
deeper level between states of affairs and elementary propositions, and at
the third and final level between objects and names. Without spelling out
the debts Wittgenstein acknowledges to the terminology of both Frege's
and Russell's philosophies of logic and language, we can, once again very
roughly, try to visualize the proposed structure of the world with the help
of a diagram.[17] The diagram represents the parallelism, but it leaves out just
how the elements are understood to interact, whether at the horizontal or
at the vertical levels.

World	*Language*
facts	propositions
states of affairs	elementary propositions
objects	names

When we read this schema upwards, that is, from the simples, through
their compoundings, into the complexes, we have the notion of the atomistic
world as a representation of reality in terms of objects as logical simples,
and the simples build up into states of affairs. (These states, we may add
from 2.06, are taken either as existent and hence positive facts or nonexistent and hence negative facts.) Accordingly, the atomistic world is not an
aggregate of things or a collection of elementary objects. Rather, the atomistic
world is the totality of facts arising from elementary states of affairs from
which objects (i.e., individuals, properties, at least formal ones, and relations) can be abstracted.

Notoriously, Wittgenstein provides no example of either objects, states
of affairs, or facts. He does however insist that facts consist of states of
affairs, their combinations and arrangements, and that states of affairs themselves consist of further unanalyzable objects. Although unanalyzed objects
that are of a certain kind can change; simple objects that are not only of

any one kind cannot change. Just what are these kinds of simple objects—unanalyzable, unchanging, and of not one kind—Wittgenstein does not say.

Now, when we look back through the complications of the atomistic account in the early Wittgenstein, with a view towards eventually parsing the object of literary interpretation as a world, we need some critical perspective. Here is one that, however partial, may provide, with a greater sense of the contour in Tractarian atomism, the criticisms this atomistic notion of the world requires.

> ... Wittgenstein's early system is basically realistic. Any factual sentence can be completely analyzed into elementary sentences which are logically independent of one another because they name simple objects. At that basic level all languages have the same structure, dictated by the structure of reality. True, different languages incorporate that structure in different ways, and so they exhibit considerable variation on the surface; but in the final analysis there are no options. The superstructures vary, but the foundations are necessarily identical. Once a name has been attached to an object, the nature of the object takes over and controls the logical behaviour of the name, causing it to make sense in some sentential contexts but not in others.[18]

While not uncontroversial, this view nicely sets the scene for the series of local and global changes that Wittgenstein himself began to formulate in 1929 and 1931 and that he also articulated more fully in the *Investigations*.[19]

The local and particular changes in Wittgenstein's views were many but at least three need highlighting. He came to see that the truth-functional analysis of properties was exaggerated in that, unlike the definition Russell had provided for the definite article, certain properties such as color impressions could not be analyzed this way at all.[20] Moreover, the understanding of names in his early theory of meaning was inadequate—"names do not simply attach themselves to things. . . ."[21] Further, the early theory of language, even without considering the picture theory, exhibited two key related failings. The senses of signs need not be determinate and far reaching, nor need the senses of each factual sentence be separated from that of others—the doctrines of separatism and far-reaching sense both needed overhauling.

More globally, three general changes were to be introduced. Perhaps the biggest problem in the *Tractatus* version of atomism was the lack of specification for the nature of the objects underlying factual sentences. Wittgenstein seemed unable or unwilling to choose between simples as material points, or simples as sense-data. This problem had to be solved. Objects had to be seen as not necessarily devoid of internal complexity if the further problem of color incompatibility was to be dissolved in such a way that, despite "this is red" and "this is green" being logically incompatible, both could be taken as elementary propositions. Moreover, the idea of one unique language had to be rejected. As David Pears writes, "what he was rejecting in 1929 was the idea of a unique language, perfectly mirroring the essential nature of phenomena and providing the complete analysis of ordinary factual discourse."[22] Finally, the very strict restraints Wittgenstein had imposed on the doctrine of showing in the *Tractatus* needed to be greatly loosened. Showing had to be understood as operative in many different language games covering the gamut of human activities and not restricted just to the ways in that only elementary sentences display the simple possibilities they assert.[23] Thus, the atomic notion of the world gradually gave way under the successive critiques that Wittgenstein himself brought against it.

INTERPRETATION AND MODALITIES

With these elements of the atomic notion of the world as well as its criticism freshly in mind, what conceptual resources might still be on hand here for our concerns with specifying the object of literary interpretation as the world? The basic difficulty that an atomistic account presents for our concerns is that nothing can be said about the world of Valéry's poem—the whole, the sun-world and the sea-world—that, within the very strict constraints of the atomistic account, makes sense.

Yet talk of Valéry's world is not meaningless. For after all, whatever the objections may be, at least some of the many suggestion of his interpreters are meaningful. Rather, on the atomistic view, talk of Valéry's world is nonsensical. The reason goes back to the peculiar ways the correlations between language and the world were said to obtain. For at the most fundamental level, whatever facts are embedded in their states of affairs that would be pertinent for poetic matters, these facts still lack any correlation with whatever names could be suitably embodied in elementary philosophical propositions. Literary matters, like philosophical ones, stand outside the limits of the atomistic world.

However, we need not accept this doctrine given some of the problems already mentioned—its quite problematic reliance on an obscure notion of a "picturing relation" between language and the world, its insufficiently critical dependence on now dubious Fregean and Russellian views about propositions and states of affairs, and the unwelcome consequences of its putting even most philosophical matters and not just aesthetic, ethical, and religious ones beyond the pale. Rather, instead of accepting the atomistic version *tout court*, we can notice its peculiar suggestiveness in pointing to some nonelementary states of affairs as showables, if not sayables.

A first move then would be to supplement an atomistic account of the world with a much less restricted doctrine of what can be shown. The suggestion here comes to the idea that poetic worlds as novel states of affairs existing already as part of the one actual world, but in the form of still unactualized possibles, can continue to be construed as properties of entities and not just of propositions when their proper discussion is understood in terms of what philosophical discourse can not so much utter as exhibit in uttering. The salient cases here are those of fictional entities and fictional events in philosophical poetry, such as those in the choral odes of Sophocles, the cosmological visions of Lucretius, the *Paradiso* of Dante, Shakespeare's speculative dark romances, the dramatic explanations of conflictual states of mind in Racine, the nature mythologies in parts of Goethe's science, and of course the high modernist poetry of an abstract suffering in Valéry's "Le cimitiere marin."

Beside this needed reminder to specify those kinds of discourse where talk of worlds can be described in other than merely propositional ways, a second lesson comes clear on reconsidering the atomistic account of the world. For, in its striking and persistent attentiveness to what the atomistic version calls "facts," and the facts' combinations in complex states of affairs—embedding arrangements of objects as logical simples—the atomistic view opens up the prospect of construing simples in poetic worlds in less abstract terms than those states of affairs a conceptual framework quantifies over in making modal claims. The question here is whether literary invention, such as Valéry's, can be understood in less general terms than those on which modal realism insists.

In particular, if we are to capture more faithfully some of the many ways in which, as yet, unactualized fictional possibles already preoccupy our reflections in the ongoing present—subscribing for example to Valery's understanding of the whole as a play among mind, body, and world—why not construe these states of affair in what may be called quasi-modal terms, such as virtuality and intermittence?[24] Here, we would say that these future states are to be understood as falling into and out of the actual world to the degree that they are virtual states of affairs that are intermittently actual and intermittently possible.

We need to anticipate here the idea that the term "actual" pushes the notion of the actual world too far. Consider for example the expression "I" in another stanza from Valéry's poem:

Ah for my self, to my own self within,
Close by a heart, at the source of the poem,
Between emptiness and the pure event,
I await my grandeur's echo from within,
That bitter, gloomy and resounding cistern
Ringing in the soul a still future void.

Now someone can be said to be pushing the notion of the actual world too far when he or she construes the actual world as including, rather than standing as a counterpart to, possible worlds in indexical expressions like "here," "now," and "I." The term "actual" points us in the direction of certain states of affairs that include, among their many components, the reference of "actual." More specifically, our focus should be on a metaphysical and not just on the semantic version of this claim, to wit, the claim that what the adjective "actual" points to is the relation between the real world and the things existing within that world.

We need then to construe the reference of the adjective "actual" in larger terms than a possibilist alone would ("I and my surroundings") so as to include "the ways things are." Thus, while endorsing the indexical analysis of "actual" in some possibilist vision of the world, we need to detach that analysis from its dependence on any commitments to possible worlds and their parts really existing outside the domain of the one actual world, and from their construal as nonredescribable and irreducible, logical primitives.

This move allows us to parse the overly general element in the actualist version of poems like Valéry's "Le cimitiere marin" as novel states of affairs that consist in those abstract objects we call ways of relating some future philosophical dispositions of actual rational agents as readers. For now we can take these "ways of relating" as actual in the double sense of real things existing in the real world and as including in their reference not just the parochial and its regional surroundings of philosophical interpreters but the universal ways things are. Here nothing need stand outside the scope of those as yet unactualized dispositions of rational agents acting in the future, nor need any human being, however remote in language, culture, space, and even future times, be excluded either.

Yet the composite metaphysical notion of a world that would allow us good enough rational grounds for thinking through talk of worlds as basic objects of interpretation, if it now can accommodate possibles within one world only while integrating a sophisticated indexical interpretation of the actual and its manifold references, still lacks some metaphysical purchase on our concerns. For, as a strictly modal vision, this story of the world seems over-committed to talk of actuality and possibility. In particular, as a *de re* modal vision, this account does not yet address the difficult question of whether, in the case of fictional possibles, modality in some way must attach not only to entities but to the propositions as well.[25] So in a final move here, we also need to retrieve some of those features of an atomistic vision of the world we considered in the context of Wittgenstein's own second thoughts about the *Tractatus*—some nonelementary states of affairs as showables and as quasi-modal intermittent virtualities.

Each of these final steps, you will object, requires much more discussion.

Accordingly, I would like to return to the main issues here later. But for now good reasons urge us to entertain the idea that construing the world as the basic object of interpretation depends in some strong ways on construing the world with the help of those nonpropositional and more than merely strictly referential accounts of how things stand. Such accounts enable us to exhibit, if not to say, just how the virtual ways philosophical dispositions of rational readers and interpreters may be directed to the appearance of genuinely novel states of affairs in as yet unactualized fictional domains.

Still, as we shall see later, the idea of fictional worlds in the contexts of European high-modernist poetry and especially the important differences between fictional and possible worlds, must be scrutinized more closely yet. But before pursuing such matters further, we need to ask: to what extent do such philosophical attempts to account for the object of interpretation in such cases as Valéry's extraordinary poetry go against the grain of Valéry's own intellectual convictions? In light of the earlier comments made by Valéry about for example, the "real," what are the modernist poet's characteristic objections to philosophical attempts to reflect on poetic matters, even to construe the object of interpretation as, in some philosophical and not just literary senses, a world?

POETICS, AESTHETICS, AND PHILOSOPHY

Valéry's repeated attacks on philosophy are well-known. His *Cahiers*, for example, are punctuated with mordant remarks about philosophy. "Presque toute 'philosophie' consiste," he writes, "dans la transformation d'un mot . . . en un excitant d'arrêt, une résistance, une difficulté, un obstacle—devant lequel piétine indéfiniment le 'penseur'" (28:502). Or much earlier on the same theme: "La philosophie croit au mot en soi—et ses problèmes sont des problèmes de mots en soi . . ." (13:502). "Philosophie," he writes elsewhere, "où les questions mal posées" (19:89); and "la plupart des problèmes philosophiques sont tels qu'ils s'évanouissent si vous les énoncons" (11:265).

Valéry thinks philosophy misuses language. Philosophy tends to succumb to one or another or both of the dangers with language Valéry was always quick to analyze. To move from poetry to poetics and then to philosophy is to move from a domain where words are repeatedly anchored in their contexts to one were abstractions balloon away endlessly. When we turn to philosophy, Valéry suspects, the important questions that both theory and a poetics address become nothing more suspect than verbal quibbles. In short, to move from a poetics to a set of philosophical reflections is to empty a poetics of its legitimate contents.

Valéry puts this point forcefully in the *Analecta*, in 1926. "La philosophie . . . parle de tout," writes Valéry, "par oui-dire. Je n'y vois point de permanence de point de vue, ni de pureté de moyens. Rien ne peut être plus faux que le mélange (par example) d'observations internes et de raisonnements, si ce mélange est fait sans précaution et sans qu'on puisse toujours distinguer le calcul de l'observé (*Oeuvres* II, 713). This is of course the case with philosophy as Valéry sees it.

Valéry's most well-known comments on philosophy however occur in his studies of Leonardo da Vinci. These comments provide more nuance than the occasional remarks do. They demonstrate that Valéry's criticism of philosophy cannot be reduced, as some have thought, to the charge of misusing language.

Like science and in the same way, philosophy claims to be impersonal. Thus in the marginal comments that Valéry added in 1930 to his original text of 1895 we read: "Voilà le vice essentiel de la philosophie. Elle est chose personnelle, et ne veut l'être. Elle veut constituer comme la science un capital transmissible et qui s'accroisse. D'où les systèmes, qui prétendent n'être de personne" (*Oeuvres* I, 1164). Valéry links the notion of impersonality in the sciences with a number of other issues such as verifiability, predictability, universality, and so on. However, despite his lifelong interest in the sciences, Valéry does not explore this similarity. He chooses instead to reinforce his counter-claim that philosophy is essentially personal although unwittingly so.

Whatever demands philosophy justifiably makes upon us do not arise from the subject of its deliberations, but from the forms of these deliberations." . . . toute philosophie," Valéry writes, "est une affaire de formes. Elle est la forme la plus compréhensible qu'un certain individu puisse donner à des connaissances que peut posséder cet homme" (I, 1238). This stress, however, on form rather than substance needs occasional qualification. For whether Valéry means what he says here, in 1930, is not entirely clear.

Ten years earlier, in his "Avant-propos à la Connaissance de la Déesse," he seems to leave the possibility just barely open that something more than form may be at issue in genuine philosophical problems. Philosophy, he writes, "si l'on déduit les choses vagues et les choses refutées, se ramène maintenant à cinq ou six problèmes, précis en apparence, indéterminés dans le fond, toujours réductibles à des querelles linguistiques et dont la solution dépend de la manière de les écrire" (I, 1273). Despite the suggestion of being no more than quibbles, these problems retain a certain interest. Valéry continues: " . . . dans cette fragilité et dans ces querelles mêmes, c'est-à-dire dans la délicatesse de l'appareil logique et psychologique de plus en plus subtil qu'elles demandent qu'on emploie; il ne réside plus dans les conclusions . . . Notre philosophie est définie par son appareil, et non par son objet" (I, 1273–1274).

The consequences Valéry draws from these more positive views of philosophy are not so well-known as those he drew from the negative critiques. Yet, once we think about the consequences at all, the positive points are obvious. Thus, in the original Leonardo text, he writes of "metaphysics" (for which we may legitimately substitute "philosophy"): "Seule, une interprétation esthétique peut soustraire à la ruine de leurs postulats plus ou moins cachés, aux effets destructeurs de l'analyse du language et de l'esprit, les vénérables monuments de la métaphysique" (I, 1247). Toward the end of his life, in the 1937 lecture, the same idea recurs: " . . . la plus authentique philosophie n'est pas dans les objects de réflexion, tant que dans l'acte même de la pensée et dans sa manoeuvre" (I, 1336).

Valéry, thus, does not recommend that one take the step beyond poetics into philosophy for two reasons. First, because philosophy, provides no genuinely new resources for pursuing the proper subject of poetics in his sense: what seem to be resources (say, a critical reappropriation of the atomistic notion of the world) are empty mystifications. And second, because the only genuine questions philosophy may manage to address can already be understood from the perspectives of poetics. For philosophy is a matter of form just as much and no more so than poetry itself is.

If Valéry refuses to explore his poetics into a philosophy, why does he not choose instead to explore this poetics with the help of an aesthetics?

At the beginning of his 1929 text, "Léonard et les philosophes," Valéry acknowledges the apparent attractions of aesthetics. "Il faut avouer," he writes, "que l'Esthétique est une grande et même une irrésistible tentation. Presque tous les êtres qui sentent vivement les arts font un peu plus que de les sentir; ils ne peuvent échapper au besoin d'approfondir leur jouissance" (I, 1235). Is this something more than appreciation that characterizes aesthetics.

When criticizing philosophy Valéry talks of the philosopher's desire to understand everything. He distinguishes between ethnics and aesthetics. "Il va donc méditer," Valéry writes of the philosopher, "de se construire une science des valeurs d'action et une science des valeurs d'expression ou de la création des émotions—une éthique et une esthétique—comme si le Palais de sa Pensée lui dut paraître imparfait sans ces deux ailes symétriques dans lesquelles son Moi tout-puissant et abstrait put tenir la passion, l'action, l'émotion, et l'invention captives" (I, 1238).

The comment suggests an account of what Valéry thinks aesthetics is. Yet, despite Valéry's insistence elsewhere on subordinating expression and creativity to a particular species of action, the comment curiously situates action in the ethical domain. Aesthetics must be distinguished from poetics then. For only poetics effects this subordination properly, whereas aesthetics gets the priorities wrong.

If, however, we imagine for a moment some kind of identity between Valéry's poetics and his reflections as an artist, a more basic difference appears between poetics and aesthetics. "Ce qui sépare le plus manifestement l'esthétique philosophique de la réflexion de l'artiste, c'est qu'elle procède d'une pensée qui se croit étrangère aux arts et qui se sent d'une autre essence qu'une pensée de poète ou de musicien . . . (I, 1243). Valéry's point is that both philosophical interests and aesthetic ones are fundamentally different from the interests of poetics and poetry.

Aesthetics, for Valéry, is a philosophical discipline centered on conceptual issues concerned with the arts. Poetics, by contrast, is not a philosophical discipline at all. Moreover, poetics attends to more than just conceptual issues; for example, poetics also scrutinizes empirical matters. For the philosopher, that is the practitioner of aesthetics, is not observant enough. " . . . il se figure mal l'importance des modes matériels, des moyens et des valeurs d'exécution, car il tend invinciblement à les distinguer de l'idee. Il lui répugne de penser à un échange intime, perpétuel, égalitaire, entre ce qu'on veut et ce qu'on peut, entre ce qu'il juge accident et ce qu'il juge substance, entre la 'forme' et le 'fond,' entre la conscience et l'automatisme, entre la circonstance et le dessein, entre la 'matière' et 'l'esprit'" (I, 1243–1244). In short, Valéry thinks aesthetics is a narrower discipline than poetics, and, like philosophy itself, aesthetics is also a naive discipline.

Aesthetics not only misses what is essential in the literary artwork; it cannot do otherwise. Valéry writes: "on ne peut pas résumer un poème comme on résume un 'univers.' Résumer une thèse, c'est en retenir l'essentiel. On voit combien cette circonstance rend illusioire l'analyse de l'esthéticien" (I, 1224; emphases omitted). Valéry reinforces this point, although not without a certain irony regarding himself sumarizing his earlier view, when he writes further on: "en un mot, si l'esthétique pouvait être les arts s'évanouiraient devant elle, c'est-à-dire—*devant leur essence* (I, 1245).

If the first of Valéry's attempts to distinguish poetics from aesthetics by invoking a prior distinction between aesthetics and ethics is problematic, the second and third attempts are not very convincing either. For the description of philosophical aesthetics that Valéry provides can arguably be construed as more of a caricature than a characterization. If Valéry's account of the purposes of aesthetics, in terms of necessarily providing summaries of artworks, is already too narrow, it is also tendentious.

Valéry tries again to differentiate between aesthetics and poetics in his "Discours sur L'Esthétique" at the Second International Contress of Aesthetics in 1937 in Paris. This time he tries to make the distinction turn on the subject of pleasure.

The kind of pleasure we recognize in the arts, Valéry holds, is difficult to describe satisfactorily. One reason for this is the conceptual opposition between pleasure and pain. For Valéry whether these are real relations, pleasure and pain would have to be "indéfinisables, incommensurables, incomparables de toute façon. Ils offrent le type même de cette confusion ou de cette dépendance réciproque de l'observeur et de la chose observée qui est en train de faire le désespoir de la physique théorique" (I, 1298).

Despite these difficulties, however, psychologists and philosophers, Valéry thinks, have managed to provide us with some kind of persuasive definition of pleasure in the more general and usual sense, but they have failed to attend carefully enough to the distinctive kinds of pleasure in the arts.

What then is artistic pleasure? Unlike the pleasure that has been made into the object of diverse sciences with all the arguments of finality and the propagation of the race in view, artistic pleasure cannot be explained either by its utility or its abuses. For artistic pleasure has to do with what Valéry calls effective modifications in perception, and not just with sensation. Valéry provides a long description.

> "Un plaisir qui s'approfondait quelque fois jusqu'à communiquer une illusion de comprêhension intime de l'objet qui le cause; un plaisir qui excite l'intelligence, la défie, et lui fait aimer sa défaite; davantage, un plaisir qui peut irriter l'étrange besoin de produire, ou de reproduire la chose, l'évenement ou l'objet ou l'état, auquel il semble attaché, et qui devient, par la une source d'activité sans terme certain, capable d'imposer une discipline, un zèle, des tourments à toute une vie, et de la remplir, si ce n'est d'en déborder,—propose à la pensée une énigme singulièrement spécieuse . . . (I, 1299).

Valéry understands artistic pleasure then as necessarily including an element of chaos. This chaos derives from what he calls "le désordre instantané des choses observables" (I, 300). The central distinction between aesthetics and poetics is that the former, as a philosophical discipline, must either overlook this necessary, ineradicable, and recalcitrant element, or rationalize it away with the help of metaphysical categories like substance, accident, quality, and so on. Aesthetics must either blink or rationalize: Valéry thinks that aesthetics rationalizes.

The pleasure peculiar to the arts is rationalized as the pleasure of the beautiful. By contrast, poetics refuses both alternatives; further, poetics critizes the second with particular vigor. "Le plaisir, enfin, n'existe que dans l'instant, et rien," Valéry writes, "de plus individuel, de plus incertain, de plus incommunicable. Les jugements que l'on en fait ne permettent aucun raisonnement, car loin d'analyser leur sujet, au contraire, et en vérité, ils y ajoutent un attribut d'indétermination: dire qu'un object est beau, c'est lui donner valeur d'énigme" (I, 1301).

Why Valéry refuses to adopt either a philosophical or an aesthetic stance to the obscure matters at the center of his poetics is then relatively clear. Both would impose an order that, despite the dissembling of the philosophers, is finally only fictive. Both would impose an order on indefinable, even inexpressible causes of events and states of affairs—the origins of those disparate mental acts that are orchestrated into the making of poems. Valéry's poetics then is deliberately nonphilosophical; it cannot be understood as a branch of philosophical aesthetics. But his own objections to philosophy, as we have noted, have serious difficulties of their own. Moreso, his talk of a "fictive order" is more resourceful than he realized.

CONCLUDING REMARKS

Returning to the difficulty of specifying exactly what to take to be the object of interpretation in such works of high-modernist poetry as Valéry's "Le cimitière marin," we find both resources and liabilities.

In the details of a suitably critical philosophical account of the high-modernist philosophy of logical atomism, we have a series of richly unfolding suggestions about the elements and interrelations of a starkly abstract atomistic notion of the world, "black shadows on white backgrounds" we might say, just like those on Wittgenstein's architectural masterpiece, the house he built for his sister in Vienna's Kundmanngasse. These suggestions, moreover, are both varied and detailed enough to invite further philosophical reflection on their suitability for reconsideration on some description as the proper object of interpretation—the object of interpretation, say, taken as the poetic world of the poem.

Yet moving toward such a philosophical appropriation and adaptation of the conceptual resources for literary interpretation still sedimented in the details of logical atomism runs directly counter to many serious objection to philosophical speculation on the part of intellectual poets as Valéry. Even when we try to address those objections on the part of the poets, we are left with a sense of forcing our views unduly and prematurely.

NOTES

1. Paul Valéry, "The Graveyard by the Sea," trans. D. Paul, in *The Collected Work of Paul Valéry*, vol. 1 (Princeton: Princeton University Press, 1971), pp. 215–219.
2. See "Au sujet du *Cimitière marin*," *Nouvelle revue francaise*, March 1, 1933; later reprinted as a Preface to G. Cohen, *Essai d'explication du "Cimitière marin"* (Paris: Gallimard, 1933; repr., 1946).
3. Paul Valéry, *The Art of Poetry*, trans. D. Folliot, in *The Collected Works of Paul Valéry*, vol. 7 (New York: Pantheon, 1958), p. 142.
4. Cohen, pp. 47–48.
5. Cohen, pp. 67, and 60–70 passim.
6. Paul Valéry, *Oeuvres*, ed. J. Hytier, vol. 1 (Paris: Gallimard, 1957), p. 864.

7. On his "trinity," see especially his course at the Collège de France, "Corps, Monde, Esprit."

8. See the catalogue, *Paul Valéry: Pré-Teste: Manuscrits inédits* (Universite de Paris: Bibliothèque Littéraire Jacques Doucet, 1956), item n. 93, "Gênes-Octobre," a version of "Nuit de Gênes" which Valéry's daughter, A. Rouart-Valery published in facsimile in 1964. The early reflections are especially interesting. They can be found in the manuscript collections of the Bibliothèque Nationale (hereafter BN), especially in the manuscript volumes entitled, "Proses Anciennes 1887–1895," "Proses Anciennes: Articles 1897–1900," and "Articles 1897–1900." I am grateful to the BN and to the curator of the Paul Valéry papers, Florence de Lussy, for permission to consult these and other manuscripts. Cf. F. de Lussy, *Charmes d'après les manuscrits de Paul Valéry: Histoire d'une métamorphose*, 2 vols. (Paris: Lettres Modernes, 1990).

9. See BN manuscript, "Proses Anciennes 1887–1895," pp. 265ff. for some related reflections on the difficulties of trying to live in a purely intellectual way. Earlier in the same manuscript Valéry writes, in 1891: "ce soir, je veux en ces lignes vaines que dicte la caprice avec les songeries se prévoir l'invisible étoile—cette âme lointaine et par mon âme désirée" (103).

10. Valéry describes what led up to the writing of "M. Teste" in his "Preface pour la traduction suedoise de la soirée avec Monsieur Teste," dated, September 1934. See BN manuscript, "Monsieur Teste," vol. 2: "J'ai écrit M. Teste il y a quarante ans, dans une phase terriblement voluntaire de ma vie dont je venais de bouleverser toutes mes valeurs en les soummettant au contrôle le plus impitoyable de la conscience de moi-même. Je n'imaginais guère que cette oeuvre de fantaisie et de cruauté fictive et profondement vraie, dû avoir une carrière si prolongée...." (139 his).

11. J. Levaillant, *Genèse et Signification de "La Soirée avec Monsieur Teste"* (Paris: Klincksieck, 1971), p. 94.

12. Among the many prefaces Valéry wrote to exhibitions of paintings, see in particular *Berthe Morisot (1841–1895) Catalogue* (Paris: Musée de L'Orangerie, 1941). See also his passionate interest in Edgar Degas whom he dared to describe only after Degas's death. For some of Valéry's own painting, see de Mann (1948), especially the water color, "M. Teste à l'Opera" with Valéry's inscription, "Il ne regardait que la salle." An excellent collection of Valéry's drawings and paintings is on permanent exhibit at the Musée Paul Valéry, Sète, France.

13. Scientific images abound in Valéry's words, many coming from his earlier reading. See for example, the French translation of Clerk Maxwell in two volumes (Paris: 1885–1887) which was presented to Paul Valéry and signed by Gide, in *Paul Valéry: Pré-Teste: Manuscrits inédits*, cited above. Valéry also bought the translation of Lord Kelvin's *Conférences scientifiques et allocutions* when it appeared in Paris in 1893, a book to which he referred when he met Lord Kelvin in London the next year. Further details can be found in the National Library of Scotland catalogue, *Paul Valéry* (Edinburgh, 1976). This catalogue also includes J. Middleton Murray's review of *La Jeune Pargue* from the *TLS*, August 23, 1917.

14. Cf. BN manuscript, *Proses Anciennes*, "Petites Proses 1892–1893": "Le monde est ma force. Je sens qu'il me produit et accompagne ma voix" (Folio 261; see also folios 262 and 263).

15. L. Wittgenstein, *Tractatus Logico-Philosophicus*, trans. D. F. Pears and B. F. McGuinness (London: Routledge, 1961), p. 7.

16. *Tractatus*, pp. 11–15.
17. Cf. A. Grayling, *Wittgenstein* (Oxford: Oxford University Press, 1989), here slightly
    rearranged. The roughness of these approximations can be appreciated by re-
    flecting on, notably, Cora Diamond's "Throwing Away the Ladder," in her book,
    The Realistic Spirit (Cambridge, MA: MIT Press, 1991), pp. 179–205.
18. D. Pears, *The False Prison: A Study of the Development of Wittgenstein's Philoso-
    phy*, vol. 1 (Oxford: Oxford University Press, 1987), p. 88.
19. For a brief and lucid account of the transition here between the early and the
    latter Wittgenstein see, among others, P. M. S. Hacker, "Thought, Language,
    and Reality," *TLS*, February 17, 1995.
20. L. Wittgenstein, *Philosophical Grammar*, ed. R. Rhees, trans. A. Kenny (Oxford:
    Blackwells, 1974), p. 211.
21. Pears, 1989, p. 193.
22. Pears, pp. 69, 96, 99, and 194.
23. Pears, p. 193.
24. See P. McCormick, *Fictions, Philosophies, and the Problems of Poetics* (Ithaca:
    Cornell University Press, 1988), pp. 286–93.
25. On de dicto/de re ambiguities see L. T. E. Gamat (pseud.), *Logic, Language, and
    Meaning: Intensional Logic and Logical Grammar*, vol. 2 (Chicago: University of
    Chicago Press, 1991), pp. 178–87.

9

The Philosophy of Symbolic Forms and *Perspective as Symbolic Form*

Allister Neher

Intellectuals with allegiances to neo-Kantian philosophies have often tried to extend the critical project to realms of experience that were not addressed in Kant's writings. In Germany during the nineteenth century and the early part of the twentieth century, the foundations of the emerging discipline of art history were under constant dispute as practitioners battled over which philosophical orientation could best secure art historical research. One notable figure in this debate was Erwin Panofsky, who in the early years of his career pursued such questions as: could one investigate art as a realm of experience with its own conditions of possibility?, delimited by *a priori* concepts with a role analogous to the one that Kant assigned to the categories in the formation of scientific knowledge. Panofsky also posed questions, inspired by critical concerns, about the representation of space in the visual arts.

One topic that occupied him was whether linear perspective has any special epistemological status in the representation of reality, which is of interest not only for the history of art, but also for the history of modern techniques of viewing and their role in the constitution of everyday experience. (After all, the procedures of perspective construction have an intimate relation to the development of photography, film, video, and computer imaging, all of which have assumed a prominent place in contemporary self-understanding). This chapter is not about the primacy of linear perspective nor its effect on modern image-making techniques. It addresses a more basic question about Panofsky's seminal work *Perspective as Symbolic Form*[1] and its neo-Kantian orientation; namely, what could Panofsky mean in claiming that perspective is a symbolic form? This question is preparatory to taking up any of the larger issues raised by the work.

147

Panofsky published his ambitious study *Perspective as Symbolic Form* in 1924, and it has since become a classic of art history and remains a central text in discussions of perspective.[2] This compact and dense essay addresses singly and in their interconnections a skein of historical and theoretical issues in a manner that veers between brilliance and suggestive obscurity. Accordingly, summarizing the main lines of argument and principal themes of this compressed work becomes an interesting exegetical task in itself, one that I shall not take up in introducing the topic of this chapter. Although in order to provide a context for my arguments, I would like to begin with an overview of some of the more prominent themes that have made Panofsky's study engaging and contentious.

Put very generally, Panofsky's central contention is that the system of linear perspective that was developed during the Italian Renaissance, and that dominated Western art until the late nineteenth century, is not the "natural" and only correct way of representing three-dimensional space pictorially, but only an artifice suited to certain Western modes of apprehending the world. Futhermore, Panofsky maintains, that the form of spatial organization inherent in a work of art is a direct correlate of the cosmology and modes of perception of the age to which it belongs.

The two eras that Panofsky singles out for special consideration, in support of these claims, are antiquity and the Renaissance. He argues that, in the art of these eras we can discern two very different and fundamentally opposed methods of perspective construction that are derived from distinct reckonings of visual experience, from distinct emphases on the elements of visual experience. Panofsky supports this assertion by appealing to a text based on a misguided nineteenth-century optical theory: Guido Hauck's *Die subjektive Perspektive und die horizontalen Curvaturen des Dorischen Styls.*[3] Hauck discusses two dissimilar ways in which we determine relative visual size. The first way, which he names collinearity, refers to what could be commonly called focal vision, seeing things in clear focus because one is attending to the object and light rays are entering the eye in such a way that they predominently strike the area around the *fovea centralis*. In such circumstances straight lines are perceived to be straight lines. Now, according to Hauck (and let us not forget Panofsky), the kind of method most in harmony with representing this visual situation on a two-dimensional surface is that which is embodied by Renaissance linear perspective. The other way, conformity, refers to the perception of features peripheral to the visual field. In this situation, perception of relative size supposedly accords with the size of angle subtended when straight lines representing visual rays are drawn from the outer edges of the object of vision to the eye. In such circumstances, Hauck maintained, straight lines appeared to be curved and became increasingly curved the further they were removed from the center of focus.[4] Panofsky goes on to argue that an awareness of this phenomena and an attempt to incorporate it in representation can be discerned in certain telling efforts at two-dimensional depiction that have survived antiquity. That this could be the case is supported by an examination of relevant philosophical and theoretical texts, from Euclid's *Optics*, for instance, we discover not only that the ancients measured relative size according to visual angles, but they also lacked the Renaissance's conception of an infinite, homogeneous space, and, hence, that they could not have conceived of a pictorial surface as a plane intersecting a visual cone that has its apex in the eye of the viewer, which is how it was conceived of during the Renaissance. The assumed conclusion is that in the history of civilization there has been a certain relativity of vision—most strikingly evident in these two eras—and that different peoples have apprehended the world around them in differing terms, which we see in the forms of spatial representation developed by them and in what we could loosely call their scientific and cosmological texts (it is not clear if these differences in vision are mainly, or only partially, due to varying emphases on the purportedly common elements in perception, as in the collinearity/conformity distinction). Anyway, these considerations prompt Panofsky to refer to the different approaches to perspective as different "symbolic forms," a term he borrows from the German philosopher Ernst Cassirer.[5]

All of Panofsky's arguments supporting these claims are far from convincing and often incomplete. It is not surprising that his ideas about the relativity of spatial representation have been the major targets of his opponent's attacks.[6] What strikes me as unusual though about the debates that Panosky's essay has been embroiled in, and here I approach my topic, is the dearth of discussion on what he means by claiming that perspective is a *symbolic form*. It is after all the title of the work and, hence, should be of some consequence and offer more than an indirect hint about the context and direction of his thoughts.

It's not that no one has commented on his use of the term, nor has anyone ventured to reflect on why he might have chosen to employ it, but the reflections that have been offered are noticeably thin and no real effort has been made to determine how the idea of a symbolic form, which was taken over from Cassirer's philosophy of culture, informs Panofsky's project.[7]

What is typically said about perspective being a symbolic form? Consider a representative contemporary situation. Picking up William V. Dunning's book, *Changing Images of Pictorial Space*, we discover that he defers to Michael Kubovy's book, *The Psychology of Perspective and Renaissance Art*, on this question. Here Dunning goes-on to say, "In his book on *The Renaissance Rediscovery of Linear Perspective*, Samuel Edgerton wrote a masterly exposition of Panofsky's seminal article "Die Perspektive als 'symbolische Form'," and that on the matter of perspective being a symbolic form Kubovy is now going to quote Edgerton (a move that I have seen more than once).[8] So, what does the oft deferred to Edgerton have to say? He begins by claiming that, "Unfortunately, Panofsky never explained definitively just what he meant by the phrase "symbolic form,"[9] but he perseveres, and the result is worth quoting at length:

> The symbols that man uses to communicate ideas about the objective world have an automony all their own. Indeed, the human mind systematizes these symbols into structures that develop quite independently of whatever order might exist in the natural world to begin with. . . .
>
> The real thrust of [Panofsky's] essay was not to prove that the ancients believed the visual world was curved or that Renaissance perspective was a mere artistic convention, but that *each historical period in Western civilization had its own special "perspective,"* a particular symbolic form reflecting a particular *Weltanschauung*. Thus linear perspective was the peculiar answer of the Renaissance period to the problems of representing space. . . .
>
> In the 15th century, there emerged mathematically ordered "systematic space," infinite, homogeneous, and isotropic, making possible the advent of linear perspective. . . . Linear perspective, whether "truth" or not, thus became the symbolic form of the Italian Renaissance because it reflected the general world view of the Italian people at this particular moment in history.[10]

To anyone familiar with Cassirer's "Philosophy of Symbolic Forms" and the Kantian critical project on which it is based, this won't do at all. Moreso, such nebulous, unsubstantiated conjectures, born from a vague cultural relativism and coupled with an obscure pseudo-Hegelian tone, are clear evidence for why the role played by the concept of symbolic form in Panofsky's essay has not received systematic treatment.

The remainder of this chapter will present an outline for such a treatment, a sketch of a reasonable reading of what it could mean to call perspective a symbolic form. I am *not* going to argue that the reading I give is one that could be extracted from Panofsky's essay, for that is a torturous task and would evolve into great length, indeed. Besides, in order to address what Panofsky might have meant by claiming that perspective is a symbolic form, one would first have to have developed a determinate idea of what the term "symbolic form" means and how it could be applied to something like perspective, which is what I intend to do. All the same, my account fits with Panofsky's text—it has been pursued with that in mind. It has also been pursued under the conviction (often contested) that Panofsky's use of the term was not unreflective or gratuitous, that he knew very well what it meant and that he was familiar with its philosophical provenance. Anecdotal evidence provides a very strong rhetorical foundation for this claim, given that Panofsky and Cassirer were friends and colleagues for quite a long time, and worked together on joint projects.[11] So then, on to the philosophy of symbolic forms and its background.

In the *Critique of Pure Reason* Kant tried to put an end to the fruitless, dogmatic controversies of traditional metaphysics and establish a firm foundation for philosophy by determining the nature and limits of our cognitive powers (or "reason," in the widest sense that he gave to the term). He did this by giving philosophy a new orientation, one that replaced previous conceptions of an unmediated relation between the subject and the world, with another that saw the knower as having a constitutive role in claims to knowledge. All empirical knowledge for Kant orginates in sensibility, through which we have intuitions (sensory experiences) that are determined by the forms of intuition, space and time, which are brought by us to experience, to structure, and constitute sensibility. Knowledge also requires the application of concepts to experience. The concepts that we apply to appearances are, if they are empirical concepts, such as "cat" and "black," concepts that have been derived from experience and are then reapplied to it by the understanding in making judgments about the world.

However, there are other concepts that we apply to appearances to determine those that are not derived from experience these are the pure concepts of the understanding or "categories," and they too are brought to experience by the understanding, order to structure it and make knowledge of the world possible. The categories are *a priori* concepts that are embodied in the form of our judgments. According to Kant there are a total of twelve categories, the two most familiar are "causality and substance" and "attribute," and like the forms of intuition they allow us to make synthetic *a priori* judgments; that is, they permit us to judge and know *a priori* and with necessity such universal principles as that every event has a cause. They can do this because our understanding forms the phenomenal world, the world as it appears to us, and thus makes it so (for Kant, all we can ever have knowledge of is the phenomenal world; the world of things as they are in themselves, the noumenal world, is unavailable to cognition and is only thinkable—or better, only a limiting concept). The categories form the boundaries of our world, they delineate the realm of possible experience.

There is something more that is required to explain how a judgment such as "the cat is black" connects with and matches the phenomenal world. More precisely, we have to answer how the category involved in the judgment fits (or rather, forms) what is given in intuition; for the *a priori* concepts that we call the categories are even more general than the empirical concepts involved, as they are universal and abstract from all experience. What effects this connection, for both empirical concepts and categories, are "schemata"; a schema is like a rule that stipulates the conditions a manifold of intuition must meet so that it can fit a category. In all instances, the schemata relate to the categories through temporality. Hence, in our judgment "the cat is black", where the category of substance and attribute is involved, the schema concerns the thought of something that endures in time.

Kant referred to his philosophical approach as critical or "transcendental," not because it concerns itself with realms beyond experience (what he would call the "transcendent") but, as he said, "it is occupied not so much with objects as with the mode of our knowledge of objects in so far as this mode of knowledge is to be possible *a priori*."[12] For Cassirer, the heart of the Kantian critical philosophy, that which deserves to be preserved in moving beyond Kant, is the transcendental method, which Cassirer elucidates as follows:

> His transcendental method has to assume "the fact of the sciences" as given, and seeks only to understand the possibility of this fact, its logical conditions and principles. But even so, Kant does not stand merely in a position of dependence on the factual stuff of knowledge, the material offered by the various sciences. Kant's basic conviction and presupposition consists rather of this, that there is a universal and essential *form* of knowledge, and that philosophy is called upon and qualified to discover this form and establish it with certainty. The critique of reason achieves this by reflective thought upon the function of knowledge instead of upon its content.[13]

As we know, in the *Critique of Pure Reason* Kant's focus was on providing a transcendental treatment of, as Cassirer would put it, the form of empirical knowledge, an inquiry into the conditions of possibility of the knowledge that we achieve through everyday and scientific investigations of the world. One of the cardinal features of Cassirer's neo-Kantianism is that he tries to extend the transcendental method to other ways in which human beings apprehend and form the world, turning the critique of reason into a critique of culture:

> The Philosophy of Symbolic Forms is not concerned exclusively or even primarily with the pure scientific, exact conceiving of the world; it is concerned with all forms assumed by man's understanding of the world. It seeks to apprehend these forms in their diversity, in their totality, and in the inner distinctiveness of their several expressions. And at every step it happens that the "understanding" of the world is no mere receiving, no repetition of a given structure of reality, but comprises a free activity of the spirit. There is no true understanding of the world which is not thus based on certain fundamental lines, not so much of reflection as of spiritual formation. In order to apprehend the laws of this formation, we have above all to distinguish their different dimensions.[14]

What was definitive about Kant's "Copernican Revolution" was that he realized that there is no unmediated access to the "Real" in itself, that this is in fact an obstructive conception and that in order to understand the nature of human knowledge we must grant ourselves a constitutive role in the fashioning of reality. Accordingly, we must shift our attention from ontological concerns about the elements of a reality independent of us to epistemological questions about the principles of formation involved in our construction of it. As is apparent in the noted quotations, Cassirer wanted to make this shift not only for empirical knowledge but also for all the other ways in which we form the world into recognizable realms of experience with their own laws of formation. These realms are identified by Cassirer as symbolic forms. He typically lists language, myth, art, and science, and often history and ethics, as prime examples of distinct symbolic forms that must be approached as Kant approached the science of his day in the *Critique of Pure Reason*, i.e., they must be taken as givens, and our inquiries into them must be directed toward discovering what the conditions of possibility are for them as they present themselves as individual forms of apprehension. However, unlike Kant who believed that Newtonian mechanics and Aristotelian logic were finished, static, and enduring achievements whose adequacy would not be questioned, Cassirer knows that our symbolic explications of the world, the givens that we are to study, are constantly in transformation. Indeed, this is something that he is keenly alert to and charts with great patience and insight in both his historical and theoretical studies (a distinction that is often collapsed in Cassirer's writings). He also does not privilege or rank symbolic forms, they are equally important organs of reality, although he does track how some have developed through possibilities realized by others (as physics and mathematics derived their initial categories from natural language) and have achieved a greater autonomy from the sensory and a more complete and complex symbolic articulation.

In the quotation taken from *The Problem of Knowledge*, Cassirer says Kant believed "that there is a universal and essential *form* of knowledge, and that philosophy is called upon and qualified to discover this form and establish it with certainty." For Kant in the *Critique of Pure Reason* this concerned the realm of empirical knowledge, for Cassirer it concerned all forms of apprehension. One might have doubts about the possibility of unity in such a situation, but Cassirer didn't think that this extention would end in a fragmented world of independently articulated symbolic forms—the demand for a universal form of knowledge would have to be transformed in order to discover what unity there could be amongst them. Cassirer believed that the diverse symbolic forms are manifestations of the same basic human function and that "a philosophical critique must formulate the universal conditions of this function and define the principle underlying it."[15] This function is the symbolic function, for "all these spheres produce freely their own *world of symbols* which is the true vehicle of their immanent development . . .,"[16] all thought, not just scientific thought, "is sustained by the *symbolics* and *semiotics* on which it is based."[17] Hence, the symbolic function is that which mediates the various symbolic forms, revealing and respecting their individual differences and at the same time disclosing more general principles of symbolic formation that unite them.

A key to understanding Cassirer's theory of the symbol is the Kantian notion of schemata (once more, that which matches intuitions and concepts in connecting understanding and sensation).[18] In criticizing both pre-Kantian idealism and empiricism, Cassirer argues that they both fail in their attempts to address the question of how a sensuous particular, such as a spoken sound, can convey a purely intellectual meaning because they have in their own ways instituted a dualism that divides the intelligible from the sensuous.[19] Even Kant, he says, "in a passage which constitutes the purely methodological climax of the *Critique of Judgment,* once again sharply develops the antithesis between the *intellectus archetypus* and the *intellectus ectypus,* between the intuitive, archetypal intellect and the discursive intellect 'which depends on images.'"[20] Indeed, one could say that Kant needed the notion of schemata because he insisted on such a division; something had to bridge the gap (which is of course what schemata can do once they are defined as mediating forms that are both sensuous and intellectual). The crucial step for Cassirer then is to overcome the misleading and inhibiting dualism that separates the intelligible and the sensuous.

Kant's separation of the understanding and sensation was made to facilitate the exposition of his transcendental analysis; he did not believe that the activities of these "faculties" could be isolated and studied in the ordinary workings of consciousness—they always worked in unity with the other constituents isolated in the *Critique* (imagination and schemata, for instance). It was Cassirer's insight that these elements could find their natural reunification in a reformulation of the notion of schemata, which in turn could be articulated in a theory of the symbol that unites the functions of sensibility and understanding. Let us begin to introduce Cassirer's theory of the symbol by considering his concept of the symbol or sign (he uses the words interchangeably), which he defines in the following passage:

> In [the concept of the symbol] we have attempted to encompass the totality of those phenomena in which the sensuous is in any way filled with meaning, in which a sensuous content, while preserving the mode of its existence and facticity, represents a particularization and embodiment, a manifestation and incarnation of a meaning.[21]

Or, in Carl Hamburg's slightly more concrete translation, the notion of a symbol encompasses "the totality of phenomena which—in whatever form—exhibit 'sense in the senses' and in which something 'sensuous' is *represented* as a particular embodiment of a 'sense'."[22] We can see from the language Cassirer uses that he is intent on formulating a definition that requires the interpenetration of 'sense and the senses', how he presents his case for this is the topic we shall pursue shortly. Probably the first thing that strikes anyone who is familiar with more recent work in semiotics is the unusual generality and apparent vagueness of Cassirer's definition. This is deliberate, and it speaks to his desire to begin with a conception that does not force a specific, potentially constrictive model of the symbol or sign (for instance, one appropriate to linguistics) on all the other signifying practices engaged in by human beings.[23] Moreso, if the various symbolic forms are to be analyzed immanently, then the hope is that investigations into their unique conditions of possibility will reveal both the distinctive features of their symbolizing capacities and the structural commonalities that unite them with other symbolizing activities.

Cassirer has provided one such essentially complete immanent analysis of the symbol in *Substance and Function*,[24] which is his treatment of scientific signs. *Substance and Function* predates the volumes of *The Philosophy of Symbolic Forms*, but it sets out many of the features that will define Cassirer's theory of symbolization and that will provide the structural commonalities that underlie other signifying practices. Most important is perhaps the idea of function, which is central to Cassirer's attempt to unite understanding and sensation in his treatment of scientific symbols.

Cassirer uses the idea of function to overcome the inadequacies he perceives in the traditional account of concept formation that we have inherited from Aristotle. According to Cassirer, the central problem with this approach is that it presupposes that which it is suppose to explain. The principal idea is that general concepts are created by abstraction: amidst the diverse properties assigned to objects, likenesses are noticed over time and abstracted from the differences to form a general concept such as "triangle." Cassirer replies that the "similarity of things, however, can manifestly only be effective and fruitful if it is understood and judged *as such*. That the 'unconscious' traces left in us by an earlier perception *are* like a new impression in point of fact, is irrelevant to the process implied here as long as the elements are not *recognized* as similar."[25] Such an account has an initial plausibility because it presupposes a function, a logical operation for identification that groups together phenomena according to a principle of similarity.

Cassirer's conception of function is indebted to Russell's work on the logic of relations. Relations can be stated as propositional functions, i.e., in the logical form $f(x, y)$ where f stands for the relation under consideration and (x, y) stand for the elements to be related. A propositional function is not itself a proposition, but "only sets up a general schema which must be filled with definite values before it can achieve the character of a particular statement."[26] Cassirer holds that class concepts such as "electron" and "polyhedron" should also be analyzed as relations stated as propositional functions. In other words, "What holds the class together, according to the theory developed here, is the circumstance that all the members united in it are thought of as variables of a determinate propositional function: it is therefore the propositional function and not the mere idea of a quantity as a pure collective that becomes the core of the concept."[27] In general, concepts understood as propositional functions are rules that determine how phenomena are related in experience and how, accordingly, experience is constituted. It is this kind of rule determining similarity that is presupposed in the traditional account.

We can see as well now that the propositional function is a perfect example of a sensuous-intellectual form of the sort sought after by Cassirer, for it combines in an unbreakable unity a rule or principle, f, with potential elements in sensation, (x, y), which have no determinate identity apart from that given to them in the relation. Propositional functions then stand at the center of Cassirer's theory of the concept as he states it for scientific symbols or signs. But what about other symbolic forms? Cassirer contends that this is a perfectly good approach for signs in natural language, for understanding, e.g., ordinary class concepts such as "black" or "cat." However, in keeping with his desire to analyze the various symbolic forms immanently, and not impose a particular model on their unique principles of formation, he does not try to force such an account on, for instance, myth or art. Nevertheless, he does believe that the general idea can be carried over to other symbolic activities. For in Cassirer's vision any mode of apprehending the world involves intellectual determinateness, all experience has unity, and though it may not come from the unity of the scientific concept, it is still the unity of a "relation by which a manifold is determined as inwardly belonging together."[28] It is this general idea of functional relation that is at the heart of Cassirer's theory of the symbol, and it is central to what he has in mind when he speaks of form.

The task then is to uncover the sensuous-intellectual relational forms (and their structural frameworks) that constitute experience in the other symbolic forms, to disclose the other ways in which we can have "sense in the senses." One of the difficulties involved in realizing this task is that the symbols of other modes of apprehension can be more resistent to dissection; one of the differences between science and art is that the analysis of scientific symbols clearly reveals the sensible and intelligible aspects that are united in the function; the structure of the concept is readily apparent. In art the two aspects are so closely bound together that they can hardly be distinguished. In art and other forms the sensuous substratum is "so essential that it sometimes seems to constitute the entire content, the true "meaning" of these forms . . .—the worlds of art and myth seem to consist entirely in the particular, sensuously tangible forms that they set before us."[29] This is one of the obstacles to a tidy exposition of what it might mean to call perspective a symbolic form, and when it works in collusion with standard semiological models it becomes intractable.

So, if perspective is a symbolic form we know at least that the general features of the above discussion will go into its characterization—and that in itself is a significant advance on what is usually said, though there is much more that needs to be teased out of this cryptic phrase. To do that I should begin by addressing an easy question about the appropriateness of Panofsky's use of the term 'symbolic form.' It is routinely said that Cassirer does not employ it in a way that fits perspective; this is true, if one holds onto his usage with unflinching literalism. We find the term 'symbolic form' employed in essentially three ways in Cassirer's writings: first and foremost he uses it to refer to general cultural divisions, i.e., myth, religion, science, language, art, etc.; second, it sometimes functions as an equivalent to symbol or sign; and third, it is applied to what for Kant would be the forms of intuition and the categories.[30] Perspective of course doesn't fit into any of these divisions. To me this seems to be of little consequence. Cassirer's usage is provisional and heuristic; for instance, I don't think that we would want to be so uncharitable as to say that he actually believed that the world is portioned into neat cultural components labeled myth, science, art, and so on, and that these are complete and independent parcels of human experience— indeed, his noted historical studies seem to reveal the opposite. Besides, it is not these general divisions that guide Cassirer's work but the actual practices that we loosely accept as falling under them. Although it is true that he believes that there are certain principles that are, e.g., characteristic and formative of all activity that we would call scientific, i.e., "The particular must not be left to stand alone, but must be made to take its place in a context, where it appears as part of a logical structure, whether of a teleological, logical, or causal character,"[31] these principles result from an investigation of the formative aims of working scientific theories and practices, and not from some reified general concept of "science." It is from the level of human practice that Cassirer draws his material, and it would be a natural extension of the term 'symbolic form' to apply it to, in Cassirerian language, working functional arrangements of symbols that have distinct identities according to their own principles of formation. So, just as Newtonian mechanics and Riemannian geometry could be described as symbolic forms that fall under the general symbolic form "science," Goethean color theory and Albertian linear perspective could be referred to as symbolic forms within that greater symbolic form identified as "art." We are now in a position to speak more directly about this.

It is central to Kant's doctrine of empirical knowledge that "appearances . . . are not given in themselves, but only in . . . experience, being mere representations, which as perceptions can mark out a real object only in so far as the perception connects with all others according to the rules of the unity of experience."[32] Cassirer, as we know, argues similarly that signs or symbols do not copy an independently given reality, and that all apprehension of the world is mediated, not just by symbols, but by *arrangements* of symbols, for nothing "means" without being part of an interconnected whole. This is a common enough semiotic principle, though in semiotics it has usually been explicated in terms of a model provided by natural languages or artifical formal systems. Hence, as Hubert Damisch and others have pointed out, if it is to this kind of system that perspective is to be referred, then it is hard to see how it could be studied semiologically.[33] But, as was said earlier, this is not something we are forced to resign ourselves to; like Cassirer, we can try to interrogate recalcitrant symbol systems immanently, using only the most general semiological principles for guidance.

At the most basic level, in order to have a signifying structure one needs to have elements and rules of combination (a syntax/semantics distinction is not going to be delineated here, in part because at this stage it is not clear how one would make it, but also because giving into this distinction in its familiar form would be to prematurely surrender to standard semiological models). What could be the elements of Albertian linear perpective? Speaking broadly, and not very precisely, we could suggest lines and shapes. This is a rather large and open class, but I think it can be used to at least indicate the direction in which we might go in conceiving of perspective semiologically (at least in Alberti's formulation). The next step will make this clearer. Consider the notion of a semantic field. That is, an arrangement in space or time, or both in which a symbol takes on a different meaning depending on its location in the field, its place in the arrangement.[34] A good example of a semantic field is a musical staff, where a circle, which stands for a whole note, represents a different tone depending on its placement on the staff (or above or below it). This seems to have an immediate application to perspective constructions. In musical notation it is the staff that is the structure that determines the value of the note. Similarly, the determining structure in a painting in Albertian perspective results from the interrelation of the bounded painting surface, the horizon line, the vanishing point, and the distance point. The choice of configuration involving these four conceptually primordial components constitutes the structure that will give value to an element placed on the flat painting surface (and will transform the painting surface into a picture plane). The same line placed in different locations can assume very different meanings, e.g., in being lower or higher than the horizon line it is either above or below the beholder's eye level and can be interpreted as closer or further away from the ground plane in the image. Obviously, the same could be said for the employment of other lines: a line starting at the top right-hand corner and reaching the vanishing point will be taken as being above the beholder's head and extending to ground level, whereas the same line starting in the lower left-hand corner and reaching the vanishing point will be taken as running parallel to the ground surface, and so on. Likewise for the placement of a shape, which will be evaluated as nearer to or further from the beholder, depending on its location on the painting surface within the structure that has been set up. The four conceptually primordial components are not all there is to the determining structure; for in the Albertian construction positing them immediately induces a grid that maps the entire painting surface. This grid is not a secondary feature imposed on the conceptually primordial elements but is, as I said, immediately induced by them; it literally *materializes* with their positing, an evident inference from visual axioms. It is of course the gradient created by the grid that provides the finer determining structure that allows an exact estimation of how far a group of similar shapes are from each other and from the beholder, or allows similar shapes of different sizes to be seen as resting at different distances (here lies what little truth there is in calling perspective the rationalization of sight).

Evidently, making marks on a flat surface is not sufficient in itself to create a perspectival effect; afterall, house pets and young children don't see pictures as illusions of spatial depth. One must be taught to take the configuration of marks in a certain way, to know the principles according to which the elements mean. Underlying this meaning relation is what Cassirer calls symbolic pregnance, "the way in which a perception as a sensory experience contains at the same time a certain nonintuitive meaning which it immediately and concretely represents."[35] Cassirer illustrates this through the example of a simple line, which can serve as the vehicle of sense for various functions of meaning: it can be taken, apprehended, and evaluated, as an aesthetic ornament, a geometrical construction, a mythical symbol that embraces the distinction between the sacred and the profane, the representation of a trigonometric function, and so forth. In each different modality of signification it becomes a sign, a representation of sense in the senses, through a network of relations that determine its function; it is never given in itself but always and only as part of a greater structure of meaning.[36] Each greater structure of meaning, each symbolic form (in the extended sense given to the term above) is grounded in a basic principle(s) of formation.

In the case of perspective, this principle of formation, however we choose to specify it in the end, will concern the establishment of relations between designated elements that will serve as conventions for the representation of three dimensions on a two-dimensional surface. From this basic principle are derived the rules that govern the perspective construction and our reading of it, e.g., all receding lines that are in nature parallel to one another, and not perpendicular to the beholder, will be drawn to converge at an implied vanishing point; all lines that are receding, level lines in nature will be drawn so as to end on the horizon line; and so on for all the rules that regulate determinations of depth and scale. These, and the further principles they logically imply, are the rules of combination for the elements of the semantic field. So we have then the basic elements of a signifying structure.

This is fairly detailed exposition of what the concept of symbolic form means for Cassirer, attempting to indicate in conjunction with it that perspective has all of the features that are central to this concept. The next question to address would be whether Panofsky's use of the notion fits the characterization I have given. I have already indicated that it will—his approach is for the most part compatible with everything Cassirer says and with my extrapolations made from Cassirer's account. Even though, as many have observed, Panofsky does not employ the concept explicitly, the way he frames his study and chooses his subjects indicates that he is operating implicitly with this concept of symbolic form; and indeed, given all that time he spent with Cassirer, it would be surprising if he didn't.

It should be said, if it needs to be said, that such an account (sketch that it is) would not by itself be an adequate treatment of the signification of space in painting—not even quattrocento painting under the sway of Alberti's *Della Pittura*. To begin with, one would need a corresponding analysis of color and value relations, and a comprehensive theory of the use of iconic signs— signs which signify on the basis of resemblance—in two-dimensional media (and of course one would have to pay some attention to those pesky issues that surround the subject and the social world). But this is a start. Some determinate sense has been given to the idea of perspective as a symbolic form— which is more than can be said for the account that I quoted at the outset.

NOTES

1. Erwin Panofsky, *Perspective as Symbolic Form*, trans. by Christopher S. Wood (New York: Zone Books, 1991).
2. A most impressive study by Hubert Damisch, *L'Origine de la perspective* (Paris: Flammarion, 1987), recently trans. into English by John Goodman as *The Origin of Perspective* (Cambridge: The MIT Press, 1994).

3. Guido Hauck, *Die subjektive Perspektive und die horizontalen Curvaturen des Dorischen Styls* (Stuttgart: Verlag von K. Wittwer, 1879).
4. Hauck believed that we alternated between collinearity and conformity as modes of vision. However, because we attempt to achieve unified vision, collinearity got the upper hand, as it corresponds to our belief that straight lines appear straight.
5. Ernst Cassirer, *The Philosophy of Symbolic Forms. Volume 1: Language; Volume 2: Mythical Thought; Volume 3: The Phenomenology of Knowledge*, trans. by Ralph Manheim (New Haven: Yale University Press, 1955).
6. Some critics have even raised doubts about the intelligibility of his assertions: "While the present writer has considerable misgivings with regard to a number of Panofsky's arguments and conclusions, it must be pointed out that he does not always find it easy to understand what, from an optical, physiological and psychological standpoint, Professor Panofsky, and the other art historians who have been influenced by his thesis, do exactly mean." M. H. Pirenne, *Optics, Painting, and Photography* (Cambridge: Cambridge University Press, 1970), p. 93.
7. Two notable contemporary exceptions are Michael Ann Holly, *Panofsky and the Foundations of Art History* (Ithaca: Cornell University Press, 1984) and, once again, Hubert Damisch, *The Origin of Perspective*. I find Holly's discussion inattentive to the philosophical background of the idea of symbolic form. Damisch, on the other hand, is apprised of the philosophical connections, but he does not think that they are of great import in evaluating Panofsky's essay: "In truth, these questions [about the semiological status of perspective] do not seem to have interested Panofsky, whose intention was, as he says quite openly, "to extend Ernst Cassirer's felicitous term [i.e., 'symbolic form'] to the history of art." The fact is, however, that, far from making reference to it from the start, he only introduces it after extended developments, supposedly based on psychophysiology, that directly contradict Cassirer's arguments because they take the retinal image, which has nothing to do with the symbolic order, to be the touchstone of perspective construction. As for the definition he uses, which holds that perspective is one of those "symbolic forms" by means of which "intellectual meaning becomes so closely linked to a concrete sign as to indistinguishable from it, it is sufficiently vague and generalized to justify any interpretation one would like." Damisch, op. cit., pp. 12–13.
8. William V. Dunning, *Changing Images of Pictorial Space: A History of Spatial Illusion in Painting* (Syracuse: Syracuse University Press, 1991), p. 38. Michael Kubovy, *The Psychology of Perspective and Renaissance Art* (Cambridge: Cambridge University Press, 1986), 164–5. Samuel Y. Edgerton Jr., *The Renaissance Rediscovery of Linear Perspective* (New York: Basic Books, 1975).
9. Edgerton, op. cit., p. 154.
10. Block quote as it is presented in Kubovy, op. cit., pp. 163–4 (from Edgerton, op. cit., pp. 156–8 and 161).
11. For a survey of the personal and professional connections uniting Panofsky and Cassirer, see Dimitry Gawronsky, "Ernst Cassirer: His Life and Work," in *The Philosophy of Ernst Cassirer*, ed. Paul Arthur Schilpp (LaSalle: Open Court, 1949) in conjunction with Holly, op. cit.
12. Immanuel Kant, *Critique of Pure Reason*, trans. Norman Kemp Smith (Atlantic Highlands: Humanities Press, 1923), p. 59.
13. Ernst Cassirer, *The Problem of Knowledge*, trans. William H. Woglom and Charles W. Hendel (New Haven: Yale University Press, 1950), pp. 14–15.

14. Ernst Cassirer, *The Philosophy of Symbolic Forms. Volume 3: The Phenomenology of Knowledge*, p. 13.

15. Ernst Cassirer, *The Philosophy of Symbolic Forms. Volume 1: Language*, p. 77.

16. Ibid., p. 86.

17. Ibid., p. 86. Later on this page, Cassirer says that "if it were possible to show their [the symbolic forms] typical and consistent features as well as their special graduations and inner differences, the ideal of a "universal characteristic," formulated by Leibnitz for cognition would be fulfilled for the whole of cultural activity." About this passage and the discussion surrounding it, Damisch says that: "The philosophy of symbolic forms aims at nothing less than the application of Leibniz's "universal characteristic," based on the idea that conceptual definition of any content whatever goes hand in hand with its stabilization in a *sign*, to the totality of symbolic activity, whether linguistically based or not "(op. cit., p. 8). But it is not quite correct to identify Cassirer's project with Leibniz's "universal characteristic," for Cassirer continues in the next paragraph to criticize the epistemological foundations of Leibniz's vision; Leibniz is only the convenient starting point for the elaboration of Cassirer's position. My suspicion is that Damisch uses the Leibniz connection as an unstated argument to devalue the philosophy of symbolic forms and, hence, to remove the need to consider its role in contemporary discussions of the questions raised by Panofsky's text.

18. This interpretation was first suggested by Charles W. Hendel in his Introduction to *The Philosophy of Symbolic Forms. Volume 1: Language*, pp. 12–15.

19. Also *pace* Damisch and the philosophy of symbolic forms as a type of Leibnizian "universal characteristic," for Cassirer this is just the point at which Leibnizian idealism falters.

20. Ernst Cassirer, *The Philosophy of Symbolic Forms. Volume 1: Language*, p. 113.

21. Ernst Cassirer, *The Philosophy of Symbolic Forms. Volume 3: The Phenomenology of Knowledge*, p. 93.

22. Carl H. Hamburg, "Cassirer's Conception of Philosophy," in Schilpp, op. cit., p. 78.

23. If he could have joined modern debates about whether linguistics should provide the general model for semiological studies, Cassirer would have argued vehemently against such an approach. In a passage on expression and the expressive function, just before the quote on the concept of the symbol, he says that "if we define the concept of symbolism in such a way as to limit it to those cases in which precisely this differentiation between mere image and the thing itself stands out clearly [e.g., as in natural languages] and in which this differentiation is emphasized and elaborated, we shall find ourselves beyond any doubt in a region [e.g., expressive phenomena] to which this concept can have no application."

24. Ernst Cassirer, *Substance and Function and Einstein's Theory of Relativity*, trans. by William Curtis Swabey and Marie Collins Swabey (New York: Dover Publications, 1953). This analysis is amplified in the third volume of *The Philosophy of Symbolic Forms*.

25. Ernst Cassirer, *Substance and Function*, p. 15. The version of the account being addressed here is Mill's.

26. Ernst Cassirer, *The Philosophy of Symbolic Forms. Volume 3: The Phenomenology of Knowledge*, p. 295.

27. Ibid., p. 295.

28. Ibid., p. 298.
29. Ernst Cassirer, *The Philosophy of Symbolic Forms. Volume 1: Language*, p. 86.
30. For a detailed discussion of these divisions, see Carl H. Hamburg, op. cit.
31. Ernst Cassirer, *The Philosophy of Symbolic Forms. Volume 1: Language*, p. 77.
32. Immanuel Kant, *Critique of Pure Reason*, p. 442.
33. Damisch, op. cit., pp. 23–4.
34. The general idea behind the notion of a semantic field is not foreign to Cassirer's conception of the symbol and I think implicit in his semiotics: "Understood in this light, space is by no means a static vessel and container into which ready-made "things" are poured; it is rather a sum of ideal functions, which complement and determine one another to form a unified result. Just as in the simple temporal "now" earlier and later are expressed as the basic temporal directions, similarly in every "here" we posit a "there." The particular place is not given prior to the spatial system but only in reference to it and in correlation with it. *The Philosophy of Symbolic Forms. Volume 1, Language*, p. 101. See the discussion surrounding this passage.
35. Ernst Cassirer, *The Philosophy of Symbolic Forms. Volume 3: The Phenomenology of Knowledge*, p. 202.
36. Ibid., 200ff.

10

What Computers Cannot Do: Two Strategies

Dagfinn Føllesdal

Phenomenology is often appealed to in arguments concerning what computers can and cannot do. There are two strategies for doing this, one common and one not so common. I shall start by discussing the most common strategy and then pursue the not so common one, which I regard as the more basic one.

THE LIFE-WORLD

The more common strategy takes its starting point in the life-world and argues that it has various features that make it hard to program into a computer.

To properly understand the life-world with all its nuances we must see it within the context of Husserl's philosophy. I will therefore start with a brief survey of the key ideas in Husserl's phenomenology and then show how the life-world is an integral part of his phenomenology.

PHENOMENOLOGY AS A STUDY OF THE SUBJECTIVE PERSPECTIVE

Phenomenology is an attempt to study in a systematic manner our different subjective perspectives, our different ways of experiencing reality. In the sciences one is searching for objectivity: one tries to secure that one's observations are independent of who makes them. They should preferably consist of reading numbers off a measuring scale or making other kinds of registrations that are affected as little as possible by the observer's subjective perspective. One does not deny the existence of a subjective perspective, but regards it as a disturbing element when one is making scientific observations. Therefore one tries to arrange experiments and observations in such a way that the influence of the subjective perspective becomes as small as possible.[1]

Phenomenology is the most advanced attempt I know to develop a theory of the subjective perspective and a method for studying it. We do not get a satisfactory understanding of other persons merely by knowing what impulses they are exposed to and how they move. It is far more important to know how they experience themselves and their surroundings. The impulses that reach us from the outside are insufficient to uniquely determine which object we experience, as is easily seen in the duck/rabbit case, where the same figure is seen now as a duck, now as a rabbit. All perception is like this, Husserl said. Normally, we are not aware of it, but even in normal perception the physical impulses that reach our senses are insufficient to uniquely determine what we perceive, as is seen in every case where we discover that we have been misperceiving. As soon as we recognize our mistake, we restructure what we perceive.

THE NOEMA—INTENTIONALITY

Since the physical impulses that reach us are the same, whatever makes the difference in the situation must be coming from us. This factor Husserl called the *noema*. The noema is a structure. Our consciousness structures what we experience. How it structures it depends on our previous experiences, the whole setting of our present experience and a number of other factors. If we had grown up surrounded by ducks, but had never heard of rabbits, we would have been more likely to see a duck than a rabbit when confronted with the duck/rabbit picture; the idea of a rabbit would probably not even have occurred to us.

The structuring always take place in such a way that the many different features of the object become connected with one another and are experienced as features of one and the same object. When, for example, we see a rabbit, we do not merely see a collection of colored patches, various shades of brown spread out over our field of vision. We see a rabbit, with a determinate shape and a determinate color, with the ability to eat, jump, and so on. It has a side that is turned toward us and one that is turned away from us. We do not see the other side from where we are, but we see something that has another side. Husserl expresses this also by saying that our consciousness is characterized by *intentionality*, it is always directed toward an object. That seeing is intentional, or object-directed, means just this; the near side of the object we have in front of us is regarded as a side of a thing, and the thing we see has other sides and features that are co-intended, in the sense that the thing is regarded as more than just this one side. The noema is the comprehensive system of determinations that gives unity to this manifold of features and makes them aspects of one and the same object.

Here the word 'object' must be taken in a broad sense. It comprises not only physical things, but also, as we have just noted, animals, and likewise persons, events, actions, and processes. When we experience a person, we do not experience a physical object, a body, and then infer that a person is there. We experience a full-fledged person; we are encountering somebody who structures the world, experiences it from his or her own perspective. Our noema is a noema of a person; no inference is involved. Seeing persons is no more mysterious than seeing physical objects; no inference is involved in either case. When we see a physical object we do not see sense data or the like and then infer that there is a physical object there; our noema is the noema of a physical object. Similarly, when we see an action, what we see is a full-fledged action, not a bodily movement from which we infer that there is an action.

The noema is a key notion in Husserl's phenomenology, not only in his theory of perception, but in his analysis of all aspects of human consciousness. The noema is just Husserl's attempt to characterize the subjective perspective. Two people can face the same thing, but nevertheless experience them quite differently, as different as duck and rabbit. But even where they agree on what kind of an object they see, there may be enormous differences between the ways they see it. We all slide into routine ways of experiencing the surrounding world and ourselves. What characterizes a great artist is in part the ability to see and experience things, events and persons in new ways, in part the ability to mediate this experience to others. Those objects that are being experienced need not be new and exceptional. They are often everyday and common. It is not the object, but the experience which is central.

CONSTITUTION

Objects are intended as having a great number of properties, normally, as in the case of a material object, many more than can ever be exhausted in our experience of it. "Objects are *constituted* through our consciousness," Husserl says. This does not mean that we create them or bring them about, merely that the various components of the noema are interconnected in such a way that we have an experience as of one full-fledged object. All there is to the object, hence, corresponds to components of our noema. In the case of physical objects, the inexhaustible character of what is experienced is a characteristic anticipation in our noema and, hence, an important feature of what it is to be a physical object.

THE WORLD, THE PAST, AND VALUES

We constitute not only the different properties of things, but also the relation of the thing to other objects. If, for example, I see a tree, the tree is conceived of as something that is in front of me, as perhaps situated among other trees, as seen by other people than myself, and so on. It is also conceived of as something which has a history: it was there before I saw it, it will remain after I have left, perhaps it will eventually be cut and transported to some other place. However, like all material things, it does not simply disappear from the world.

My consciousness of the tree is in this way also a consciousness of the world in space and time in which the tree is located. My consciousness constitutes the tree, but at the same time it constitutes the world in which the tree and I are living. If my further experience makes me give up the belief that I have a tree ahead of me because, for example, I do not find a tree-like far side or because some of my other expectations prove false, this affects not only my conception of what there is, but also my conception of what has been and what will be. Thus, in this case, not just the present, but also the past and the future are reconstituted by me. To illustrate how changes in my present perception lead me to reconstitute not just the present, but also the past, Husserl uses an example of a ball which I initially take to be red all over and spherical. As it turns, I discover that it is green on the other side and has a dent:

> ... the sense of the perception is not only changed in the momentary new stretch of perception; the noematic modification streams back in the form of a retroactive cancellation in the retentional sphere and modifies the production of sense stemming from earlier phases of the perception. The earlier apperception, which was attuned to the harmonious development of the "red and uniformly round," is implicitly "reinterpreted" to "green on one side and dented."[2]

This restructuring of the past has consequences for the programming of computers:

(1) MALLEABILITY OF STORED INFORMATION:

When new information is fed into a computer, this information should not just be added to the storage, but should for many purposes affect what is already there. It should modify it and change it in ways that it will often be very difficult to program into a computer.

So far I have mentioned only the factual properties of things. But, according to Husserl, their *value* properties are constituted in a corresponding manner. The world within which we live is experienced as a world in which certain things and actions have a positive value, others a negative. Our norms and values, too, are subject to change. Changes in our views on matters of fact are often accompanied by changes in our evaluations and conversely.

(2)   NORMS AND VALUES AND THEIR INTERWEAVING
       WITH COGNITIVE FACTORS

> **A computer that is supposed to emulate what people do, would have to contain items that, like norms and values, influence what "action" the computer takes. These items would have to be interwoven with the "cognitive" items in such a way that changes in items of one kind may bring about changes in items of the other kind.**

HORIZON

When we are experiencing an object, our consciousness is focused on this object, the rest of the world and its various objects are there in the background as something we "believe in" but are not presently paying attention to. The same holds for most of the inexhaustibly many features of the object itself. All these further features of the object, together with the world in which it is set, make up what Husserl calls the *horizon* of that experience. The various features of the object, which are cointended, or also-meant, but not at the focus of our attention, Husserl calls it the *inner horizon*, while the realm of other objects and the world to which they all belong, he calls the *outer horizon*:

> Thus every experience of a particular thing has its *internal horizon*, ... the anticipation of determinations which, insofar as they pertain to this object of experience, are now expected; in another respect it is also an aiming-beyond the thing itself ... to other objects of which we are aware at the same time, although at first they are merely in the background. This means that everything given in experience has not only an internal horizon but also an infinite, open, *external horizon* of *objects cogiven*. ... These are objects toward which I am not now actually turned but toward which I can turn at any time. ... all real things which at any given time are anticipated together or cogiven only in the background as an external horizon are known as real objects (or properties, relations, etc.) *from the world*, are known as existing within the one spatiotemporal horizon.[3]

To take a simple example of an item belonging to this outer horizon: if we ask a person who is entering a room what her expectations are, she may mention something about friends she expects to meet, a lecture she is coming to hear and so on. It is highly unlikely that she would mention that she expects there to be a floor in the room. Yet, as we see how confidently she steps in, we have every reason to believe that she expected that there would be a floor here. She did not think about it, her attention was directed to other things, but she had a disposition that she acted on. And if I had asked her whether she expected there to be a floor in the room, she might have wondered why I asked such a trivial question, but she would probably have answered yes.

Expectations and beliefs are dispositional notions. We count as beliefs not only thoughts that we are actively entertaining, but also those that we rarely think about, for example, that $2 + 2 = 4$. We do have a problem when we try to delimit exactly what beliefs we have. The method of questioning is not reliable. On the one side, it gives too much. Remember how in the *Menon* a skilled questioner uncovers that the slave boy has the most unexpected geometrical beliefs. Plato took this as evidence for his theory of *anamnesis*. On the other, it yields too little. As Freud and others have taught us, we often sincerely deny that we have beliefs that seem all too apparently to underlie our actions.

BODILY SKILLS AND NON-COGNITIVE STATES

The most reliable criterion, that we often fall back on, is to assume that people have those beliefs that best explain their actions, including their verbal activities. However, then a further problem is that the states we appeal to in order to explain people's actions are not exclusively cognitive states. Also various physical states are needed, and skills of various kinds that it is often hard to classify as mental. Thus while our arithmetical skills are presumably mental, our skills in swimming or walking can hardly be classified as mental. Then we have tricky intermediate cases, such as one's keeping a standard distance to partners in a conversation, where the standard may vary from culture to culture. Is keeping this distance a matter of a tacit belief that it is the proper distance? Or is it a matter of a bodily skill which is gradually acquired as one grows up in this culture? What about the way we sign our name?[4] Obviously, cognitive activities are involved in the process that brought us to sign it the way we do. We had to learn the alphabet, we had to learn our name, and so on. Also, in our semiautomatic way of signing it, bodily skills are involved to a great extent. Various personality traits play a role, as do certain general traits of our culture.

Opinions concerning examples such as these may vary. One of our problems is that we have no clear-cut way to settle such issues, lacking a precise definition of what is to count as mental, or what is to count as physical. However, there is obviously an interplay here, both in the process that leads to the skill and in the skill itself, and any satisfactory theory of intentionality must heed such an interplay. The noema may still be defined as a structure, but the anticipations that are related through this structure are not merely the anticipations involved in seeing, hearing, and the like, but also the anticipations involved in kinesthesis and bodily movement, where when something "goes wrong" we are aware of it. We are familiar with this experience of "going wrong" from cases of misperception: we cannot always tell exactly what went wrong, but we are aware that something went wrong.

Husserl started out in the *Ideas* and other early works with a strongly cognitivist attitude: the anticipations in the noema are of a purely cognitive kind. However, in manuscripts from 1917 on, he focused more and more on the role of the practical and the body in our constitution of the world. He never worked out the full implications of this for his conception of the noema, but it seems clear that he would consider our anticipations as not merely beliefs, but also as bodily settings, which are involved in kinesthesis and also play an important role in perception and in the movements of our body. In numerous passages, Husserl talks about practical anticipations and the role of kinesthesis in perception and bodily activity. A consequence of this is the following:

(3)   BODILY STATES AND SKILLS

In order to imitate humans, a computer would have to emulate not only cognitive, but also bodily states and skills.

THE "ICEBERG"

What is particularly important about the horizon, is its hidden nature. As we noted, the horizon is that which is not attended to. Usually, as in the case of the floor in the room example, we have not even thought about it. Typically, we cannot even recall when we first acquired the corresponding "belief" or "anticipation." According to Husserl, there may never have been any occasion when we actually judged there to be a floor in some particular room. Still we have come to "anticipate" a floor, not in the sense of consciously expecting one, but in the sense that if we entered the room and there were none, we would be astonished. In this example we would easily be able to tell what was missing, in other cases our "anticipations" are so imperceptible that we just may feel that something has gone awry, but we may not be able to tell what it is.

Words like "belief" and "anticipate" are clearly not the proper ones here, since they have overtones of something being conscious and thematized. Both English and German seem to lack words for what we want to get at here: Husserl uses the words *"antizipieren,"* *"hinausmeinen,"* and *"vorzeichnen."*

This creates a special problem for attempts to make a computer imitate humans:

(4)   THE HIDDENNESS OF THE STRUCTURE

> **The structure we impose upon reality is normally hidden to us and therefore not easily mapped and put into a computer.**

A main aim of phenomenology is to make us reflect upon the way the world is constituted by us and thereby make this hidden structure accessible. Through a special reflection, the "phenomenological reduction," phenomenology will take us out of our natural attitude, where we are absorbed by the world around us, into the phenomenological, transcendental attitude, where we focus on the noemata of our acts, on our structuring of reality. In this way we can study the rich and complex structure of anticipations we have concerning the world. However, that our anticipations are accessible to us through reflection does not mean that we can survey them easily. There are two main difficulties:

(5)   THE RICHNESS AND NON-SYSTEMATIC NATURE
      OF THE STRUCTURE

> **If we make this structure of anticipations accessible through reflection, we find it tremendously rich. To map it would be an infinite task, to speak with Husserl. Further, we lack a systematic way of cataloguing all that we find. Also, here, as in all other realms, mistake is always possible, both in our registering what is there as well as in describing it properly.**

THE SECOND STRATEGY

Most phenomenological discussions of what computers can and cannot do focus on the various features of the life-world I have listed, and discuss how far computers can get without insuperable difficulties. Hubert Dreyfus, in particular, has explored the limitations that Feature 3, "Bodily States and Skills," imposes on computers, and has tried to determine what they can do and what they cannot do.[5]

However, there is a quite different way of looking at computers that leads to a much dimmer view on what they can do. This is based on the observation that computers have no consciousness. This observation can easily be regarded as question-begging: Is not the question of whether computers have consciousness just a question of what they can do? And what is consciousness anyway? Husserl has an answer to the latter question: to have consciousness is to have intentionality, to give structure or meaning to the world, to bring about that there be objects in the world, rather than the mere physical boundary conditions that are compatible with any number of different ways of reifying our surroundings.

On this view, a computer can do nothing. It cannot even compute. In order for the physical processes that take place in a computer to be computations, they have to be taken in certain ways; they must be construed as computations. Even the construal of them as computations can be done in numerous different ways. In order to bring this point home, let us consider the simple case of a slide rule. Here one rod is moved against another until lines on the one coincide with lines on the other. One and the same physical movement may be interpreted as addition, or as multiplication, depending on how one reads the scales. There is nothing intrinsic to the physical movement of the rods that makes it any of these operations.

Similarly, in an electronic computer, there is nothing in the oscillations of the circuits that intrinsically make them computations, far less any specific computations. It all depends on how we structure them. The physical flicker permits numerous different interpretations. Of course, not all physical processes can equally readily be interpreted as computations. That is why we build computers. However, what goes on in them, is not by itself computation. It becomes computation only when interpreted in a certain way. This interpretation is what requires consciousness.

This, then, is the dim view we end up with: It is wrong to say that computers can do certain things, but not others, or that they can play simple games but not games that require ingenuity, or that they can perform purely cognitive task but not such that require bodily skills. They cannot do even what we usually think they are good at, namely compute. They can do nothing; the physical processes that go on in them are not doings. In computers there is neither doing nor is there a doer.

NOTES

I am indebted to Hubert Dreyfus, Izchak Miller, David Smith, Ronald McIntyre, and John Searle for numerous discussions over the years concerning the issues examined in this chapter, in particular those connected with the role of the body (point 3). I am also grateful to the Axel o Margaret Ax:son Johnson Foundation for support of this and other work.

1. See my "Intentionality and Behaviorism." In L. J. Cohen, J. Los, H. Pfeiffer and Klaus-Peter Podewski, eds., *Proceedings of the 6th International Congress of Logic, Methodology and Philosophy of Science*, Hannover, August 22–29, 1979 (Amsterdam: North-Holland, 1982), pp. 553–569.
2. *Erfahrung und Urteil*, §21a, p. 96=p. 89 of Churchill and Ameriks's English translation (Northwestern University Press, Evanston, IL., 1973).
3. *Erfahrung und Urteil*, §8, pp. 28–29, Churchill and Ameriks, pp. 32–33.
4. This example came up in conversations with David Wellbery.
5. In particular in *What Computers Can't Do* (New York: Harper and Row, 1972).

Part 4

Transcendental Philosophy and the Emotions

11

Empathy, Persons, and Community

Dallas Laskey

In recent decades, studies in transcendental philosophy have taken the form
of a search for transcendental arguments designed to ground, or otherwise
legitimate, some fundamental principle or category. This kind of investigation has appealed to philosophers of different orientations. Concurrent with
the interest in transcendental arguments, there has also appeared mounting
criticism and suspicion. Quine's arguments[1] against the analytic-synthetic
dichotomy have led to a disenchantment with the *a priori*; philosophers
following Quine's naturalism[2] generally disbelieve in the possibility of ever
finding principles that can be taken in such an unrestricted manner.

There are other forms of transcendental philosophy which are not engaged in the search for transcendental arguments and that deny their very
possibility. Edmund Husserl, for example, introduced a version of transcendental philosophy which concentrated on finding faithful descriptions of
experience which were free from the usual metaphysical or ontological arguments current in the empiricist tradition.[3] This philosophy, although open
to criticism, is not open to the kind of criticism that has been directed to
transcendental arguments, and offers some distinct advantages when dealing
with problems of self and society.

It is my intention to show that transcendental phenomenology provides
a positive and fruitful framework for the study of empathy and related issues. Where empirical studies had tended to trivialize the role of empathy
in the problem of understanding the actions of other persons and groups,
transcendental phenomenology restores empathy to a central position by
bringing into clear focus the intentional structures which link human subjects with other subjects and with their surrounding world. Empathic understanding provides us with provisional knowledge about the states and
behavior of other persons and groups; such knowledge claims are not tested
according to the procedures of the natural and social sciences, but have
their own methods appropriate to the data involved. Empathy is also a factor

174

in bringing about intersubjective agreement. Finally, empathy is essentially involved in the constitution of self and society, and is the source of what might be called "the moral point of view."

To develop these claims in more detail, I will first show the limitations of empirical empathy and then turn to an analysis of transcendental empathy. When this has been concluded, I will consider the role of empathy in intersubjective agreement. Finally, I will show how empathy plays a fundamental role in morality.

EMPIRICAL STUDIES OF EMPATHY

Empirical studies have almost without exception denied both a cognitive role to empathy and a valid method of verification for its claims. It is usually assigned a function *outside* the scientific process, possibly as a source of hypotheses which can then be scientifically tested. This is no accident, because the empirical perspective with the present assumptions simply is not suited for certain kinds of problems in the social sciences and humanities. To show this, let us turn to the arguments deployed against empathy and empathic understanding by the positivists at mid-century in what has been termed the Erklarung-Verstehen debate. K-O Apel[4] distinguished three different historical phases of this debate in an important study, but I will restrict myself to the first place where the issues are more sharply contrasted.

Let us consider the arguments of Theodore Abel,[5] because of their clarity and historical importance. To his credit, Abel examines three concrete cases for detailed scrutiny; but it is clear from the outset that he redefines the concept of Verstehen (empathic understanding) to meet the demands of his own empirical orientation. Empathy is wrested from the hermeneutic tradition where it functioned, and was described in a framework and a language quite foreign to it. In the philosophy of Wilhelm Dilthey, for example, empathy was situated in a holistic framework where subjects and their environing social world were inextricably enmeshed. Empathic understanding referred to the acts of imaginative feeling initiated by a subject towards the behavior of societies that were alien—the focus was on the meaning or significance of the strange behavior with the intent of understanding that behavior as it might appear to a native. However, Abel,[6] working from a positivistic and behavioristic orientation, redefines Verstehen as:

> the postulation of an intervening process "located" inside the human organism, by means of which we recognize an observed—or assumed—connection as relevant of "meaningful." Verstehen, then, consists of the act of bringing to the foreground the inner-organic sequence intervening between the stimulus and a response."

In Abel's perspective, nature is contrasted to experience so that the former is objective and physical while the latter is subjective and mental. Empathy is a subjective phenomenon postulated as existing between the two objective phenomena of stimulus and response. Having set it up this way, it is easy to show that there is no reliable technique by means of which we can objectively attribute feeling states to persons, nor is there a reliable technique for associating feeling states and observed behavior. Similarly, there are no *objective maxims* linking the feeling-state provoked by an impinging situation. Such behavior maxims are alleged to be generalizations from direct personal experience and derived from introspection and self-observation. Described in this manner, it is clear that empathy is *outside* the scientific process and cannot serve as a means of discovery. Verstehen (empathic understanding) is rejected as a scientific tool of analysis,[7] but it is given a subordinate role outside science where it can "serve as an aid in preliminary explorations of a subject" (p. 685). In this capacity it is like a hunch that leads to hypotheses that can later be tested scientifically. Thus, as described, it can neither add to our store of knowledge nor admit of adequate testing.

Other empiricists follow substantially the same arguments. C. G. Hempel, whose influential article, "The Function of General Laws in History"[8]—one of the great classics of our century—follows Abel in taking empathy our of its original hermeneutic framework where it exercised an important cognitive role, and considers it as a psychological phenomenon possessing heuristic value only. What really counts for Hempel is the question of the truth or validity of these claims, and this can be settled only through the procedures of natural science. Richard Rudner put the matter very clearly in the following:

> What is at issue is whether empathic understanding constitutes an indispensable method for the validation of hypotheses about social phenomena (p. 93)[9]

Statements reached by empathic understanding just could not satisfy the demand for public verification, being linked with the personal and the subjective.

To get at the heart of the problem, one should turn to some of the assumptions operating in the empiricist perspective, which are adequate for the study of physical nature, but are superficial or irrelevant for the study of human action. In the first case, the empiricist makes the objective/subjective distinction in a contrastive or opposed manner, so that the terms are *mutually exclusive*. To attain the empiricists's ideal of objective knowledge of physical nature, it is necessary to eliminate systematically all traces of subjectivity. The distinction creates a dualism in which the world of physical nature stands over against the experience of the subject. In the language of J. L. Austin,[10] the objectivity side of the distinction "wears the trousers" for it assumes preeminence; subjectivity is derogated and every effort is made to exclude it. This results in what I call a defective theory of subjectivity; it is defective because it is not based on a disciplined study of subjective experience, but postulated from assumptions and beliefs that are part of the Cartesian tradition. As formulated above, the only possible relation between the objective and the subjective is a one-way causal relation, the physical world being the cause or source of subjective experience.

Within the empirical perspective, the focus is on the things and processes of the external objective world; the ontological direction is to focus on the objective data that are real and existent, and in causal relations. What lies within the domain of subjectivity is not real; there is a constant flux of inner experiences and an absence of order. Strictly speaking, there are no subjects in such a world; it is easy to see that physicalism is a logical consequence of such assumptions. The framework is such that objective events are considered only in relation to other objective events in a causal connection.

On the other hand, the hermeneutic tradition employs a different way of making the objectivity/subjectivity distinction. Here it is not contrastive and mutually exclusive, but rather *mutually implicative*; the objective is always tied to the subjective processes that produce it. Objective and subjective are correlates; where the distinction is interpreted in terms of intentionality, the objective and subjective are intentional correlates. Each requires the other and it makes no sense to take one without the other. The distinction does not carry the ontological implications of empiricism, for the focus is on meanings and values rather than on things and events in the world. Meanings and values arise from the various intentional acts of subjects in their respective contexts. Empathic understanding is initiated by subjects in order to understand the meanings and values implicit in the actions being considered for investigation. It is especially useful when an alien or native culture is being studied and the behavior is strange to the outsider. Empathic understanding yields hypotheses about meanings and values that are subjected to tests within and peculiar to the hermeneutic tradition. In the empiricist perspective, the focus is on causality and causal explanations; in the hermeneutic perspective, the focus is on meanings and values; these are intentional phenomena requiring an *intentional analysis*, not a causal explanation.

In retrospect, it would seem from this account that the two viewpoints are radically different in fundamental concepts, kinds of objects dealt with, types of explanation or accountability, and ways of testing claims. Empiricists, employing a defective theory of subjectivity, dismissed empathic understanding as psychological and beyond the cognitive process. The tradition of Verstehen, however, features an entirely different conception of subjectivity and a different sense of order—intentional order. Consequently, it seems reasonable to say that the early positivists were simply attacking a straw man, and to say that empathy fell outside of the scientific process was to say nothing interesting or important.

In view of the reason advanced, I would conclude that empathy is bound to be trivialized and not understood in any empirical investigation working with the prior assumptions. Thus, I turn now to a consideration of a transcendental perspective where more interesting and important claims about the nature and function of empathy are possible.

TRANSCENDENTAL EMPATHY

In a critique of the experimental psychology of his time Husserl noted the following:[11]

> ... there is a fundamental error of this psychology that should be brought out. It places analysis realized in empathetic understanding of other's experience ... on the same level with an analysis of experience ... proper to physical science.

Reformulated in modern language, one can say that it is important not to confuse the psychological processes at work in empathy with those processes at work in empirical inquiry. The empiricist is not in a position to know this, let alone to challenge it, for an investigation of subjective processes is not a legitimate part of his perspective. To find this out, an analysis of consciousness must be instituted, and this is the point where one turns to Husserlian phenomenology for the appropriate framework. The strength of this perspective lies precisely in the fact that its whole focus is on the subject. It is not an empirical investigation of the world, but an experiential study of the various intentional acts and objects in their respective horizons or contexts. What is so unique about Hüsserlian phenomenoloy is the effort made to set aside or bracket the assumptions integral to the normal empirical standpoint. It studies the acts of meaning and the meant, quite apart from the objective references normally associated with them. Furthermore, the study is focused on the intentional order of experience, rather than the causal order; thus it becomes possible to trace the intentional links binding subjects to one another and to their environing world. This, then, is the suitable framework for the study of empathy.

Empathy and empathic understanding involve complex intentional structures ranging across various levels of experience which play an essential role in the understanding of human behavior. They are acts, initiated by subjects, which possess a complex intentional structure; they can be analyzed in terms of noetic, noematic, horizontal, constitutional, and evidential structures. In *Formal and Transcendental Logic*,[12] Husserl observed that the intersubjectivity problem was in reality a nest of problems having a certain order, and that it was imperative to deal with them in the right order. A similar observation could be made about the problem of empathy, for it involves levels of functioning both at the conscious and the unconscious (active and passive genesis). I cannot do justice to the complexity of the problem in this chapter, but will sketch some of its main features.

It can be affirmed initially that empathy is not exclusively a specific kind or class of feelings, but that it is a complex intentional act involving cognitive, affective, and volitional dimensions all *interwoven* in a synthetic unity. The objects to which empathic acts are directed also cover a wide range, even including ideal objectives of the imagination. One can empathize with beliefs of others, with desires, feelings and emotions, strivings, values and norms, and so on, almost without limit. Empathy is closely related to a variety of other intentional acts, including perceptions, memory, anticipation, and imagination. What has often been overlooked is the fact that empathy lies at the heart of so many fundamental activities of the subject, and reaches out in so many ways to the wider context of human motivation.

Husserl looked to the kinesthetic processes in the body for a preliminary understanding of empathy. Here it often functions below the level of consciousness as we initiate various bodily acts . . . when we move our legs, when we change our position, when we adjust our hearing or vision, when we feel or probe . . . We become aware of our kinesthesias in the sense in which we direct or control our bodies; these acts are not in the mode of the 'I think' but in the mode of 'I am doing' or 'I can'. Through such acts we become aware of our animate organism as the "carrier of acts in intentional lived processes"[13] It is at this level of functioning that we gain first approximations of ourselves as subjects, both constituting and constituted. Although there is much more to be explicated at this level, this is but the first stage in elucidating the structure of transcendental empathy.

The next structure useful in the clarification of empathy is that of "appresentation." In the *Cartesian Meditations*, Husserl describes appresentation as a kind of making copresent, an intentional process in which we supply what is not immediately present to experience, but which is intentionally related to it.[14] Appresentation consists of what is presented to our consciousness and what we thus add to it; as such, appresentation is not an inference or even a thinking act. It is that intentional structure which accounts for that "transfer of sense" from a primordial experience to all other experiences of the same type. Appresentation "awakens" or "calls forth" the appresented element (what we add) to what is presented in experience. It is at work in every recognition of subjects, where what was originally constituted is now transferred to a new instance. In every case of meaning or

understanding there is such a transfer. At a higher level, we are all familiar
with the way the transfer takes place; when we are presented with an animate organism, we appresent those features that are not given originally
but which are intentionally implicated. The relevance to the problem of
empathy is easily evident where we are presented with a particular pattern
of behavior and we appresent (add) the intentional life along with it.

A similar structure involved in empathy is called "pairing" and is the
most important structure in passive synthesis. Husserl described it as follows:[15]

> Pairing . . . is a *universal* phenomenon of the transcendental sphere . . .
> [and] is a *primal form of that passive synthesis* which we designate as "*asso-
> ciation*," in contrast to the passive synthesis of "identification."

In a pairing association, two data are given as one phenomenologically, so
that they are always constituted as a pair. Just as my ego and its intentional
life is paired with my animate organism, so in the case of other animate
organisms an ego and intentional life is paired with them.

Now we have reached a fundamental stage in the exposition of empathy,
but one which has seldom been fully appreciated. As previously noted, empathy
is rooted in the lived body, where the source of a hidden "if-there" relation
is located. This has to do with the process by means of which we are able
to shift imaginatively our position to that of another. My animate organism
has a central "Here" as its mode of givenness, while every other body has
the mode "There." It is through the mechanism of the kinesthesias that the
"There" can be changed into a "Here." By a free modification of my
kinesthesias, particularly those of locomotion, I can change my position in
such a manner that I can convert any "There" into a "Here" and vice versa.
When I thus change my position from a "Here" to a "There" I can perceive
from that position and experience the correspondingly different modes of
appearance that pertain to it. I can thus apperceive an other as having
those experiences that I would have if I were there. This feature of empathy—the imaginative ability to anticipate the experience of the other in
his (her) position—is subject to confirmation or disconfirmation to some
extent, but never a complete fulfillment by presentation. Verification is,
thus, *mediate*, but future experiences can provide further opportunities
to confirm or disconfirm. This kind of activity is one that is capable of
being learned, and individuals vary considerably in their ability to empathize in this manner. It is important to remember that this is a fairly
low level of functioning, for to imaginatively anticipate what something
looks like from another's perspective is a long way from being able to anticipate what another person is believing, yearning for, feeling, striving for,
and so on.

What complicates the account so far is the *horizontal* character of all intentional acts. The horizons, built up in the personal biography of the individual as well as the horizons implicit in the social contexts in which the action takes place, contain factors that contribute to the sense of one's experience. We are not faced here with discrete, separable acts, but on the contrary, with acts essentially tied to their horizons. Thus, in the case of empathic acts at the level of consciousness it becomes even more difficult to initiate acts that will attribute or transfer sense to the other's experience because of the difference in horizons. The risk of attributing sense to other's situations is frequently hazardous, and such an ability varies greatly in any population. Nevertheless, because of the main universal features of intentional life, and the similarity of the experiences facing most people, it is possible to gain at least some approximation of the other's intentional life. One can become more skilled in this matter, confirmation that is appropriate to this kind of appresentation.

How is verification possible? Husserl noted that even at the level of passive synthesis the sense or meaning attributed to another animate organism continues to prove itself by virtue of its changing but necessarily *harmonious behavior*.[16] The harmonious performances referred to are just the sequences of intentional activity where the noetic acts become progressively fulfilled in a coherent fashion. Simply and perhaps inaccurately stated, it is just that our anticipation and predictions about other people are continually verified; were it not so, we could make no sense (attribute no meanings accurately) of the other person's behavior. At higher levels of consciousness, the problem is more complicated, but one still looks for syntheses of verifications of the various intentional acts we set in motion.

The problem is more complicated when we are dealing with attributions of affective and volitional acts to others—as when we assign feelings, emotions, attitudes, strivings—but again experience is our guide. We all have our successes and failures in reading off from the behavior the appropriate intentional acts. Such transfers of sense carry with them many unfulfilled elements, and it is necessary to initiate sequences of similar intentional acts so as to reach some credibility. The cognitive worth of our judgments clearly lies in whether or not they can be fulfilled in evidential performances. It is important to conclude that empathic judgments are fallible and requireconstant checking. The experienced politician who can determine the want and needs of his supporters, the skilled nurse who seems to know what to do to make her patient comfortable, and the dedicated social worker who identifies with the suffering and the helpless, are all examples of successful empathy. Likewise, failure in the ability to attribute sense to the actions of other results in eventual isolation on the one hand, and oppression on the other. But this is a problem that cannot be explored further in this chapter.

INTERSUBJECTIVE AGREEMENT

The role of empathy in intersubjective agreement has not been discussed extensively in the literature, notwithstanding its importance. Let me get to the issue without further ado, by posing the transcendental question: how is intersubjective agreement possible? Note that one must pose it in the transcendental perspective; the reason for this, is that it concerns a relation between subjects and there must be a place for subjects in the framework. If you pose the question in the empirical perspective, then you can only get a *de facto* answer. One can report that "Community C, comprising members a, b, c . . . assented to hypothesis X at time t, in such and such a place, under particular circumstances, and so on. But this is a sociological observation that agreement was reached; it has nothing to say about the validity or truth of the agreement. Conceivably the community could be mistaken. The normative dimension is unaccounted for. Kant raised transcendental questions so that he could deal with the normative question of the objective validity of the syntheses under examination. Empirical questions get empirical answers.

Let us return to the transcendental question and ask how it is that subjects can come to an agreement? What is it that is the object of agreement? More so, what makes the object of agreement true, or highly credible? It is a question of subjects finding certain evidences in their own experience, and then being able to attribute such experiences to others, such that each person claims that all the other members of the consensus share the same experience of having their specific intentions fulfilled. Given the fallibilistic character of empathic claims, one can easily see the difficulty: it is one thing for a given subject to claim that a given hypothesis is correct or true—it is another thing to assign such a significance to the experience of others. Yet there is such a thing as a shared experience—a group experience of an earthquake, a graduating class, a common illness, a commitment to a specific political party, and so on. In shared experiences, people are able to project the same or a common intentional object, in spite of differences in age, sex, color, size, and so on. What is needed for the solution of the problem is a doctrine of "ideal objectivities"[17] or common intentional objects. Although such "ideal objectivities" always occur with their respective horizons, nonetheless, it makes sense to consider them as enjoying a kind of independence and autonomy. In natural science, logic, and mathematics one deals constantly with such ideal objectivities. The essential references to subjects that are carried by such ideal objectivities are not restricted to particular subjects, but rather a reference to any subject. In other words, it is the kind of intentional object reached through a specific kind of intentional act that is instituted.

Let us assume for the moment that this notion of "ideal objectivities" is acceptable; then the notion of shared meanings is plausible. Subjects can now reach assent or consensus, if they can perform the same intentional acts and get the same intentional objects; thus each one has a validating experience. The problem is to recognize this and to recognize that others have the same sort of experience; in other words to compare and share results. All of these are intentional activities and subject to the claims of evidence. So it is, therefore, that intersubjective agreement is possible. The sharing of a particular cognition with others is clearly an empathic act of great sophistication, but not altogether uncommon in human experience.

EMPATHY AND COMMUNITY

It is one thing to be able to understand the acts and actions of other subjects, and quite another thing to do anything about it. In normal empathic acts of understanding the behavior of another, it is not necessary to be experiencing what the other is experiencing. For example, in understanding another's joy or sorrow, it is not necessary to be feeling these emotions. To know that another is believing that such and such is the case is not to be presently believing the same thing. This is an instance of what has been called the "distance" of the observations from the other's predicament. Psychotherapists have often drawn attention to this phenomenon. To understand empathically is not to be experiencing the same things (beliefs, feelings, volitions, and so on) of the other, but to make faithful attributions of meaning and value to the other's conduct . . . to transfer meaning or significance with some degree of credibility.

The basic step to morality requires another step—from the mere understanding of the other's situation to a participation in the other's intentional life and conduct. This means that the observer must assist in the fulfillment of the other's intentional life . . . to help them realize their intentional acts. Here, one literally participates in another's life with the objective of helping in the realization of their objectives. The obvious question arises at this point—suppose the other has beliefs, desires, strivings values which are opposed to our own? How could we possibly help to fulfill another's values which we did not respect? Husserl's answer to these questions was that there was a *vital qualification*—all intentional acts must comply with the question of evidence. Evidence was itself an international experience, and referred to those ideal cases where there was a coincidence or identity between noesis and noema. One could participate in another's intentional life only in so far as the other's intentions and objects were on the way to adequacy (coincidence of noesis and noema). Husserl took the norms of correctness (evidence) to be the same for all intentional life whatsoever.

He seemed to be driven by a messianic desire in his own case for a kind of rigorous self-purification of all beliefs, desires, strivings, and so on through the evidential performances necessary to bring them to adequacy. No belief was to be accepted, no desire, no striving that could not meet the test of evidence. Given this strict criterion for all aspects of intentional life, then the question of participation in the life of another would meet the same tests.

The conception I've sketched captures a basic conception of morality by virtue of the movement from the self to other selves. Husserl pointed out that the model of the *solus ipse* was an absurd abstraction stemming from a defective theory of subjectivity. Human subjects are all inextricably bound together by intentional links; the task of phenomenology is to show how these links function in the constitution of both self and society. The very nature of the intentionality of experience links us to others and to wider and wider circles of community. It is empathy that reveals to us the binding ties to all forms of life, and the step to morality moves us toward greater community. An ideal community is implicit in the teleological character of our own intentional life. Just as we strive for greater accuracy and reliability in our beliefs, desires, and strivings, so we move toward an ideal society which is brought together in tighter bonds of community through the caring and participation in the life of others.

NOTES

1. W. V. O. Quine, "Two Dogmas of Empiricism," *From a Logical Point of View* (Cambridge, MA: Harvard University Press, 1953).
2. W. V. O. Quine, "Epistemology Naturalized," *Ontological Relativity and Other Essays* (New York: Columbia University Press, 1969).
3. Edmund Husserl, *Cartesian Meditations*, trans. by Dorion Cairns (The Hague: Martinus Nijhoff, 1969).
4. Karl-Otto Apel, *Understanding and Explanation: A Transcendental-Pragmatic Perspective*, trans. by Georgia Warnke (Cambridge, MA and London, England: The MIT Press, 1984).
5. Theodore Abel, "The Operational Called Verstehen," *Readings in the Philosophy of Science*, eds. H. Feigl and May Brodbeck (New York: Appleton-Century-Crofts, Inc., 1953).
6. Theodore Abel, ibid, p. 682.
7. Theodore Abel, ibid, p. 685.
8. C. G. Hempel, "The Function of General Laws in History," *Readings in Philosophical Analysis*, eds. H. Feigl and W. Sellars (New York: Appleton-Century-Crofts, Inc., 1949).
9. Richard Rudner, "On the Objectivity of Social Science" *Understanding and Social Inquiry*, Thomas A. McCarthy, ed. (Notre Dame, London: University of Notre Dame Press, 1977).
10. J. L. Austin, *Sense and Sensibilia* (New York: Oxford University Press, 1964).

11. Edmund Husserl. *Phenomenology and the Crisis of Philosophy.* trans. by Quentin Lauer (New York: Harper Torchbook, 1965).
12. Edmund Husserl, *Formal and Transcendental Logic*, trans. by Dorion Cairns (The Hague: Martinus Nijhoff, 1969).
13. Edmund Husserl, *Cartesian Meditations*, §43–50.
14. Edmund Husserl, ibid, §50.
15. Edmund Husserl, ibid, §51.
16. Edmund Husserl, ibid, §52.
17. Edmund Husserl, *Phenomenological Psychology*, trans. by John Scanlon (The Hague: Martinus Nijhoff, 1977), §9.

CONTRIBUTORS

David Carr, Professor of Philosophy at Emory University.

Dagfinn Føllesdal, Professor of Philosophy at Stanford University and at the University of Oslo.

Erazim Kohák, Professor Emeritus of Philosophy at Boston University and Professor of Philosophy at Charles University.

Dallas Laskey, Professor of Philosophy Emeritus at Concordia University.

Rudolf Makkreel, Professor of Philosophy at Emory University.

Joseph Margolis, Professor of Philosophy at Temple University.

Peter McCormick, Professor of Philosophy at the University of Ottowa.

J. N. Mohanty, Professor of Philosophy at Temple University.

Allister Neher, Professor of Philosophy at Dawson College CEGEP in Montreal.

Tom Rockmore, Professor of Philosophy at Duquesne University.

Vladimir Zeman, Professor of Philosophy at Concordia University.

INDEX